Drawn from Me...
Drawn from ...

'*Drawn from Memory* re-creates a vanished age with unusual clarity . . .
Mr Shepard makes it all delightfully real; text and pictures combine
with the happiest effect.'

The Times Literary Supplement

'Although I may have shared childhood with Mr Shepard, I never
shared his talent with pen and pencil. He can make a receding line of
simple Georgian railings exciting and lovable: he does it often and often
again in this delicious book.'

Illustrated London News

'Anyone who has even the fewest recollections of the later years of the
last century cannot fail to be charmed by Ernest H. Shepard's enchanting *Drawn from Memory* . . . Mr Shepard's account of his early days is as
simple as it is pleasant, and as revealing as his art becomes in maturity.
In fact, this is one of those books that have all the marks of a classic.'

Country Life

Drawn from Memory
Drawn from Life

The Autobiography of
ERNEST H. SHEPARD

A Methuen Paperback

A Methuen Paperback

First published in 1986
by Methuen London Ltd
11 New Fetter Lane, London EC4P 4EE

Drawn from Memory first published in 1957
Drawn from Life first published in 1961
by Methuen and Co Ltd
Drawn from Memory copyright 1957 E. H. Shepard
Drawn from Life copyright © 1961 E. H. Shepard

Printed in Great Britain
by Richard Clay (The Chaucer Press) Ltd
Bungay, Suffolk

British Library Cataloguing in Publication Data

Shepard, Ernest H.
    Drawn from memory; Drawn from life: the
    autobiography of Ernest H. Shepard.
    1. Shepard, Ernest H.   2. Illustrators—
    England—Biography
    I. Title
    741'.092'4   NC978.5.S52

    ISBN 0-413-14400-3

CONTENTS

CONTENTS

Drawn from Memory

TO
MY WIFE NORAH
AND
TO THE MEMORY
OF
MY SON GRAHAM

PREFACE

THIS story tells of the period of my childhood when I was seven to eight years old. I was born in St John's Wood, at No. 55 Springfield Road, and I can remember the nursery there and the garden at the back. Each morning my father would come in and dance me round before he went to business. I can also remember the cotton frocks that I wore with plaid bows on my shoulders and a plaid sash round my middle; under these I wore little drawers, rather tight and scratchy for small legs. Getting ready for a party, Mother would frizz my hair with a curling iron.

We moved to No. 10 Kent Terrace when I was about four years old, and it was there that I spent the happiest days of my early boyhood, with Mother and Father, my sister Ethel and my brother Cyril. I was the youngest of the family and we were all devoted to Mother. She had a sweet and gentle nature and her beauty was enhanced by the colour of her hair—the colour of ripe corn, as I heard it described by an admirer.

It was soon after this story ends that she was taken ill. We children did not realize the seriousness of her illness and enjoyed pushing her wheeled chair on our walks round the Park. Her early death cut short our happy family life. We tried to put a brave face on it for Father's sake, and I remember telling my brother that I would not cry any more because Mother would not have liked it. It was years before the cloud seemed to lift and the natural buoyancy and happiness of youth revive itself in me.

When my own children were growing up I told them the story as I tell it here, recalling the incidents, one by one, as they came back to my mind. They would ask to have more about the Aunts, or the Farm, or perhaps Martha and Lizzie. I think that their first visit to a pantomime must have been just as exciting as mine was, but, when I described my pantomime feelings, my son asked that I should one day 'write it all down and make a story of it'.

The drawings of the people and places are as I remember them. Both No. 10 Kent Terrace and No. 53 Gordon Square look today very much the same from the outside as they did seventy years ago. Standing on the Terrace, as I was a few days back, I almost expected to see Lizzie's face appear at the area steps, telling me to bring in Septimus and wash my hands for dinner. I was once again just a little London boy.

E. H. S.
February 1957

Chapter One

SEPTIMUS

A COLD wind was blowing down Park Road as we three children, with Martha our nursemaid, passed St John's Wood Church and, crossing over, came in sight of the flag-staff on the roof of the public house on the opposite side of the road. A flag had been hoisted, a light blue flag, and it meant that Cambridge had won the Boat Race. Ever since I could remember, both my

'It was a light-blue flag'

brother Cyril and I had looked forward eagerly to the race, though we had never seen it. We were staunch Oxonians; the only reason for this was that our favourite uncle Willie, the clergyman and St Paul's master, who was father's eldest brother, had been at Balliol College. My sister Ethel, on the other hand, was for Cambridge; she would give no reason for her preference, and we boys always suspected it was because she thought light blue the prettier colour. In any case, there it was: Cambridge had won this year; there was no doubt of it.

Sunk in gloom, I trailed along behind the others, and as they passed the spot where road crosses canal, I stopped and hauled myself up on the wooden paling. I knew that by peering over the top, I could see the canal, dark and sinister, below. It was just possible I might see a corpse floating on the water, such as the old messenger man at the corner of the Terrace had seen. But even that consolation was denied me, and in obedience to a call from Martha I turned and trotted after the others. I was still brooding over this when I caught up with my brother and sister, and Cyril was able to remind me that there would be another race next year, which Oxford might win. Much comforted by this thought, I dismissed the subject from my mind before we reached our home at No. 10 Kent Terrace.

The house is still there. It stands in the middle of the row and is ornamented with stucco columns in front and a small balcony to each drawing-room window.

The Terrace lies back from the main road and has a garden in front. There used to be railings all round, but these have now been replaced by a wire fence. The railings were unclimbable by small boys, and too close together for them to squeeze through. There was a lock on the gate, for which we had a key but it was very stiff to turn. The garden was untidy, with some big trees and a lot of sooty shrubs, but it was an excellent place to play in because no one ever disturbed us there.

I was rather proud of the front door of our house, for it was distinguished by having two stained-glass panels which my father had designed. One was called 'Night' and the other 'Morning'. 'Night' had an owl in it, which enabled me to tell it from 'Morning'. Behind the front door there was a little hole where the key of the garden was kept.

'With the hapless doll attached'

The front dining-room was separated by folding doors from the smaller back part, which we used as a playroom. Over the fireplace in the front room was an overmantel of wood, with shelves, also designed by Father, and filled with a collection of blue and white Nankin china, a type of ornamental pottery then in vogue.

The hall was paved with tiles and the staircase was of stone with iron banisters. It was wide, and open enough for us to play our favourite game of parachute descents. This pastime had been a craze with Cyril and me ever since we had

'Sailed majestically down'

been taken to the Crystal Palace and had seen a certain Professor Baldwin make the perilous descent from the main transept. Lit up by limelights and accompanied by the din of a brass band and the thunder of drums, he had sailed majestically down, to arrive in the arena in tights and spangles, and to bow his thanks to a delighted audience. When we came home we set about emulating him, but wisely decided to try the experiment first with Ethel's dolls. Ethel was older than we were and her interest in dolls was waning, so she took the conscription of her dolls in good part. This was fortunate, for the casualty rate was high. Woe betide the wretched victim if her head was made of china or wax! We soon found that an umbrella was of little use as a parachute; it became unmanageable and stuck. Then we tried handkerchiefs of various types and sizes, one of which was decorated with a coloured picture of the Professor himself; but even these proved unsatisfactory. Poised at the top of the stairs, leaning over the banisters and holding the contraption with the hapless doll attached, I would launch it while Cyril waited below, prepared to avert calamity. The only doll to survive was Minna, grubby, tough, and made of leather.

The Terrace was paved with flagstones, and had gas lamp-posts with $\boxed{\begin{array}{c}\text{IV}\\\text{G.R.}\end{array}}$ on the base, which Martha told us meant a king. There were round iron coal-hole covers at regular intervals, and these would make a loud clank, clank when ridden over by Septimus.

Septimus was my pride and joy. He had arrived, carefully packed, on the tenth of December, my seventh birthday, and been christened Septimus by my father. The horse was a gift from my Godmother-Aunt. Cyril and I always thought there must have been some direct divine influence working on my behalf to guide Aunt Alicia on this occasion, leading her away from the more useful gifts; and that the Angel Gabriel, disguised as the shopwalker in Mr James Shoolbred's store, had led her to Septimus where he stood, with eyes dilated and distended nostrils, pawing the air with his two forelegs as though yearning to discard his three wooden wheels. It was some days before

I mastered him, but after that I would carry him down the front steps and pedal along the Terrace, 'clank, clank', to the end and back again, my little legs spinning round till Septimus and I stopped for lack of breath, or the face of Lizzie, the cook, appeared at the area steps to say that dinner was ready. Tethered to a lamp-post, Septimus would then await his master's pleasure.

There was generally someone with whom to pass the time of day

'The Angel Gabriel, disguised as the shopwalker'

on the Terrace. If it wasn't one of the tradesmen's boys it was Ellen the milk-woman. Ellen had been my nurse before Martha came, when Cyril and I were of very tender age. She had been with us until she married, and used to push us in the double perambulator. We sat side by side and squabbled most of the time. The pram was like a wide chair on three wooden wheels, the smaller wheel being in front. It had a canopy hood which folded up like an umbrella made of green material with a fringe which I enjoyed picking off. There was an apron to cover our legs, with a strap across our middles. It furnished a very bumpy ride, especially when crossing roads, which were badly metalled in those days. Almost the first thing that I can remember is trailing round the Park and being lifted from the pram to feed the ducks by the ornamental water.

'Tethered to a lamp-post'

Sometimes we would go as far as the Zoo and look through the bushes so that we could see some of the animals in their cages and hear their various noises or the raucous shriekings of the parrots. Then we would pass the Botanical Gardens and come to the Enclosure, a slice of the Park reserved for the residents who lived in the houses opposite. The Enclosure had oak railings along the road side which were sufficiently widely spaced to allow anyone as small as myself to squeeze through. It had been a game with Cyril and me, until he grew too big, to sneak through and, avoiding the eye of the Park Keeper, run along inside. Dodging from bush to bush, one could go quite a distance. If spotted, one broke cover and made for the railings. The Keeper, in his top hat and with a stick under his arm,

'Trailing round the Park'

was too dignified to run after us and would content himself with shouting.

Ellen was a sturdy woman and made light of the long walks. When she left to get married, she took a job at the dairy. Carrying the cans of milk, she came round the Terrace in the morning and afternoon. She had two cans, slung on a wooden yoke across her shoulders and over her plaid shawl. She would put down the cans, and tip some milk into the waiting jugs from a tin measure, any that was spilt being quickly lapped up by our black Sambo and the other cats who always followed her. If Martha or Lizzie were there she stayed for a gossip. Her husband was named Jack. According to Martha, he never would work and sometimes beat Ellen. He was an ill-conditioned, lanky fellow, who was to be seen, more often than not, leaning against the palings by the Windsor Castle.

'All the cats would follow her'

Once a week the dustmen came round. They had a grey horse which seemed permanently to wear a nosebag, and which moved slowly along the Terrace, pulling the open four-wheeled cart. The horse would stop every now and then while the men, who wore leather flaps at the back of their hats, clattered up and down the area steps and emptied their baskets into the cart. Martha and Lizzie always went round shutting doors and windows against the flying dust, and if I were out on the Terrace on Septimus, I had strict orders to bolt indoors quickly. The same thing applied when the coalman came. I would watch him from the dining-room window as he tipped the coal sacks into the hole with a distant sound of rumbling from below. Then one day I thought I'd like to see what happened when the coal came down, so I sneaked downstairs, slipped past the kitchen and dived into the cellar. I could hear the coalman above heaving the sacks about, then down came an avalanche of coal and I was nearly choked. Covered with coal dust, I found the door and staggered out, to find myself face to face with Lizzie. She told me I ought to be ashamed of myself, and led me upstairs, where I was undressed, scrubbed, and threatened with direst penalties should I ever do it again.

'Reminded me of a respectable stork'

At the top of the Terrace was a high wall, behind which were the grounds of Hanover House. There are large blocks of flats there now, where once were pleasant gardens. It was by the high wall that there sat, day in and day out, the old messenger man. He sat on a box with his back against the wall so that he commanded a view of the whole

Terrace. Beside him in a canvas bag was his lunch. He appeared to spend his time sleeping, but he would spring to life if any householder

'Had once given him a penny'

appeared at a front door to wave or call to him. His mission in life was to do odd jobs or to 'run' errands, though he had never been known to break out of a walk. He was tall and lean and wore a threadbare grey tail coat which was too small for him. He always reminded me of a respectable stork. In a spasm of generosity I once gave him a penny, which the old man pocketed after dubiously spitting on it. He always knew where to find a cab when one was wanted and repeated whistling had failed to produce it.

'The butcher's boy'

I suppose the most popular caller, anyhow among the cats, was the cat's-meat man. He came twice a week with his hand cart, which was decorated with painted boards on each side reading, 'Purveyor of choice meat for cats and dogs.' The meat was cut in slices and stuck on a skewer. It cost about threepence.

The butcher's boy was the pick of the tradesmen. He came round the Terrace in a smart little pony cart with a very well-groomed pony, brown with white stockings, and harness as clean and bright as new pins. The boy sat perched up on his driving seat, wearing his striped blue apron and with his hair plastered down with mutton fat. The pony trotted very fast and would pull up sharply. The boy would then run round to the back and shoulder his meat on a wooden carrier. He was down the area steps and up again in a jiffy, the pony starting before he was fairly back on the box. None of the other tradesmen was half so smart. The baker had only a hand cart with a basket hanging at the back.

Then there was, of course, our own particular policeman. He often came round in the dusk of an evening. Slow of movement he was, but wise, and given to good advice.

Park Road, with its wide pavements, was almost countrified then, and we got to know all the shops. First after the Windsor Castle was Chaplin's the fishmonger. Then came Kensit the greengrocer, with Mrs Kensit stout and motherly in her bonnet. Further along was Mr White the chemist, with large coloured glass bottles in his window and a strong smell of medicine as you passed the shop. Beyond that was the upholsterer and cabinet maker, Mr Grahame, who had a broad Scots accent. Maltby, the tailor, had an important-looking coat of arms over his shop, and at the end, built into the wall, close to Clarence Gate, was the little dressmaker's shop with its two round-topped windows and door between. Then, just at the top of Upper Baker Street, was what Martha called the Victoria Wining Shop, where a friend of hers served behind the counter. At the upper end of Park Road, on the opposite side, where is now a big garage and block of flats, by the top of Upper Gloucester Place, stood Coles the linen draper. Quite an important shop it was, with windows full of the latest fashion in hats and a fine display of long lace curtains. Mother was never allowed to leave the shop without having her attention drawn to 'Our latest line, fresh from Nottingham.'

Nearly all our shop assistants in those days were young men, even in the drapers' and the chemist's.

Behind Coles' shop, where are now the marshalling yards of British Railways and the approach to Marylebone Station, was an acreage of small and pleasant Georgian houses, as there are to this day around Lord's Cricket Ground. They had brick-walled gardens and quiet roads. It was there, in a tiny white house in Boscobel Place, that father and mother lived after they were married. Mother often told us how happy they were there, and what heart searchings the faithful Lizzie suffered before leaving grandma to come to them.

We passed all the shops as we three children, in charge of Martha, went to school in Upper Baker Street. Ethel went to the Church of England High School for Girls, and we boys to the Kindergarten attached.

The Kindergarten was down a yard, where now stands British Railways Lost Property Office. The yard was paved with concrete and served as a playground. We had invented a sort of football adapted to this ground. Played with a rubber ball, it included certain hazards such as drain pipes, and there were penalities for going out-side into Baker Street. At the lower end of the yard was a high brick wall, but, by climbing on a stack of timber, we could look down on Baker Street Underground Station and see the trains steaming in and out. It made our clothes dirty, and Miss Parkman would come out when she saw us there and clap her hands and in we would have to go.

There were three mistresses, Miss Parkman, Miss Turner and Miss Gardner. I liked Miss Turner best. We had morning prayers up in the big schoolroom, and Canon Holland came once a week to talk to us. There was a boxed-in staircase leading to this classroom, and the door at the top was firmly shut when prayers had begun. When we were late we had to wait, in silent shame, in the dark, to emerge

25

and be admonished after prayers were over. On the whole Cyril and I liked going to school; the work was not too hard, and there was plenty of time for play; also we had made several friends, and there were some grand toys in the cupboards for wet days. 'The Fighting Cocks', real feathered birds operated by wires, were a special treat and only allowed out under strict supervision. Then we were encouraged to make gifts for our parents; paper cards would be decorated with coloured wools after being pricked in patterns; drawing was encouraged, but coloured chalks were not popular as they always made a mess.

'The fighting birds'

The school house, which was on three floors, had been a workshop. All the kindergarten children gathered in the big downstairs room for morning break. There was eager competition for the post of 'Bun-buyer' which, ever since the disaster to the bag of hot buns that had burst in the middle of the street, had fallen to the lot of one of the eldest. After the pennies had been collected, the bun-buyer would go to the baker's across the road and come back with a bag full of steaming hot buns. It was the fashion among the boys to flatten their buns by pressing them, sometimes under foot, to gain an effect of size.

The classroom where I was taught was on the top floor, and was presided over by Miss Gardner. There were benches and long desks, but we were not trusted with ink-wells and always used pencils or slates. There was a big stove, which one tried to get near in cold weather. Among the pupils were Nigel Playfair and his sister Audrey. Then there was Willie Rayner, whose father was a doctor in Dorset Square. Cyril and I often went with Willie and some of our other

'Duly flattened'

friends to play cricket in Paddington Recreation Ground. We had a bat and a ball but had to use our jackets for a wicket, until one day a friend of Willie's turned up and brought some stumps. His name was George, a tall youth in white flannel trousers, whose father, George Grossmith, was acting in *The Mikado*. George said he wanted to be an actor too.

Among all the girls it was Helen Clowes whom I liked best. Helen had something wrong with her spine and had to lie on a board all the time. We boys would try to get the end seat so as to be near

27

her, to hand her books or pencils. She had dark curly hair and grey eyes and was very quiet. She would say 'Thank you' in a gentle voice for the small services she was rendered. She was only at school a short time, and one day Miss Parkman called us together and told us that Helen had died.

Afternoon school ended early, and sometimes Mother came and fetched us. This was a special treat, as it meant that we might get a bus ride to Oxford Circus and help her to do some shopping. Cyril and I found the women's shops very dull, but these expeditions generally ended by our going to Elphinstone's, the teashop in Regent Street, where we could get cream and other delicious cakes, or better still, ices. ·

It was getting on for Easter when a large parcel arrived at No. 10 Kent Terrace. From the fact that this was hastily put away out of sight by Mother, Cyril and I suspected it might possibly be a present for us. Mother's great friend Gussie had been known to give liberally before now, and a large Easter egg might contain anything, even a steam engine with rails for it to run upon—things I had always longed for. After I had gone up to bed, I lay in my combinations and pondered, while Martha was airing my nightshirt over the gas-jet. She passed the garment backwards and forwards over the globe, casting strange shadows on the ceiling like clouds in the sky. I questioned her closely. 'Martha, have you seen it? What shape is it? Is it heavy, and does it rattle?' But it was no use. Martha, intent upon her airing, would give me no answer beyond 'Now, Master Ernest, don't you go asking me a lot of questions. You know what curiosity did to the cat.' As a matter of fact I didn't, but I had to give in. Tucked up in bed I thought of every possibility, and when Cyril came up too I tried to get an opinion from him. But he had brought up his stamp album and was too much excited over a stamp that his

'Where you could get cream cakes'

uncle, Mother's brother, had sent him from Natal to bother with Easter Egg speculations.

When I woke on Easter morning it was some time before I remembered, then I hopped out of bed. It seemed a long business

'Airing my nightshirt over the gas'

washing and dressing, and it was not till after breakfast that we had our presents, and the parcel was produced and opened on the dining-room floor.

It *was* a great big egg, gaily coloured and decorated with a gold frill round the join in the middle. Inside was a red box with a black and gold label: 'Pontoon Train. Made in Germany.' Wrapped up in paper were soldiers in blue uniforms with spiked helments, little horses with harness that would take off, and little carts filled with tiny wooden planks and surmounted by boats. It was all very exciting.

Dear Gussie had given us a 'train', but it was the wrong kind. Nevertheless, Cyril and I spent many happy hours with the blue soldiers. We built a bridge with the wooden planks and the boats; then our whole army, horse, foot, artillery, black savages and all, marched solemnly across. It was at dinner time that Mother brought

'Pontoon Train. Made in Germany'

up the awful question of 'Thank-you' letters. She said we must get down to it and write ours before we forgot. This was a horrible task which Cyril and I both hated and always put off as long as possible. It was all right if Ethel was there. She was older and full of brilliant ideas. She would have the thing done in no time, and it would only remain to be copied out, but that afternoon she had gone along to the Lloyds' to practise the Toy Symphony. So Cyril and I settled down in gloomy silence to make the best of it. I had made several false starts when I decided that I needed inspiration, and what better way of achieving that than a ride on Septimus? So I fetched him from his stable at the back of the house, carried him down the front steps, and proceeded to rattle up and down the Terrace.

What with the fresh air and the excitement of the ride I forgot all about my letter and was only recalled to earth when Mother appeared at the front door and called a halt. She asked if I had written my letter. I could only answer that I had done some of it. She looked worried and asked: 'How much?'

'Well, not very much.'

'We'd better go in and see,' she said.

So I tied Septimus to his lamp-post and in we went. Cyril was deep in his stamp album, and by the look of satisfaction on his face I guessed that *his* troubles were over. Mother bent over the table and picked up the ink-stained results of my labours. With furrowed brow she read out: 'Dear Gussie I hope you are quite well . . .' She looked at me sternly for a moment, and then burst out laughing. 'It's not very much, is it?' she said. Then: 'Perhaps we had better do it together.'

This we did, and it was the grandest 'Thank-you' letter I had ever written. When it was finished, addressed and stamped, I was able to remount Septimus and ride him, in triumph, to the pillar-box at the corner and post both our letters. It required a certain amount of horsemanship to keep Septimus under control while doing this, for he was apt to shoot away from underneath when I was reaching up to the slot, but by turning the front wheel sideways he could be kept quiet. Then I waited at the corner, as I always liked doing, to watch the traffic go by.

There were not many buses, but in the hot weather their horses would be given a drink at the trough in front of the Windsor Castle. I could see this from the end of the Terrace. One day a man riding a high bicycle fell off, right over the handlebars. Mr Chaplin, the fish-monger, ran out and helped him up and then sat him on a chair and mopped his head with a rather fishy sponge.

Once a week all three of us had a music lesson. We had violins of different sizes and were taught by Mr Cruft. He had a long beard and talked about Herr Joachim. His son is now teaching the violin to young people.

It was dreadfully tedious having to play scales and my fingers never seemed to be in the right places, but it was better when I was promoted to Boccherini's *Minuet*. By that time Ethel could rattle along with *The Caliph of Baghdad*. We boys were not to be allowed

'My little fingers never seemed to be in the right place'

to play our fiddles in the coming Toy Symphony, and it was only after the most urgent appeals that Cyril was given the warbler thing, filled with water, that he blew into, while I got the triangle.

Soon after Easter, after the Miss Dicksees had been to tea, Mother told us that there were plans for Father and herself to go abroad, and that Polly, Minnie, and Frank Dicksee might join them in a trip to France. This was all very well for them, but oh how I hated it when Mother was away! I had been known to express myself very forcibly on the subject. On one occasion, at a tender age, I lay on my back in the middle of the high road in Ripley and kicked and yelled till the whole village was roused.

'Kicked and yelled in Ripley'

Cyril and I were filled with suspicion about this new trip and brooded darkly upon what was to be our fate while our parents were away.

Chapter Two

THE AUNTS

THE Aunts lived in the corner house in Gordon Square, a very big house with a portico in Gordon Place. It had been built by my grandfather, an austere gentleman who was quite bald and always wore a wig. He felt the cold and generally wore, in addition to his overcoat, a plaid shawl wrapped round his shoulders. This, in combination with the wig, caused much amusement among the younger elements at Lloyd's of which he was a member. The Aunts told how they watched the new house being built from their back windows in Tavistock Square, and how Grandfather kept an eagle eye on the proceedings. The old man died soon after it was finished, and his widow lived there with her grown-up daughters till she too died. I remember her, in her stiff black silk dress, with a white cap

'He felt the cold'

and side ringlets, giving me spoonfuls of crystallized coffee sugar. But that was before our story begins.

There were four aunts. The eldest, Aunt Alicia, was my God-mother. Aunt Annie was an invalid who spent the day lying on a couch, which it was difficult not to bump against; she had a nurse

35

who kept a canary, called George, in a cage outside her window. Then there was Aunt Fanny, the smallest but by far the most energetic; and finally Aunt Emily, stout and short of breath. There were a lot of maids, and Mrs Lamb, the charwoman, and Henry, the odd man who cleaned the knives and boots and didn't seem to be quite right in the head, or, as Aunt Emily more delicately expressed it, 'was a little touched'.

'Giving me spoonfuls of crystallized coffee sugar'

It was the Aunts who suggested that we three children should stay with them in the Easter holidays while our parents went abroad with the Dicksees. Though stoutly opposed by Cyril and myself, the visit was arranged, and promises were wrung from us to behave well and make the best of it.

We said 'good-bye' to Martha and Lizzie and Black Sambo with gloomy hearts. I came near to open revolt when I was told that to

aunt Fanny

'By far the most energetic'

aunt Emily

aunt Alicia

'Stout and short of breath'   'My godmother who always felt the cold' take Septimus was out of the question. We and our bags were finally stowed in a four-wheeler.

Things began to look brighter when we arrived at Gordon Square and found that the morning-room had been set aside for our use and we were to have tea there, with buttered scones, by ourselves. Then,

'A stone urn for visitors' cards'

the front door of the house had narrow windows on either side through which one could peep at visitors outside. In the hall was a hard and forbidding chair for the use of the less respectable callers. There was also an elaborate mahogany hat-stand with two men's hats (Father's cast-offs) to strike fear into the hearts of such burglars or other Lawless Men as might effect entry by the front door. On one side stood a great sideboard with a marble top, supporting a stone urn for visitors' cards. On the wall above was an albatross's head with mothy plumage and faded glass eye. Someone must at one time have had an urge to brighten the scene, for on the wall hung an incongruous framed picture from a Christmas number showing a little girl sitting up in bed giving pink biscuits to a dog. The stairs, which led up and up, had ornamented iron banisters. The dining-room was painted a dull green and was rather dark, with large bookcases; an enormous mahogany sideboard took up almost one end of the room, and on the walls were: (1) a mezzotint of the Duke of Wellington, (2) an engraving by Landseer with a lot of game lying about and a man who looked like the Prince Consort, and (3) several Martin engravings of Biblical scenes. All the furniture

'More proper to have a hip bath in your own bedroom'

was of solid mahogany, and not very comfortable, and there was always a slight smell of dinner.

Cyril and I found that we had separate rooms, which was a nuisance as we couldn't talk after going to bed. Taking a bath was going to be difficult too, for although a bathroom existed at the very top of the house, the water in it was never hot and it was rarely used. Ladies considered it much more delicate and proper to have a hip bath in their own bedroom.

The Aunts dined at six o'clock, and we children were given High Tea at the same time. The only drawback to this feast was that all

'A string of maids'

hands had to be clean, faces washed, and shoes changed. Afterwards there was generally a round game of cards in the drawing-room. Aunt Alicia had a horror of fire, so the only lamp allowed was one which burnt a sort of oil that had to be pumped up; but as the thing gave no light anyway, that didn't matter. There were also six candles on the table. At a quarter to nine tea was brought in. Though Cyril and I were generally already as tight as drums, we would find room for more, particularly for a specially choice brand of biscuit. Blown out and sleepy, I then went to bed. It was something of a shock when my godmother came up with me and made me say my prayers out loud. Of course I got muddled, and kept repeating myself. Finally I was told I would be given a little book suitable for a boy of my age, which gave all the prayers from A to Z. Oh dear! I had to learn several. They kept me awake at night, and I never, never got them quite right.

Down in the drawing-room at ten o'clock proper prayers were said. A string of maids filed in, led by Mrs. Edlin the cook, followed

'Time they were carried up to bed'

by Jane the parlour-maid, then Alice and Mary, and the little one at the tail. There was always a whispering outside, and a suspicion that eyes were peering through the crack of the door to make sure that Aunt Alicia had found her place in the book and was ready. On the marble slab in the hall was an array of polished brass candlesticks with glass shields and metal extinguishers. They were lit as a sign that it was time they were carried to bed.

The large Square in front of the house had a promising look, but it was disappointing when, after taking the key that hung on the hat-stand, we crossed the road and opened the gate. There was a large stretch of grass, but this had a notice 'Keep Off'. Moreover there was a man with a broom and a barrow to see that you did keep off. Then the grimy laurel bushes and shrubs led to dirty hands and clothes, which meant retaliation from the household. To climb trees was forbidden. Altogether it was a poor substitute for Kent Terrace, and we boys preferred to stay and play in the morning-room.

'Sweep the dust into two neat borders'

Near the gate at the corner of the Square a crossing sweeper had his pitch. I felt sorry for him, for his eyes were always watering, and sometimes he looked very cold. If the weather was wet and the road muddy, he swept clean a path across, and if it were fine and the road dusty, he would sweep the dust into two neat borders with a curl at each end. He wore an old bowler hat, and had a special—and newer—one on the pavement for pennies.

There were certain days when the Aunts used to shop. Aunt Fanny was the active one, and did most of this. She would take Ethel with her. Cyril and I did our best to keep out, but were trapped and conscripted more than once. First there was the dairy in Torrington Place, where large china urns with polished brass lids stood on the counter, and where we could have a penny glass of milk dipped out for us. Next door was John's, the stationers, with this week's *Punch* open in the window. Then Shoolbred's, in Tottenham Court Road. Apparently there was a

'The keeper with the goldbanded hat'

rivalry between this shop and Maples', and I could not get it clear why the Aunts would not go to Maples'. Aunt Emily, whose explanations never gave satisfaction, said it was something to do with a four-in-hand, and that it was 'raffish'. This called forth an expostulation from Aunt Alicia. 'Emily! where did you learn that horrid expression?'

Aunt Emily's attempts to ward off searching questions as to why

43

'Spend the afternoon in the drawing-room'

there were gates with a lodge attached at the corner of Woburn Square were met with little sympathy, and she had to fall back on saying it was to keep out rough people. But the keeper with the goldbanded hat didn't look equal to keeping out rough people, any more than did the beadle at Marylebone Church, or the inspector of nuisances.

On Sunday we went to St Pancras Church. It was the only occasion that I saw my godmother go out, for, like her father before her, she felt the cold, and was swathed in shawls and cloaks. When we got back to Gordon Square, Cyril and I were horrified to find our playroom had been tidied up, the few toys and games we had brought with us put away in a cupboard, and the order had gone forth that we must spend the afternoon in the drawing-room. No old *Punch* or *Illustrated London News* volumes to look at: instead, *The Sunday Magazine, Leisure Hour,* and *Sunday at Home.* The Aunts rested or knitted garments for the

'I followed the pattern most carefully'

people of Algoma. Aunt Emily had her own special activity, which was in aid of the Deep Sea Fishermen. The garments she knitted, which were of fearful and wonderful proportions, were often tried on Father, who was inclined to make derogatory remarks, while Emily, with puzzled looks, and a knitting-needle in her mouth, would say, 'Tut-t-t, very odd, I know I followed the pattern most carefully,' and, 'But then, Harry, you must remember they are very *big* men.'

45

As the afternoon wore on, the only cheerful sound was the ringing of the muffin man's bell as he came round the Square. But, alas! he was allowed to pass unheeded.

Mr Paget was the Rector of St Pancras, and the curates used to make duty calls on the Aunts. It is recorded that, on one occasion, while they were returning the call of a newcomer, and were waiting in the sitting-room, the Aunts saw on the mantelpiece a TOBACCO PIPE! And that was the end of that call.

But there were happier days when Aunt Fanny took us to the Tower of London, and I got all worked up and involved in long discussions on armour and culverins with the Beefeater, and we saw the Golden Crowns and the places where people were tortured. . . . All most enthralling.

Then there was the party at Dr Davis's. Dr Davis lived opposite. It was a real children's party, with lots of good things to eat, as well as ices, but there were some grown-ups, including a man with a loud booming voice who kept us in roars of laughter. His name was Whymper, and Mrs Davis told us he used to climb mountains.

There was no piano at Gordon Square, which was hard lines on Ethel, who was learning that instrument and was getting on very well. Normally she practised most diligently. We had not brought our violins with us as our parents were afraid the scraping would worry the Aunts. So I was surprised when my godmother asked me one day if I would like to go to a concert and hear a great violinist play. Aunt Alicia knew that I learned the fiddle; indeed I had played my 'piece' to her on more than one occasion, though I do not think she was much impressed. She had kindly thought of the concert as a special treat for her godson. I accepted the invitation with alacrity and was told that Sarasate was giving a recital at the St James Hall and that my aunt would get tickets. The concert was in the afternoon,

'On the mantelpiece a TOBACCO PIPE!'

and I went with Aunt Fanny. I had never been in a concert hall before and was rather disappointed with its general appearance. I had expected a stage and scenery, a gaily decorated curtain and lime-lights, and here there was just a platform with a very large piano. There were banks of flowers on either side, but that was all.

However, I ceased to worry about this when the great man began to play. I know that I was deeply moved. It was a revelation to listen to the music that he got from his fiddle, and to watch his delicate white hands fingering so perfectly. I could not explain what I felt when I tried to thank my godmother afterwards. I never, never dreamt that such music was possible, and I felt quite hopeless about my own efforts.

Sitting in the drawing-room after tea, our Aunts would tell us of their childhood. Aunt Alicia, being one of the eldest, remembered more than the others. She told us how the family had lived on two top floors of the big house in Tavistock Square. With no form of heating, the rooms were icy cold in winter. Hot-water bottles were unknown, and, except for an occasional bed-warmer for delicate little Mary or Annie, they had to freeze. The marvel is that they survived at all. At certain times the children were taken downstairs to see their parents, which meant endless cleaning, tidying, and dress-ing up in little starched underclothes and low-necked muslin frocks with short sleeves. Most of their lives were spent in a large, cheerless playroom, which was never warm enough. Then the daily walk was purgatory. No running wild in the Square, but a prim little procession of underclad children with blue noses, chapped wrists and ankles, who were glad to get indoors again. In the summer they were just as uncomfortable, though not so cold, for the holland dresses that they wore were hard and scratchy.

There were eleven children, seven girls and four boys. Aunt

Mary, the eldest, died before I was born, as did Richard (a very dapper-looking Uncle, to judge by the family album), about whom the Aunts were inclined to be sentimental. It was suggested that his early death was due to a disappointment in love. There were many sighs, and he was generally referred to as 'Poor Richard'.

My godmother, Alicia, came next, then Willie, our favourite Uncle. Aunt Ellen, the fourth, had left the maternal home some years before, to go off and live on her own in Bournemouth. Tended by a Scots maid called Ganson, who came from the Shetland Isles, she lived to a great age.

Then came Annie, the invalid; Robert, my godfather, whom we rarely saw; Fanny, who possessed as much energy as all the others put together; my father, the youngest son; and Emily the youngest child of all, always rather short of breath.

Before Gordon Square was built, my grandfather had built a house in Guildford, on Guildown. There the whole family went for their summer holiday, year after year. Richard Shepard, his brother and my great-uncle, had also built a house on Guildown Road, so that the two families were much together at that time. There are photos, again in the family album, of croquet parties on the lawn of Guildown House, including one of my great-aunt, a woman of character who could never be persuaded to face the camera. It shows her standing in bonnet, shawl, and crinoline: back view.

We children were glad when, at the end of twelve days, we heard that our parents were back. Eagerly we packed our things and went out in the Square in the morning. As Cyril and I came back into the house for midday dinner we sensed an air of gloom. Indeed Aunt Alicia was lying down in her room, and Aunt Emily was distinctly snappish. We had a dreadful feeling we might be to blame and I tried to think over my conduct of the last few days. We kept out of the way in the playroom till Father came. He greeted us, and then went upstairs.

He was gone some time, so I crept up to the landing to listen, and came back to report that they were all talking very seriously. I had

'Sitting on the dustman's knee'

heard Aunt Alicia say: 'Do you think we should send for William?' Presently Father came down and, carefully closing the playroom door, burst into laughter. Then he revealed the awful truth.

Only that morning Aunt Alicia had descended into the kitchen and found the cook sitting on the dustman's knee.

50

Chapter Three

SCARLATINA

My parent's friendship with the Dicksees was of long standing, for Mother had known them as a child, and their father Thomas Dicksee had painted a portrait of Grandma. Frank was an Associate of the Royal Academy and was considered to be one of the rising artists. He had a studio on Campden Hill, at the top of Peel Street. My brother and I, dressed as choir boys, were his models in a big picture he was painting. The studio was up a rather narrow flight of stairs. His housekeeper, a kindly woman, made us feel at home during the sittings.

Before Sending-in Day for the Royal Academy my parents were invited to Show Sunday at Frank Dicksee's studio. They took, besides my sister, us boys, which was rather a rash thing to do. We were severely tidied up and packed into a four-wheeler. When we reached the studio we found a lot of people and carriages. There was not much room to pass on the stairs, but I was forging ahead when the door at the top opened and a lady came out followed by an old gentleman. He had white hair, a white beard, and a florid face, and obviously I was in his way. My mother clutched my shoulder and drew me back to allow the old man to come slowly down. As he passed he bent down and gave me a smile. Mother, in rather a breathless voice, whispered, 'That was Robert Browning, the poet,' which, I fear, did nothing to impress me at the time. Up in the studio we were announced by a man in a brown coat and brass buttons.

'Collapsed with a mighty crash'

In the crush it was rather hot and stuffy and difficult to see the pictures, so Cyril and I found our way to the back, where we knew there were two suits of armour on stands. These we proceeded to investigate. Presently we undid certain straps. It was a most interesting business finding out how the various pieces fitted together, and it kept us amused for quite a time. Until, that is, I tried to climb up to reach the helmet. This was too much. The stand collapsed with a

'Mostly concerned with battle scenes'
Drawn by me in 1887

mighty crash and the assembled company turned round and stared at us lying among the debris. My poor mother, covered with shame, gathered us up and we were ignominiously taken home.

Some of my early efforts at drawing were shown, with a certain pride, by my father to his artist friends. Father had quite decided that I should be an artist when I grew up, though I myself considered an artist's life to be a dull one and looked for something more adventurous. There was a box full of these drawings which my father had saved. They came to light many years later, and showed that I was gifted with a somewhat lively imagination, mostly concerned with battle scenes.

It was on the first of May that I had one of the frights of my life. I was playing alone in the Terrace garden when I heard the jingling of bells and went to the end of the garden to investigate. A motley group of men rigged up for 'Jack-in-the-Green' was turning into the Terrace. One fellow, completely covered with greenery, so that only his legs were showing, was jigging up and down. Another had

'Jack-in-the-Green'

his face smeared with paint to represent a clown, and a third, in striped cloth coat and trousers, with a huge collar and a blackened face, was beating a tambourine. But the one that really frightened me was a man got up as a woman, in a coloured, ill-fitting dress, a wig made of tow, and showing brawny arms above dirty white gloves. Brandishing a tattered parasol, he, or she, held it out to catch coins thrown by passers-by or from the houses. Fascinated, I watched their progress from behind the bushes. Then I made a bolt for home. But I had left it too late. As I emerged from the gate the man-woman spotted me and came prancing up, calling out, 'What have you got for Jack-in-th'-Green, little gentleman?' Petrified with fear, I ran

'I was up in a jiffy'

back into the garden, and made for the sloping tree we always climbed. I was up it in a jiffy, but the dreadful creature, grinning like a satyr, followed me into the garden and started to dance around, while the others clattered and banged and shouted encouragement from the gateway. I was fast losing my reason when a welcome face appeared at the area steps—it was Lizzie. She took in the situation at a glance and up she came. Her indignation was more for the state of my clothes than anything else, but the enemy gave way before her and, blowing kisses and still dancing, the troupe passed on. I must have been almost hysterical when I was taken in and washed, and I never could bear the sight of a man dressed as a woman after that.

I do not know if I was in a weak state, but not long after that I was taken ill. It was by no means a serious illness, but enough to upset the routine of the household.

One Sunday evening I did not feel well. Cyril and I had been playing in the Terrace garden during the afternoon—our usual game of making swords out of iris leaves and having fights with them—and Father and Mother and Ethel had gone out to supper. As it was Martha's evening out we boys went down and sat in the kitchen. Lizzie was stitching in her armchair, and Cyril was nursing Sambo. I felt drowsier and drowsier; such a headache came on and I began to feel very hot. I told Lizzie that I did not want my supper. This made her look up. 'Why, Master Ernest, how flushed you look!' she exclaimed. When I said I wanted to go to bed, she realized something was genuinely wrong. I was packed off to bed in the back room upstairs and given lemonade to drink. There I felt hotter and hotter and thirstier and thirstier and oh, how my head did ache! When Martha returned she came upstairs and sat beside me. She put her hand on my head and tried to make me comfortable. The blind was not drawn and I could see the three ladies on the house in Hanover

'She grew larger and larger'

Terrace, beyond the mews; made of plaster, they stood on the cornice in classical attitudes. My favourite, the plump one, with the garment which only partially concealed her charms, seemed much in evidence, and, as I watched, she grew larger and larger and, detaching herself from the pedestal, began to float about in the air. Meanwhile all sorts of funny things were going on in the mews below. A tram clanged along, the top crowded with people shouting and letting off fireworks. It rushed up and down, as on a switchback, over the chimney-pots, then down to the yard and up again. Meanwhile the plaster lady floated nearer and nearer, till she drifted right into the room and stood by my bed. She seemed to be speaking. 'Why, Ernest darling!' But it was Mother's voice, and there was Mother home from her party. Now at last I could feel safe.

I was able to tell her about my head and feeling so hot. She sat down by me and put her cool hand on my forehead. After a while she went to the door and called: 'Harry, I think you had better ask Mr White to come in the morning.' I was feeling too sick to protest. This was the Mr White who had the chemist's shop in Park Road; he dispensed and doctored; and, though his cough mixtures were harmless and palatable, he had a dreadful concoction called 'White's Cleansing Powders'. They were taken in a spoonful of strawberry jam, but the jam always seemed to go down and the powder to remain stuck in the mouth. I had impressions of Mother coming in during the night in her dressing-gown and giving me lemonade. In the morning my head was not so bad, but my skin felt hot and itchy, and I didn't want to eat anything.

Mr White duly came, and a faint odour of chemist's shop came with him. He sat down by the bed and felt my pulse, looked at my tongue and examined my chest, and then said I'd got something called 'Scarlatina' and I must be kept away from Ethel and Cyril.

Sheets, saturated with carbolic, were to be hung on the landing out-side, and only Mother was to be allowed to see me, and then . . . out came the cleansing powders. It was some consolation to have a thing with such a long name.

It must have been a trying time for Mother, though it passed pleasantly enough for me. I fear I was a peevish patient. She was kind and gentle, as she always was, and would read to me by the

'Out came the cleansing powders'

hour. There was a serial called *Dolly and the Boys* which was full of all sorts of adventures going on and on, but it was a nuisance having to wait for the next instalment. I missed my brother and sister very much. It was not long, however, before I was allowed to talk to them over the banisters, provided they didn't come too close.

In bed, by myself, I lay and listened to the gurglings of the cistern in the loft, and to all the strange attendant noises that accompany any form of water circulation. I had plenty of time for rumination. When tired of drawing, I would lie back and consider some of the experiences of my short life. There was, for instance, the time that we stayed at Eastbourne. I could only just remember this, but I know that there was a balcony outside a large window on the first floor. Of an afternoon my mother and two of the Aunts who were staying

'Talk to them over the banisters'

with us would sit and do their needlework in the sunshine, while my sister, aged about seven, sat beside them on a stool. Every day about the same time there came along the sea front a man selling cockles and winkles. He was a strange figure. Pushing his handbarrow and calling his wares, he would sing, or rather recite, in a loud tuneless voice the lines that he made up as he went along. There was something different for each house. Opposite our balcony he stopped and taking off his hat to the ladies, sang:

I see a flock of sheep,
In the midst a little lamb,
I wish my Mary Ann were here,
I wish my Mary Ann.

This chant became quite a household call with us but Aunt Emily would quote it on most inappropriate occasions.

I remembered very well my first introduction to sea-bathing. Father and Mother had been in for a dip and had taken Ethel with them. Cyril and I were handed over to

the tender mercies of the Bathing Woman. This formidable female was dressed in a serge bathing dress and a straw bonnet. She had red and brawny arms and her skin looked as if it were covered with

'I see a flock of sheep, In the midst a little lamb'

61

barnacles. As she spent most of her life in the water, this may even have been the case.

Her method was simple: the more difficult subjects, like my brother and myself, were tucked under her arms, where, our tender skins suffering acutely from contact with the rough serge, we were carried out to sea. The protesting body was then ducked, not once but several times, according to how the victim took it. The more he yelled, the more the duckings, until, nearly asphyxiated, he was reduced to silence. The torturer, meanwhile, in what was supposed to be a soothing voice, repeated, 'Dippy go under, dear!' with each immersion, though her final remark to me did not sound like that. It took a lot to reduce me to silence and I was handed back to my parents with the comment: 'Well, that's the last I want to see of '*im*!'

'Her method was simple'

One other thing that happened during our stay at Eastbourne caused a short-lived excitement. My father and a fisherman named Tyrrell, who often went fishing together, took a boat out for a day's sport. They had failed to notice the red flag hoisted on the Redoubt as a warning that the local Company of the Volunteer Artillery was to engage in some target practice. Sitting with their lines out, the fishermen were startled by the sounds of gunfire followed by the whizzing of projectiles over their heads or ricocheting on the sea to plunge finally below the surface. This lively activity went on for a time, the chief actors lying on the bottom boards of their boat, until someone must have noticed their situation and given the order to cease fire. My father and Tyrrell seized the opportunity to pull for home, to find on reaching the shore a crowd waiting. The rumour had gone round that the boat had been sunk. A rumour which, by good fortune, had not reached our lodgings.

It seemed a long time before I could go out, and when this was permitted Mr White said it must not be with the others; but I had at least the consolation of riding Septimus again. I was told not to scratch, but this was a difficult instruction to obey for my skin irritated and little scales would come off. Mr White said I would not be well until this stopped.

One day Father came and said that I was to go to the seaside for a week. This was grand news, and worth a lot of illness. It was better still when he said that mother and I could go all the way to Ramsgate by steamer. I nearly burst with joy when, our bags packed, we drove in a four-wheeler to the quay below London Bridge where the paddle steamer lay ready. She was crowded, for the trip was a special excursion to see the Fleet, which was lying, so the sailors said, at the mouth of the Thames. Everything was new and exciting, and I explored as much of the ship as I could, even clambering up on the paddle-boxes and having to be hauled back. There was a notice board by the man steering: 'Do not speak to the man at the wheel.' We went past Greenwich, and a man who seemed to know all about it pointed out the old fort at Tilbury. Great ships kept coming and going, and we saw strings of barges being towed along.

Many of the passengers had baskets of sandwiches, and there were lots of bottles of beer. When Mother and I got hungry, we went down below into a stuffy little saloon and had cold meat and pickles. The steward who served us said 'she was a steady boat', no doubt to reassure us, but as the sea was quite smooth nobody seemed to be sick. As the river widened out and the shores faded away in mist there was a general stir of excitement. Someone had seen masts ahead, and a sailor was pointing to where ships could dimly be seen. Everyone tried to crowd forward to get a first glimpse of the Fleet.

The sight, as we drew near, was an impressive one. The great ships were lying at anchor, guarding the mouth of the Thames. Square-rigged iron-clads, or flatiron turret ships, they lay, bristling

'Great ships lying at anchor'

with guns, with shining yellow funnels, white tops and black hulls. Our little paddle boat passed quite close to one great ship with *Northumberland* on her stern, and there were many knowledgeable men on board talking of the advantages of this or that, and saying 'Ah, yes, *Devastation*, no, *Thunderer*—must be *Inflexible*,' and no one to tell them whether they were right or wrong. I hung on to the rails at the stern, gazing, till the ships faded from view and I thought what a lot I should have to tell Cyril when I got home again.

It must have been late in the afternoon when we were put ashore at Ramsgate, and Mother and I, leaving our bags in charge of a porter, went in search of lodgings. There were many houses with

'Apartments' in the window. We chose one that looked promising but wasn't when we got inside; it smelt musty and the woman had a very red nose. So we tried another, which we liked better. The woman who answered the door was young and cheerful, though

'Took the dog and me out for walks'

talkative. She told us she had only been in the house six months. She promised to send down and get our bags from the porter when her brother came in. She had an old mother, and a little rough-haired dog, and her name was Miss Smyth. She proved to be kind and friendly and took the dog and me out for walks. Mother and I each had a bedroom, and there was a sitting-room with a balcony looking on the sea.

Down on the front we could walk along to the little harbour, and Miss Smyth, her dog and I would go along to the end, passing an old man who had a penny-a-look telescope on a stand. One day

'The sailors were very friendly'

Miss Smyth, who seemed to know everything that was going on, came in and told us there was a warship lying off the harbour. Greatly excited I was, and Mother took me down to the front and along to the telescope man, where I paid my penny and stood on a box and had a good look at the ship. The man said she was a torpedo-boat, and when I complained that she was very small, he said, 'So is a wasp but it can sting all right.' He reckoned she would be there several days, and I pestered Mother to let us go out in a boat, as many people were doing, to see the ship close up. She promised that, as Father was coming down in two days' time, we would do so when he came.

I watched that ship in fear and trembling lest she should up anchor and slip away, and when Father did come I gave him no peace till we were safely packed in a rowing boat and launched. It was disappointing to come up alongside such a small ship. By standing on the seat, held firmly by Mother, I could get my hands on the rail and pull myself up so that my eyes were level with the deck. The sailors were very friendly and one of them took the covers off a Nordenfelt gun and showed us all the barrels, and then pulled a torpedo out of its tube, shining like a great fish, but I don't think I believed him when he said it would blow up a big ship.

We had to go home the next day, but, before we left, my father took me down to the shops to buy a new hat, my sailor cap having fallen into the water in the excitement of seeing the torpedo-boat and, after being fished out with a boat-hook, was in rather poor condition. It took us a long time to choose one. The hats they showed us either did not fit or were all wrong. At last we fixed on one, and though I did not like it, it was not as bad as the rest. It was grey, with a peak. I was doubtful about the peak, but Father said it was all right. When we arrived home and showed it to Mother, she was horrified. 'Harry!' she said, 'whatever induced you to buy a thing like that? Why, it's like . . . someone in Struwwelpeter.' I hated it from that moment, and

'I was doubtful about the peak'

would never wear it in London. I did, however, put it on to greet Ethel and Cyril just to hear what they would say.

When we reached home it was comforting to find everything tidied up, though there was still a smell of carbolic upstairs. It was nice to be able to run freely around the house again. Ethel and Cyril were out for a walk with Martha and I was allowed to go and meet them. I guessed they would come from the Park through Hanover Gate, so I mounted guard close to the Keeper's Lodge, and presently they hove in sight. I stood at the corner and waited. They were quite close to me before they recognized me, and when they did they just gaped at my hat, and we all laughed about it.

I was back at school again next day, rather proud of my ailment. It was something to have had an illness with such a big name. All the girls seemed to be talking about the new frocks they were to have for the coming Jubilee, and one of them boasted that her parents were going to take her to see the procession. The weather was growing warmer and we were able to go and play cricket in the afternoons with some of the other boys, either at Paddington Recreation Ground or else in Regent's Park. The draw-back to the latter was that there were often a lot of other games going on at the same time, and if we did not watch our ball closely it got stolen.

One day some tickets for the Zoo were sent to us, I think by a Fellow, as they were valid for Sunday mornings when the Zoo was closed to the general public. Mother took Cyril and me, and as the Keeper allowed us to go behind the barrier, we were able to see some of the animals quite close. There were no elephant rides going on, but I did not mind that; on the one previous occasion when I had been treated to a ride, I had had to sit on the elephant's head, and as I was wearing only a pair of thin flannel knickerbockers, the creature's sharp hairs came through and my poor behind was tender for days.

On that occasion, too, a small girl who was sitting on the double seat behind dropped her doll's hat. She shouted to the keeper below, who was walking in front of the elephant. 'Sorry, Miss,' he replied, 'it's gone inside.' She burst into tears.

There was a tunnel in the middle of the Zoo grounds that was a grand place for playing trains. It gave an echo as one ran backwards and forwards. The elephant went along it on the way to his house and looked far too big to get inside, but he just seemed to fit. As he passed by he picked up with his trunk any bits of biscuit or paper lying about— all 'went inside' like the doll's hat.

There was a bear-pit with a stout post in the middle, up which the bear would climb and sit at the top, with his mouth

'Sorry, Miss . . . it's gone inside'

open, waiting for buns to be thrown in. But it was always time to go home long before I had seen all that I wanted to see.

One morning at half-term my father had to visit the City to see my uncle about something, and he took me. On the way we stopped at Father's office in Great Marlborough Street, where he

worked with another architect. I was glad to see the office. It had
interesting plans and photographs of buildings hanging on the walls.
A young man who was tracing things on a big board showed me a
pair of compasses and explained how to use them. I was so fascinated
by the instrument that my drawings for some time after that had
as many circles as I could get in, all drawn with a small pair of
compasses which Father found for me. We went on from the
office by Underground to a station near the Bank of England.

My uncle was a member of Lloyd's, which was then housed in
the Royal Exchange, and, as we walked through the city streets, I
was amazed to see that every man seemed to be in a hurry. Also that
there was hardly a woman to be seen in the throng. Lloyd's was
upstairs and was filled with the same hurrying crowd. Father gave
our names in the doorway and we found Uncle Robert sitting on
a stool and throwing pellets of blotting paper about. He was rather
deaf and had to bend down and put his hand to his ear when I tried
to speak to him. When he and Father had done their talking it was
time for dinner, and Father took me to a chop-house. The floor was
covered with clean sawdust, and we sat at a wooden table in a little
partitioned cubicle. I had a most delicious chop and felt rather grand
and grown-up.

When we arrived home Ethel was having her piano lesson in the
drawing-room. Her teacher was a friend of ours; we all called her
Jessie, which was also Mother's name, though Mother was named
Harriet as well. Ethel practised most diligently and would play her
pieces to visitors without turning a hair. When the lesson was over,
Jessie would often play for us, which we found a great treat. She
lived in a small room in Mornington Crescent and I think she must
have been very poor because she never seemed to go about at all
and Mother often asked her to have a meal with us.

It was while we were having tea that the subject of an outing was raised. We children had been reading about Hampton Court Palace, and were anxious to see it. Mother then had the bright idea of us all making a day of it and taking Jessie with us. So it was arranged, and on Saturday morning we sallied forth. I remember that it was a wet day. I was very much impressed by all that we saw.

Hampton Court Palace

The grand red-brick building with its imposing gateway, wide staircases and spacious grounds seemed a fitting place for a king to live in. Once inside we went through gallery after gallery of pictures and one room full of weapons hung in patterns on the wall. The older pictures pleased me most and I studied these carefully. There was one of the Field of the Cloth of Gold, with a horse prancing just like Septimus. There was also an Elizabethan subject with a procession of knights and men-at-arms, and Queen Elizabeth herself

71

in an elaborately jewelled dress at their head. This absorbed my attention for a long time.

We had a midday meal at a shop on the green opposite the palace, and then walked across to Bushey Park to see the avenue of chestnut trees, all in full bloom. I would gladly have gone back for another look at the pictures but we had to think about getting home.

The first thing I did when we were back was to rush upstairs and get out my copybook and all the pencil ends that I could find. I drew pictures of Elizabethan processions, knights, horses, halberdiers, kings, queens and all. One drawing still survives. It was found in the box of my drawings which father collected and which lay for many years among the debris in the loft.

'One drawing still survives'
This was drawn after my visit to Hampton Court

Chapter Four

JUBILEE

Hooray! Hooray! for Jubilation Day!
'Tis only once in fifty years, so people say,
We all got mixed, and had a jolly spree,
A' going with the missus to the Jubilee!

CYRIL and I picked up this refrain from the local tradesboys, and we sang it about the house. The third line ran 'We all got *tight* and had a jolly spree', but Martha, with her strict sense of propriety, objected, insisting upon a more respectable word, so we reluctantly agreed to substitute 'mixed'. I do not think that Mother and Father would have raised the same objections, but the Aunts had to be considered.

It was early summer, and London was getting all dressed up for the great event. Along Park Road flags were sprouting, and V.R. signs with fairy lights were being fixed up. In the window of Coles the linen drapers, the usual display of long lace curtains had given place to rolls of brightly coloured material and a riot of flags of all nations. Small Union Jacks were on sale at $4\frac{1}{2}d.$ each, complete with stick. Larger flags of many countries could be bought for 1s. $1\frac{1}{2}d.$ I had saved up two shillings and sevenpence, so I felt justified in investing in one of the larger kind. As Cyril and Ethel had each bought a Union Jack, I thought a change was called for. After due deliberation I chose one in red, yellow and black. I also bought, for $2\frac{1}{2}d.$, a piece of bright red ribbon to make a bow for Septimus. The shopman could not help me in identifying the nationality of my flag, but when I got my purchase home Father told me it was Belgian and asked why I had chosen it. He went on to suggest that it should be displayed in a less conspicuous position than the others. Rather crestfallen, I

'Cyril and Ethel had each bought a Union Jack'

carried it upstairs. The window of our bedroom seemed a fitting place, and with a piece of string I tied it to the window ledge. Waving proudly in the wind, it made a brave show from the room, but the effect was disappointing when seen from the Terrace below, where it was quite outshone by the Union Jacks fluttering from the lower windows.

We heard wonderful tales of the decorations being put up in the main streets. Martha had been to see them, and we were delighted when Mother said she would take us to Oxford Street to see them for ourselves. We went after luncheon, boarding an 'Atlas' bus at the corner of the Terrace. Cyril and I were allowed to clamber up the steep steps, helped by the conductor, and were then handed along by the passengers, who sat back to back on the long middle seat. There was no railing to prevent one from falling off, only a low board, so we clung tightly as we were handed forward. I was first, and in consequence secured a place on the box seat beside the driver, where a man made room for me and fixed the tarpaulin apron.

'The effect was disappointing'

It was fun sitting beside the driver. The horses seemed to know of their own accord when to stop, though there were no regular stopping places, the bus halting where anyone might choose. The conductor stood on a little step at the back, by the door. He gave the signal to start by slapping the side of the bus with the strap by which he held on. Directly the horses heard the strap, and the driver released the foot brake, they strained forward and broke into a slow trot. The buses were painted different

75

colours, green, red, blue, or yellow according to the route, and had names like old stage-coaches. The 'Atlas' which ran up to the 'Eyre Arms' from the West End was light green, and the express 'City Atlas' was dark green. The 'City Atlas' ran in the mornings and could be watched from the breakfast-room windows bucketing past

'It was fun sitting beside the driver'

Kent Terrace, drawn by three horses at a fine gallop; the top was always filled with top-hatted men with fluttering newspapers.

A woman was never seen on top of a bus, the climb up was too steep for the long skirts worn at the time, though a young friend of Mother's called Poppy once clambered up to the consternation and horror of the inside passengers.

Inside a bus it was always rather hot and stuffy. The seats had a hard velveteen covering which stuck to the clothes, and in cold weather there was straw on the floor. The windows were adorned with coloured advertisements pasted on: 'Lamplough's Pyretic Saline', 'Rowland's Macassar Oil', 'Monkey Brand Soap'. Still, it

'To the consternation and horror of the inside passengers'.

was fun riding on a bus; but if one *had* to travel inside, a four-wheeler was better, and a hansom—a very rare treat—best of all.

We enjoyed our ride to Oxford Circus. There seemed to be such a lot going on, such a bustle in the air. At Portman Square the bus turned along Wigmore Street because of the crush and eventually stopped near St George's Hall. Crowds of people were slowly moving along; workmen were putting up boards in front of the shops; there was a babel of voices and hammering. As we pushed our way forward, Mother told us to be sure and keep close to her.

The Circus was gay with colour and bunting. Garlands of paper flowers were going up and a triumphal archway was being erected

across the top of Regent Street. Supported on striped poles it bore a large notice:

'VICTORIA!'

'ALL NATIONS SALUTE YOU!'

in gold lettering, while down the street other notices hung from house to house as far as the eye could see, saying : 'EMPIRE', 'JUBILEE', and 'BRITISH ISLES'.

78

Many of the shops had stands built in front of them, the wood-work being covered with yellow-fringed red baize. Men on ladders were fixing large wire crowns and V.R. signs on which fairy lights could be hung. On one or two of the larger shops were great stars, to be lit by gas, with 'GOD SAVE THE QUEEN' or 'LONG MAY SHE REIGN' underneath.

It was very hot and the crowd made it more so. Judging by their clothes, many of the people were up from the country. Hawkers were doing a roaring trade in favours and flags. Presently there was some excitement towards Regent Street and the crowd began to move apart. A body of soldiers marched up and stopped at the Circus. Now, I knew a lot about soldiers, and was able to inform Mother that they were not in full uniform. It was very exciting. The soldiers stopped and formed line in the middle of the street, while an officer paced out distances. The man selling flags said they were rehearsing to line the way on *the* day. It got hotter and hotter and we were very glad when Mother said we would get some tea at Elphinstone's.

We sat down at a marble-topped table and Mother ordered—(oh joy!)—ices. Glass plates with good big dollops and wafer biscuits were brought and soon eaten. Replete and happy, though very tired, we went home and were sent to bed early.

Jubilee Day dawned grey and misty, but the flyman who came to fetch Father and Mother very early, said it was going to be a hot day. The parents were going to join the Dicksees in seats to see the procession, while we were going with Martha to Regent's Park to see the Parade of the Boys' Brigade and of school children.

Mother came downstairs looking lovely in a new dress; it was striped blue and white with lace at the neck and sleeves. She wore a tiny bonnet, gay with flowers, and white gloves. She also carried a

79

'Looking lovely in a new dress'

very small parasol with a hook over her arm. I had never seen her
look so beautiful. Father was very formal in frock coat and top hat,
but he had a flower in his buttonhole. They drove off and we waved
from the doorstep as they turned the corner of the Terrace.

At ten o'clock we children sallied forth with Martha. Lizzie, with
Sambo adorned with a pink bow in her arms, gave us strict injunc-
tions to mind the crowds and stick close to each other.

'The procession came in sight'

Out in Park Road people were already streaming through
Hanover Gate, making for the Park. The Keeper at the Lodge had
new gold braid on his hat and his buttons fairly shone. Martha was
rather agitated and kept repeating her warnings to keep close to her,
which was difficult. Along Hanover Terrace the crowd was very
thick, so Martha asked a policeman to help us across to the other side.
The policeman, who was a little stout and old, said he was a Reserve,
as all the regular police were down in the West End.

The crowds began to be swollen with lots of children and these were gradually guided to where the procession was to come, so Cyril and I found ourselves in the front row. There was a lot of pushing and surging back and forth, but we managed to keep our places.

Presently the procession came in sight, led by the band of the Boys' Brigade. The drum-major, wearing a sort of busby with a plume, was a wonderful sight. He had gauntlet gloves and a sash across his chest and flourished a staff, throwing it around like a juggler. Some of the bandsmen were very young, but all were blowing away lustily and I was filled with envy of the drummers, the big drummer particularly, for he had a leopard-skin that nearly reached the ground. What fun it would be, I thought, to have a big drum and bang it along the Terrace!

When the procession had passed, the crowd began to break up, drifting into the Park to sit on the grass and refresh themselves. It was so hot that we were glad to get back home and have some cool lemonade and then lie down. Father had promised to take us out in the evening to see the illuminations.

Before I lay down, I went to the top drawer in the yellow chest and took out my copybook, the one I always drew special things in, and, with the pencil Mother had given me from a dance programme, I tried to draw some of the events of the day. Somehow, nothing would come right, the pencil would not work, suck it as I might.

I was nearly asleep when I heard the sound of horses. It wasn't just cabs or buses. It was something much more exciting. Tumbling out of bed I ran to the window in time to see Her Majesty's Royal Horse Artillery, busbies, shell jackets, yellow braid and all, with an officer resplendent in his blue and gold uniform riding in front. Behind him, on a white horse, rode a very young trumpeter. Then

came the guns, rattling along. I had often seen the gunners exercising
their horses, but never, never had I seen them in all their glory. I
knew that they were on their way back to barracks in Ordnance
Road, for sometimes our
walks took us that way
and then I would linger in
front of the sentry, stiff and
smart with his carbine on
his arm.

Here was something
worth drawing, but still the
pencil would not work. I
had given it up as a bad job
when I heard the sound
of my parents coming in.
Mother came upstairs looking rather white. She said
she had a headache, and was
going to lie down, so I had
to keep all my questions
about the Queen and the
Procession till another time.
The house was very still
after the excitements of the

'I would linger in front of the sentry'

morning, but people could
be heard singing about the streets and there was a constant murmur
of distant noise.

We were told to keep quiet because of Mother's headache, so
after lying down as long as we could, Cyril and I crept down to our
playroom. Presently I heard the organ man and went to the window

of the dining-room to look out. He was an Italian and had his organ slung on his shoulder with a stick to support it. Sometimes he had a monkey, but not today. He would come slowly along the Terrace looking up at the windows, and if he saw us, would lean over the railings, holding out his greasy hat and calling on all his saints to bless us, which they would only do if we gave him some money. At intervals he would break into song:

> Viva la Français!
> Viva l'Italia!
> Viva Garibaldi!
> Victor Emmanuele!

He sang this now with gusto and a show of white teeth, but it was hardly suitable for Jubilee Day.

'Viva Garibaldi'

It seemed a long time after tea before it got dark enough and we were allowed to start lighting our illuminations. The fairy lights in coloured glass shades had to be fitted with night-lights and carried out to put along the balcony outside the drawing-room. I insisted on lighting one of these, and made a mess of it, scorching my fingers and dropping the taper inside the glass, where it sputtered. Then I had no better luck with the Chinese lantern, which I have since found is always difficult to light. This time I set fire to the paper, and the whole thing went flaming into the area below. Further attempts were then stopped by Father. When all the illuminations had been lit, we trooped down and out of the front door to see the effect. It was not so good as the house three doors away, but still it was very gay.

Cyril and I were jumping up and down in our eagerness to get started, but first we had to sit down and eat some sandwiches and drink a glass of milk. Mother came downstairs, her headache better, and, to my joy, she said she would come with us; so off we all went.

There was a glow in the sky, and Park Road, usually rather gloomy after dark, with only a few gas lamps, was now a blaze of light. People were out in the street or else gossiping by their front doors. Coles the linen drapers had a beautiful star sign in flickering gas with V.R. at each side. Most of the houses had fairy lights along the window sills. The little dressmaker's shop near Clarence Gate had rows of candles in the windows and Maltby the tailor was particularly

'Flaming into the area below'

grand. But it was only when the bus landed us near Oxford Circus that the full glory burst upon us.

Almost every shop had some sign lighted up with lamps or gas, and a number of people in the crowd were carrying lighted Chinese

lanterns. Men and women in little groups were dancing together
to the music of concertinas, and gangs of youths were making nuisances of themselves by parading in long caterpillars and pushing their
way, singing and shouting, through the throng. There was no traffic
in Oxford Street, which was just as well, for it could not have moved;

'Dancing together to the music of concertinas'

the whole roadway was packed with people pushing slowly along,
one way or the other, or coming to a stop in front of some particularly
showy display.

It wasn't long before I, with my little legs, felt quite stifled down
among the skirts of the crowd. I was lifted up on Father's shoulders,
where I could get a splendid view of everything, but, what with the

86

day's excitement and all, I began to feel very sleepy and to nod. Mother saw this and said, 'Harry, I think it is time we went home.' No voice was raised in protest, and we began to fight our way out of

'I think it is time we went home'

the press. It took a long time to get clear and longer still to find a four-wheeler. Once safely inside, Cyril and I promptly fell asleep, and I was carried up to bed with the sounds of London celebrating getting ever fainter in my ears.

Chapter Five

WHITELEY'S FIRE

SCHOOL was very tedious after all the excitements of the Jubilee; and the end of term, though four weeks away, seemed an eternity ahead. The streets remained untidy with coloured paper and litter of all sorts, and we were told to be careful and look where we were going, as there was broken glass lying about where fairy lights had tumbled from window sills.

The Aunts' house had boasted a very modest decoration. Indeed, the atmosphere of respectability about Gordon Square seemed to prohibit much display. A few discreet flags were all that was considered proper.

We children went to see them on a Sunday in July. We went from Baker Street to Gower Street by Underground, the stuffiest and most unpleasant stretch of line it was possible to imagine, especially at that time of the year. The trains—steamers!—were dirty and were drawn by engines with two quite small extra funnels, one on each side, in addition to the one at the front. I asked a porter what these were for, and he told me that in the worst ventilated parts of the tunnel the driver could cut off the smoke and divert it through the water tanks. These were carried on either side of the boiler like a saddle, and therefore the engines were called tank engines. I would watch the trains approaching to see if the smoke were coming in puffs from the two small funnels, but it did not seem to make any difference to the atmosphere. From Gower Street to

Baker Street it was almost unbearable. Along the pavements of Euston Road, and in the middle of the road as well, were gratings through which some of the smoke found its way out. Standing on a grating, it was all hot and choking, and women never stood on them because the draught blew their skirts up.

The trains had three classes of accommodation, first, second, and

'Stuffiest and most unpleasant'

third. Some of the third-class seats were just wooden boards, with low partitions between, over which it was fun to steeplechase if there were not many passengers. When the train started from a station there was always a porter at the front end whose job it was to shut the doors. He did this with great skill, 'BANG!' 'BANG!' 'BANG!' as the train gathered speed, and he had to turn the handles too! The guard, after showing his green light and blowing his whistle, would wait for his van, then step on it as it sped past and swing himself inside, all very neatly done. We did not go very often by Underground, it was much nicer by bus.

None of our Aunts saw the Jubilee Procession, but Aunt Fanny firmly went to see the illuminations. She did so in spite of Aunt Alicia's protests and warnings that if she were not crushed or set on fire she would most certainly have her pocket picked. She and Mary the maid had sallied forth together and, to judge by the description that Aunt Fanny gave us, they had a whale of a time. They went everywhere and saw everything, and, short of dancing in the street, seemed to have joined in all the gaiety. They did not get home till midnight.

During the afternoon we spent with them we were told of the Aunts' plans for the summer, which were to stay at Highgate. They always took their summer holidays within driving distance of London, as Aunt Annie, being an invalid, could not stand long journeys, and Aunt Alicia, my godmother, had an abiding horror of trains, and more especially of tunnels. So a residence had to be found which had ten bedrooms and could be reached by horse-drawn vehicles. This year it was the Vicarage at Highgate, a pleasant house with a big garden.

All preparations were made, and, at the appointed time, Father took us along to bid the Aunts good-bye and to see them safely off. A private bus with two horses was hired, and this duly arrived at 53 Gordon Square. There it was loaded up with boxes of linen and enough stores to feed an army. Also there was Aunt Annie's invalid couch and chair, Aunt Fanny's knitting machine, four maids, two cages of canaries, and, finally, two Aunts. Aunt Fanny, alert and confident, was in supreme command, giving sharp orders to the driver while he staggered in and out of the house with the heavy boxes. She carried a little notebook and checked off the various items as they were put on board. Her skirts were girded up with strange snap fasteners, showing a pair of very neat ankles and tiny feet. She had everything under control.

Aunt Emily, on the other hand, darted in and out of the house

'Aunt Fanny . . . in supreme command'

in a state of semi-bewilderment, to see that the canaries were being handled carefully. It seemed that she had appeared, hot and fussed, fully dressed for the journey, at breakfast, though the pilgrimage was timed for 2 o'clock. A closed fly had been ordered for the two remaining Aunts, and this arrived while the loading up was in progress. Aunt Annie, the invalid, was helped in and made comfortable with cushions, while Aunt Alicia, well wrapped up, settled alongside. Finally, Jane the parlourmaid and Mrs Low the nurse were packed in. Some controversy arose over the transport of George, Mrs Low's canary. This was eventually settled by Aunt Fanny, who as chief organizer was called in to adjudicate, and the cage, with George fluttering wildly, was wrested from his protesting mistress and placed with the others in the bus.

When we heard that the journey was safely accomplished, Father went to Highgate to see the Aunts. He told us that their bus had had some difficulty in negotiating the climb up Highgate Hill, and that the horses had had to be stopped at one point. It appears that the man beside the driver got down and put the drag behind the wheel to prevent, as he said, the bus from running backwards. To start again was not an easy matter, and, on Aunt Fanny's suggestion, the maids and two Aunts got out. Aunt Fanny, in travelling array, with skirts girded up, boldly started to push. At this, some bystanders joined in, and, encouraged by cheers and their combined efforts, the bus started again. The Aunts and maids were unceremoniously bundled in while the vehicle was moving. Aunt Emily, much out of breath, barked her shin on the step. This, and the rough manner in which she had been handled, put her in a bad temper, which was not improved when they arrived at the Vicarage to find the fly waiting in the drive with the other travellers. It had taken an easier route and so had arrived first.

The house was open, but the only person who appeared to be about was a gardener. He, however, was able to assist them to get Aunt Annie, faint and weary, inside and into an easy chair. With the arrival of the bus-load of luggage Aunt Fanny was able to introduce order, and tempers were further soothed when crockery was unpacked and tea provided.

Father brought us an invitation to go and spend a day there, and he arranged that this should be a week or so later. It was a Saturday. I wore a clean white sailor blouse with a new straw hat which was very stiff and uncomfortable because the elastic cut my chin.

We went by bus to the bottom of Highgate Hill. It was very hot waiting for the cable tram, and Mother took us across the road to a shop and bought us some lemonade. Cyril and I were very interested in the cable trams. They ran on lines, and we could see one coming down the hill while the other was going up. There must have been some sort of cable under the street that kept moving, up one side and down the other, and the tram had a thing that gripped it. When one tram came to a stop at the bottom we ran forward to investigate the underside, and I was only stopped from crawling below by an agonized cry from Mother, 'Ernest! Your clothes!' Once on board, we could sit either in the open-sided compartment, or, which was better, on top, but both were very jolty. Near the top of the hill we passed under an archway high above the road, which Father said carried water.

The Vicarage smelt very much the same as Gordon Square. After greeting our Aunts we were allowed to run out in the garden. This had distinct possibilities, though much of it was tidy, with a tennis lawn and round beds with red, yellow, and blue flowers in neat rows. However, there were certain more remote places among bushes and rather untidy rockeries where one could lurk without fear of interruption from Aunts or gardeners.

Some people had been invited for the afternoon to play tennis, but then it was discovered that there was no machine for marking out the court, because, the gardener explained, the vicar did not like whitewash on the lawn. However, Father, full of resource, suggested that if yards and yards of white tape could be provided, together with plenty of hairpins, he would be able to mark the court out. Cyril and I were able to help him do this, and the lines were stretched and pegged down with hairpins. This worked well, unless of course you caught your foot in the tape, as happened to the curate during the course of the afternoon.

'Gay in a blue spotted dress'

The visitors began to arrive about three o'clock, some of them carrying tennis racquets and shoes, and there was animation and chatter upon the lawn. Aunt Emily was gay in a blue spotted dress and a large straw hat; though rather stout, she was able and ready to enjoy the game; in fact it was her suggestion that lawn tennis, rather than croquet, should be played.

Among the guests was a boy who came with the people from next door. He was a quiet youth, very shy, and seemed rather lost among the crowd. Mother found him looking at the lines in a rather bewildered fashion, and he asked her what they were for. She explained the game to him, and then, noticing his black hair, and that he spoke with a foreign accent, asked him about himself. He was Chinese, he explained, and was staying with friends in England. Mother promptly rounded up Cyril and me and introduced us. Willie—for that was his name, at least it was that in English; in Chinese it was something much longer—was older than we were; he had long trousers, and his suit was made of some light silky-

'Watched him cut and shape some little frogs'

looking material. He spoke in a queer high-pitched voice, and sometimes had to stop and think of the right word, but all the same he was very friendly and told us stories about China. For myself, I could not believe that he was really Chinese because he had no pigtail, and I asked him about it. Very sadly he answered that it had been cut off and that he had mourned many days. When he talked about China he smiled, and his eyes seemed to disappear. He said that, though he liked being in England, he wanted to go back to his own country. We found a quiet spot behind the rockery and sat there while he talked to us. Presently he said he could make toys with paper, so I went indoors and fetched some and a pair of scissors, and we watched him cut and shape some little frogs. He had very delicate and deft hands, and it was fascinating to watch him cutting and folding the paper. The frogs, when finished and pressed on their backs, jumped most effectively. We were sorry when the time came for him to go. We would have liked to have seen him again, but we never did.

When the tea bell rang, the tennis players trooped indoors, mopping their brows and discussing the games. The curate received much sympathy about his fall, and there was a lot of concern over the green stain on his trouser leg. We boys had to 'make ourselves useful' at tea time, carrying things—cups of tea or plates of cakes to those who preferred to sit outside—so that we could not do full justice to the meal ourselves and were glad when we could get back to the rockery and play with the frogs.

It was quite late when the time came to go home. Dusk was falling and in the drawing-room the lamps had been lit. We said 'good-bye' to the Aunts and remembered to thank them nicely. It was hot and close, and there was a queer light in the sky.

As we came to the top of Highgate Hill a lot of people were gathered, talking and pointing down the hill towards London, where a great red fan of light showed above the houses. They said there was a big fire burning down there, and all were wondering where it was. Gripping Mother's hand, I had the terrifying thought that it might be our house, and it was not until we boarded the cable tram

'A great red fan of light showed above the houses'

and the driver told us it was Whiteley's shop in Westbourne Grove that my fears were partially allayed. Still, fires have a way of spreading, and one could never be sure. . . . People on the tram were all talking about it, and when we reached the bottom of the hill I almost forgot my fears when a fire engine went dashing by, brass helmets and all, with a fireman standing beside the driver shouting *'Clear the way—clear the way!'* The engine had three horses, one in front of the other pair, and Father said that the extra horse showed it must have come a long way.

We had to wait for a bus, and all the time the fierce glow seemed to get stronger. When a bus finally arrived it was quite dark.

The glow got stronger and stronger as we neared Camden Town. People were running about and shouting as if the fire were in

'Clear the way!'

the next street. I kept asking: 'Can't we go home quickly?' At last Mother turned to Father and said, 'Harry, do see if you can find a cab.' There was an empty four-wheeler standing outside a public house on the corner, so Father boldly entered the place and came out with the cabman, who, wiping his mouth, reluctantly agreed to drive us to Kent Terrace. We drove round the Park and the glow looked terribly close as we reached the top of Park Road. It was a great relief to come in sight of our house and to find that all was well, with Martha and Lizzie standing outside the front door and all the maids gossiping by the area steps. There was a distant sound of throbbing and roaring and a smell of burning in the air. Our own policeman was making his way slowly along the Terrace, being stopped and asked for news as he did so. When he came to us he said the fire had been burning for hours, that there were forty fire engines at work, and that people had been turned out of their houses owing to the heat and the fear of the fire spreading. He gave us a piece of charred wood he had picked up in Park Road.

'The smell of burning came in strongly'

It had been a long day and I was very sleepy, but I did not want to go to bed. I was packed off there, of course, but not to sleep. Cyril came up soon afterwards, and we lay watching the red flickering light through the crack in the side of the blind. Then we got out of bed and went to the window, which was wide open, and the smell of burning came in strongly on the night air. I confided my fears about fires spreading. Cyril pointed down the Terrace to where our policeman was still talking with the maids. Then only did I feel safe enough to go back to bed. But it was not till Mother came to tell us that she and Father had been out to see the fire, and had been quite near to it, and that it was a long, long way off, did I go to sleep.

It was some days before we boys were allowed to go to West-bourne Grove to see the scene of the conflagration. This was because the postman had told Martha that there was a danger of the walls falling. I kept worrying Mother until she said we might go, but not too near, and Martha was to keep us by her. Ethel agreed to come with us, but I fancy this was really because she, and Martha too, wanted to see the shops in Praed Street.

Before the Great Central Line and Marylebone Station were built, one could walk straight across from Kent Terrace, up Alpha Place, past Boscobel Place, and, crossing Lisson Grove and Edgware Road, come to Westbourne Grove. Having done this we found a barrier across the road, but by worming our way to the front we could see quite a lot. A salvage engine, the men wearing black leather helmets, was standing near. Further down was a real fire engine with some hoses stretching up and down the street. Someone said the fire was still smouldering down in the basement. The long front of the shop was a sorry sight, with part of the wall fallen and the rest blackened, with gaping windows, and charred wood and broken glass littering the roadway.

Some men were putting up a hoarding at the far end. We watched it all, and listened to the people in the crowd. One woman was telling how she and her children had been turned out in the night because they feared that the fire would spread across the street, and how the house fronts all down their road had been scorched and blistered and the windows broken with the heat. Then they talked of the firemen who had been injured, and of one poor fellow who had been killed when a beam fell and crushed his brass helmet.

'The long front of the shop was a sorry sight'

It was some time before we could be dragged away, and when we started for home we boys were sent on alone, Martha and Ethel making for Praed Street.

Off the Edgware Road we took a narrow street filled with barrows selling vegetables and fruit, rabbits and fish. It was thronged with shoppers. At the far end, before turning into Lisson Grove, we saw, up a side street, a crowd gathering and people running. It was not a wise thing to do, but we went to investigate.

'Threw herself on the policeman'

As we came near we saw a policeman struggling with a man. The policeman was not a big man, but he seemed to be very strong. Even so he was not able to hold the other fellow, who was far bigger than he. The man had a red choker handkerchief round his neck, and the policeman managed to get hold of this and twist it. This made the man lash out with his fists, and shout, 'Yer chokin' me!' Just then a woman began to scream, and the crowd parted, as she ran in and threw herself on the policeman. She kept crying out: 'They shan't take you! They shan't take you! Bill, don't let them take you!'

The crowd surged backwards and forwards and Cyril and I were forced against some wooden palings, where we stood, both very frightened but fascinated. There was a young woman farther down the street with a baby in her arms. She kept moaning and sobbing, and between her sobs she repeated, ''E 'asn't done nothing,' and ''E's been a good man to me.'

Nobody tried to help the policeman. His helmet had fallen off, and he and the man were now struggling on the ground. Both had blood on their faces. The officer wrenched his hand free for a moment and fumbled for his whistle. He had hardly got it to his mouth when the man hit him in the face. It was a cruel blow, for it crushed the whistle against his mouth. Nevertheless he blew it loudly before he had to give up as his mouth was all disfigured. With my back against the palings, I felt I was going to be sick; my hands and feet were quite cold, and I saw that Cyril's face was very white. Then, suddenly, the crowd began to melt away, for, running towards them, was an-

'Felt I was going to be sick'

other police-man. The woman tried to put herself in his way, but he brushed her aside and, as he came up, I saw him draw his truncheon from his hip. Neither Cyril nor I could look. We were close to the scene, but, frozen with terror and unable to run, we dared not turn and see what happened. We only knew that, soon after, the new policeman had the man by the choker and was dragging him up. The man kept struggling and shouting oaths and abuse, but they got him to his feet. It was a funny thing, but directly the other constable appeared, those of the crowd who had re-mained seemed to be on the side of law

'Uttering in a strident voice'

and order. They went so far as to staunch the wounds of the damaged policeman and retrieve his helmet. Then the man was led off in a rather dazed condition, and the street began to settle down. But small groups formed around the door of a house at the lower end, where a woman was uttering in a strident voice a stream of unfavourable generalizations about the police force as a whole.

My impression of the fire, drawn at the age of seven

Cyril was leaning his head against the palings. I said: 'Are you all right? Do let's go home.'

It was some minutes before we moved, and we had to go the length of the street. Immediately we had turned the corner we began to run. By the time our breath had given out we were across Lisson Grove and almost within sight of home. I asked Cyril: 'Did the policeman hit him with his truncheon?'

'I don't know. I shut my eyes.'

'So did I, but he *can't* have hit him very hard.'

Then: 'Do you think the policeman will die?'

Cyril said 'No' in a rather uncertain voice. All the same, it was a difficult thing to answer.

As we turned the corner into Park Road, we saw, to our joy, our own policeman standing at the corner by the pillar box. We rushed up to him and poured forth a torrent of words, each trying to describe the fight. He listened to us patiently, and then said, 'Now, don't you young gentlemen go and poke your noses into things of that sort. Quite likely you'd get into trouble—serious trouble.'

Which, on the whole, was sound advice.

Chapter Six

POLLARD'S FARM

THE summer holidays were well advanced when we were told we were going with Father and Mother to stay at a farm-house in Kent. We had been to the seaside several times, but had never been to the real country before, and Cyril and I were very excited at the prospect. I asked innumerable questions. The farm was called Pollard's.

'Mother, what is it like? Do they have cows?'

'Yes, darling, I expect there will be lots of cows, and we shall get nice fresh farmhouse butter.'

'But, Mother, the Dorset butter we have at home is salt and I don't like it.'

'Well, I'm sure the butter will be nice, and you'll have eggs all new laid, and perhaps home-made bread.'

'Ooh!' was all I could say to that. Then—'Mother, do they have rabbits as well as cocks and hens?'

'I expect so, and pigs as well, and they say there are hop fields, and if we stay long enough we can see them picking the hops. It is great fun; all the families in the neighbourhood come, children and all, and pick away all day. When Uncle Henry was Rector of Chid-dingstone I stayed with them and we all went picking, and I remember how sore it made my fingers.'

It was afternoon when we climbed into the train at Charing Cross. Cyril and I always enjoyed a railway journey, though it was a pity we were not allowed to lean out of the windows. After stopping at a number of stations, we began to leave behind the little houses and chimneys of the outskirts of London and the afternoon sun shone on fields and lanes. Before we reached our destination Father pointed out some hop fields. The hops were trained up poles, and Father explained how the poles were laid across canvas bags for the picking.

'Spread a tarpaulin cape over our shoulders'

Pollard's Farm was several miles from the station, and the porter who handled our luggage told us that the farm wagonette was waiting for us. There, sure enough, it was, with a youth, whom the porter called Charlie, standing by the horse's head. The luggage was piled on, and off we started. It had begun to rain a little, so Cyril and I, sitting on the box-seat, spread a tarpaulin cape over our shoulders.

As we went along, Charlie told us about the farm. He told us of a new litter of pigs, for one thing, and how Mrs Pollard had won a prize for bread at the village Show. It was all very new and exciting, especially when we came in sight of some queer-shaped, pointed roofs. 'They be oast houses,' Charlie told us, pointing with his whip, 'where they dry and pocket the hops. Like enough you'll see them doin' it—that is, if you're here at the right time.'

The road was getting muddy and the horse splashed in the puddles as we trotted along. Soon we turned into a narrow lane and saw ahead of us a red-tiled farmhouse. 'Pollard's,' said Charlie. At the end of the lane we passed through an open gate, and drove round to the back of the square-fronted farmhouse, pulling up in a spacious yard. A black-and-white rough-haired dog came out of his kennel with much rattling of his chain, and stood barking and waving his tail.

The farmhouse door was opened and a woman came out. She was very stout, with a cheerful red face. She greeted us in a friendly way, but when Father and Mother shook hands with her she was rather flustered. Wiping her hands on her apron first, she said ''Tis the flour, with me baking buns for the young people.' Cyril and I exchanged a quick look. 'Buns!'

We went in through a great kitchen where a small maid was trying to hide behind an enormous deal table. She bobbed a curtsey, and stood looking at us with her mouth open. Charlie carried in our luggage, and Cyril and I were sent upstairs to wash.

There was no bathroom, but washstands with white china jugs and basins were in the bedrooms, which were pervaded by a faint smell of camphor. We boys had a large room, the floor of which sloped, so that we felt we were going downhill when we went to the window. This had white dimity curtains. The bed, which we were to share, was very large and very soft to bounce on; there was a feather mattress in which we could feel the spikes of the feathers, when we pressed it, but it proved rather hot to sleep in. Below the window was a small, neat garden, and by looking sideways we could

'Wiping her hands on her apron'

see into the farmyard with its tiled roofs, and beyond could glimpse a wooden barn and some haystacks.

It did not take us long to wash and we ran along to have a look at Ethel's room. It was gayer than ours, with a spotted pink wallpaper and bright curtains, but was very small and grown-ups had to duck their heads under the doorway.

Lovely smells were now coming up from below as of sizzling bacon and eggs, and we clattered downstairs to the parlour, which was not often used but was now brushed up for the occasion. We were greeted by a delectable sight. The round table fairly groaned under the weight of good things. Plates loaded with buns, pots of

"'Tis home-cured'

jam, a dish of yellow butter and a large plum cake. Then there was a great round loaf, and plates of biscuits and cheese, and bottles of pickles, and in fact everything you could think of. A great brown teapot was standing on a side table. Our eyes were goggling at it all when Mrs Pollard came in with a dish full of bacon and eggs. She said, proudly, "'Tis home-cured, and I hope it will be enough.' Even Father's eyes sparkled and we boys hardly knew where to begin.

When the feast came to an end, and we had stuffed till we could stuff no more, Cyril and I lay back in our chairs. We had planned to explore the farm, but, overcome by drowsiness, decided to let that wait till tomorrow; anyhow it was growing dark. A lamp was brought in. Outside, the rain had stopped and there were distant farmyard sounds. It was all very peaceful. As I sat there a large moth flew in at the window and began to flutter round and round the lamp. I grew sleepier and sleepier. Father was reading the newspaper, and he looked up and said, 'Those boys ought to be in bed.' As this was exactly what I had been thinking, we went upstairs to our feather-bed without a murmur, and only Mother's reminder saved us from going to sleep without cleaning our teeth or saying our prayers.

When I woke up in the morning I could not for the life of me remember where I was. Strange, dark, oak beams across the ceiling, and whitewashed walls and, hanging over the washstand, an illuminated text in bright red and blue letters with convolvulus twirling round the words 'The Lord shall preserve thee and keep thee'. The dimity curtains were drawn, but it was light enough to see everything. I was sunk deep in the feather-bed, so that I could only see a bit of Cyril's shape alongside. It was fortunate that the bed was a big one, for he was apt to thresh about in the night. I pushed up my head and could see that he was still asleep.

By this time I had taken it all in, and could hear the farmyard noises outside; so I climbed out of bed and made the downhill journey to the window and pulled back the curtains, which were on large wooden rings. The clatter of these woke Cyril up, but he only said 'What?' and went to sleep again. The window was as high as my chin, so I got a chair, climbed on it and pushed open the casement. Last night's rain had made the ground smell nice, and a bright morning sun was shining. The garden plot below had a lavender hedge, and a brick path led round to the back of the house. Leaning out as far as I could, I saw that the farmyard was rapidly coming to life. Obviously now was the time to go and see what it was all about. So I woke Cyril, still very sleepy and protesting, and we struggled into our clothes.

It was very early, and before we ventured downstairs we stood listening intently on the landing. Nobody seemed to be stirring. We went downstairs to the square hall, where there were pegs on the wall with coats and hats hanging on them, and a gun standing in the corner. A big door promised a way out, but it had a heavy lock and the key would not turn, so we decided to try another way. There was another door, and this we pushed open. It led down two steps into the kitchen, which looked larger than ever in the morning sunshine. There were a lot of things we had not noticed the previous evening. There were hooks on the oak beams, and a kitchen range

'Pushed open the casement'

with gleaming brass knobs set in a chimney recess. A lavender-coloured frill hung on the mantel, which was quite high up, and above it was a wooden rack with a gun. There was an exciting square clock on the wall with a great round face and a picture of a volcano erupting in the centre. It ticked away loudly, and I asked Cyril to tell me the time, not being good at telling the time myself. It was five minutes past six.

There were pots of geraniums on the high window sill, with a tortoiseshell cat curled up between them where the sun made a splash. Cyril went across and stroked it—he was always fond of cats—and it got up, stretched itself, arched its back and purred. The clock ticked on slowly, and there was a faint buzzing of bees. It seemed as if nothing wanted to wake up.

'Tortoiseshell cat curled up'

The door into the yard was open and we went out. Beside the door were two brightly polished milk cans set upside down on posts. Across the yard we heard a man's voice. We crossed over to a gateway, from where we could see the cowshed.

'Do you think they'd mind if we went in?'

'Come on, I'm sure it's all right.'

A roofed archway gave a glimpse of haystacks beyond and the sounds came from an open door. A man's voice kept saying 'Coom oop!' 'Coom oop!' and there was a swishing sound. Then out came Charlie. He was carrying two milk pails with a wooden yoke on his shoulders. He saw us and grinned, 'You'm oop early,' he said. 'Do 'e want to see the milkin'?' To our eager 'Yes!' he replied, 'Coom across then, but don't 'e go inside.'

We stood in the doorway, and saw that the cows were standing in rows inside, while an old man in a greasy felt hat, which was pressed against the flank of a cow, was sitting on a three-legged stool with a bright pail between his knees. He took no notice of us, but

made queer grunts and noises which the cows seemed to understand.
The sound of the milk in the pail was strange and rather soothing.

'Do you think they'd mind if we went in?'

I asked Cyril if he thought we could have some milk as I was feeling very empty. 'Do you think, if we went back to the house, Mrs Pollard would give us some?' Cyril agreed it might be worth trying, so we crossed the yard again. The farmer's wife was by the door and saw us coming. 'Lor' bless 'e, 'tis early 'e are, and breakfast not for another hour! Come along in and have a bite of somethin'—but see and tidy yer boots!' she added, pointing to a broom scraper beside the door.

Our boots being satisfactorily tidied, we clattered in. 'Now sit 'e down,' said Mrs Pollard. We clambered on to chairs by the vast kitchen table and watched with eager eyes while she fetched a jug of milk and two cups. Then out came one of the round loaves, and large slices of bread and butter were cut. We both remembered to say 'Thank you!' before our mouths were full, and while we munched away I thought what a wonderful place a farm was.

'I reckon you don't get such fare in Lunnon,' said Mrs Pollard.

'It's much better than porridge,' was all that I could think of in reply. 'And I like bacon and eggs and sausages, too.'

She laughed heartily at this. 'Well, there won't be no stint o' them here,' she said, 'but mind 'e don't go spoiling your breakfast.'

'What is there for breakfast?' I was saying, when Cyril kicked me under the table.

It was close on eight o'clock when Mother came down and found us in the front garden. We had already been across the yard and made friends with the black-and-white dog whose name was Chance. He stood up and put his paws on our shoulders and never stopped wagging his tail. Now we were grubbing in the soil to make a grotto with some stones and our hands were filthy, so we were sent upstairs to clean ourselves before being allowed to sit down to breakfast. It *was* eggs and bacon, *and* fried bread, and Mrs Pollard gave us a broad grin as she brought the dish in.

Ethel joined us boys after the meal, and we went exploring all

'We both remembered to say "Thank you"'

round the farm. We soon found that no one seemed to mind where we went. The cowman, who was also the pig man, warned us to keep away from the palings round the sty, for the old sow was not

too good-tempered and had been known to
bite. There was a black hen in the yard with
one foot missing. It had been bitten off by the
sow, so the pig man said. The hen got about
quite nimbly on one leg, but we were much concerned for her and made a special bed of straw
in a corner by the barn, but she scorned this,
preferring to roost with her fellows. Later on
she became much attached to me, and would
follow us indoors and even try to mount the
stairs. Unknown to Father and Mother, I carried her upstairs and she spent several nights in
our bedroom; until one evening, going up after
we were asleep, Mother discovered her com-
fortably tucked up in bed between us. And that was the end of that.

'I carried her upstairs'

'Tucked up in bed between us'

There was much to do on fine days, and when it was raining we climbed the ladder in the barn. We had discovered that there was a little door by the hay-loft, which gave access to the place above the archway. It was very small, but if we kept low and minded the cob-webs, it made a wonderful hiding place. By peering through the cracks in the floor, we could look down on anyone passing below and we felt we were in a castle. Altogether most romantic!

Ethel had too much respect for her clothes to venture up there, but she would join us on the straw of the loft and tell us stories. I say 'stories' but it was really one story that went on and on, from holiday to holiday, winter and summer, and could be embellished and ornamented with all sorts of ideas and suggestions. Ethel was a great reader and seemed to have an endless fund of knowledge. We all became kings and queens in her story, and our friends were suitably rewarded with titles. I made a point of trying to draw everything, and would illustrate some of the more exciting passages; especially when, bowing to popular demand, Ethel allowed our combined armies to be described on their return from battle in triumph, after a shattering defeat of the common enemy, all drawn in detail. I always had several odds and ends of paper stuffed inside my sailor tunic, and these were filled with drawings. I used a pencil because that was easier to carry about, and though the point got broken pretty often, it could be sharpened, if Father were handy, with a knife; failing that, it could be bitten with the teeth till the lead showed, though the resulting point was not a very good one.

The cowman's name was Ned. He told us that he had worked for Mr Pollard's father, and that the farm had belonged to the Pollard family for ages and ages; there was no knowing how long they *had* owned it. He told us that his old Dad used to work near by, and remembered before the railway came, when all had to travel by wagon. The workers were paid very little money but were given their milk and bread and wood for firing, and when pigs were killed they had their share of the pork, which was salted and kept the year round in a barrel.

'Join us on the straw of the loft and tell us stories'

Charlie was a never-failing source of information. He told us all about the beasts and birds and seasons, and where we could go, and where we couldn't. Then there were the haystack men, who generally seemed to be on top of something. One of them (another Charlie, which was confusing, but he had red hair to make things easier) talked all the time and cracked jokes at the others.

The village was half a mile away from the farm. There was one shop which seemed to sell everything one could possibly want. It had jars of sweets on shelves, pails and brushes, saucepans, fly-papers and mousetraps hanging from beams. By the door-posts were strong hob-nailed boots and coconut matting. A display of millinery at the back included some brightly coloured country bonnets. But the fireworks left over from last year were damp and wouldn't go off.

'She chose a pink one'

One morning we went there in the wagonette with Mother, and Ethel was allowed to choose a country bonnet. She chose a pink one and tied it on with the strings under her chin. Both Cyril and I agreed that it was an improvement on the rather floppy straw thing that she usually wore. We were looking, rather wistfully, at the glass jars of sweets when the shopwoman told us that the big bull's eyes were made by an old man who lived in the village. He had a tiny cottage up the lane, and made all kinds of sweets. This was exciting news, and we begged Mother to take us there. So off we went up the lane, and came to a little cottage with a tidy garden in front. There was no other cottage in sight, so this must be it. The door was open and Mother looked in. She said, 'Good morning.' An old man appeared in his shirtsleeves. He had curly white hair and a beard. Mother said 'Good morning' again, and then 'I hear you make sweets, Mr Er—Er——'

'Bin makin' them for over twenty year, ever since the old lady died, but it ain't so easy to get the things as it war.'

'May the children see you making them?' Mother asked.

The old man considered this, and then said slowly, 'Coom along o' Monday afternoon I'll be makin',' he went on, 'an' maybe I can show 'em how 'tis done.'

'Oh, thank you very much, Mr Er—Er.' So it was arranged, and we went off in high glee, and called him Mr Er—Er— for ever afterwards.

On Sunday morning Mother took us to church. The congregation included a lot of people from the village in their best clothes, the women in tight shiny black bodices and straw bonnets or hats, and some of the older men, Mr Er—Er— among them, in clean white smocks. Mr Er—Er—'s outfit was completed by a rusty top hat. There was a mixed choir, but not in surplices, and the singing was led by a clerk with a strident voice which rather drowned the organ, but as the latter was a bit wheezy it didn't much matter.

The rest of Sunday was rather dull. No one seemed to be around. The cows came drowsing in to be milked, the bees droned, and it was all very sleepy. Cyril and I wandered about the farm. We leant over the half-door of the stables, where the big horses were, and I watched the flies go in and out and worry the poor beasts. I thought they would have been happier in the fields, where they could stand

'In their best clothes'

end to end and swish each other with their tails, as I had seen them doing. We longed for Monday.

When it came, Father had to go to London, so the wagonette was got out to take him to the station, and it dropped us children at the corner of the lane. Old Mr Er—Er— was at work in his cottage, surrounded by pots and pans. Something was boiling on the fire and there was a smell of hot sugar. He had a lump of sticky stuff which he was kneading. 'Sit 'e down and watch,' he said, 'whilst I does the pullin'.' There was a bright iron hook fixed to the rafters, and he stretched the sweet stuff over it and then pulled and pulled. Over and over again he pulled and turned and folded it and then pulled again, till it began to grow bright and shiny. Then he turned and wound it with a thin brown ribbon of sweet, cutting it into short lengths with scissors over a tin box. He gave us a sly glance. 'Ever 'eared o' bull's eyes?' he said. 'I reckon they're bigger nor you get in Lunnon.' He handed

'Sit 'e down and watch'

us each one. They were quite hot and filled our mouths. He showed us bottles and cans with other sweets. Mother had given us some money, so we were able to choose quite a lot for one shilling and ninepence. Before we left he took us into his garden and showed us some of the sweet herbs that he used to flavour his sweets. We had a lot to tell Mother when we got back to the farm.

The following day, when Father came back from London, he told us that someone who went to our school had mumps and that we could not go back to school for a fortnight or more. We could therefore stay on at the farm. This joyous news meant that we should be able to see the hop-picking, which would begin in a day or two, the gipsies having already begun to arrive; their carts had been seen on the roads.

The gipsies camped in a corner of the field. The camp was very untidy, with a bad-tempered, growly dog, and we were told not to go there; but it was difficult to resist, for the gipsies were very friendly. One woman offered to tell my fortune, but I hadn't got a silver sixpence, so I never knew what my fortune was to be. The hop field was close to the farm. *Too* close to the orchard, said Mrs Pollard, and we wondered why, till one day, early in the morning, we heard a rumpus and were told that 'they folk were stealing the apples'.

When picking began we went to the field with Mother and Edith, the little maid, who wasn't a bit shy when she got out of doors. Her young brother joined us, but he was very disobedient and rather a nuisance. How different the field looked now! It was crowded with pickers sitting round the long canvas troughs, whilst the men pulled down the poles and laid them handy. Whole family parties were at work, with their dinners packed in baskets or tied up in handkerchiefs. The gipsy folk kept aloof in their picking and did not mingle with the others. We were told that all were paid according to the amount they picked, so it was an advantage to have a large family. At intervals a man would come along and empty the canvas troughs, keeping a tally in a book, and at the end of the day the farmer who owned the field paid for the day's work. He grinned when he came to us, and gave each of us a shilling. It was wonderful to have so much money, and I couldn't decide whether to spend it on the sweet man, or marry Vera Beringer, which I had wanted to do ever since I had been taken to see her act *Little Lord Fauntleroy*. It was the first money I had really earned, and it was to be a long time before I earned any more. Mother had been right about hop picking making our fingers sore, and the smell made our eyes water as well.

We went to the farm for our dinner, but returned to the field

'Followed the cart out of the gate'

afterwards, and picked till we could pick no more. When the canvas bags were full they were piled on a cart and driven to the oast house. Charlie was driving the cart in the afternoon, and asked us if we would like to go with him to the oast house. So we followed the cart out of the gate, all three of us, and raced up the road. Running as hard as we were able we could not keep up with Charlie. Cyril, very hot and breathless, came second, I followed (explaining loudly that my brother was two years older than I). Ethel was a long way behind, although she was the eldest, because she kept stopping to pull up her stockings.

The man at the oast house said he was too busy to answer all our questions, but that if we came another day he would show us how

'Dan lowered himself in'

the hops were dried and packed. The inside of the oast house looked very interesting, and Cyril and I were impatient till the day came and we were allowed to go off in the morning. We ran all the way. The oast house was a round building with a pointed roof and ladders leading to the top. It was divided into floors. The hops were dried by being spread on a sort of wire frame. A man with a wooden rake kept turning them over and over. Down below some small fires were burning with a blue flame; these were fed with yellow stuff which the man, on being questioned, said was sulphur. It made my throat tingle. Presently, when the hops were dry enough, they were gathered up and taken to another floor. This had a round hole in the middle, with a great long sack fixed in it. 'We calls that the pocket,' said the man. 'An' you watch how we presses 'em. Dan!' he called, 'are 'e ready?' Dan had a very old felt hat with a wide brim, which he turned down so that you could only see the lower part of his face. Then they tipped some hops into the long sack, and Dan lowered

'To see things from below'

himself in after them, slowly disappearing, until only the top of his hat could be seen. ''E does the treadin',' explained the man, and Dan began to tread, working round and round, while more hops were poured in over his head.

Gradually Dan began to reappear, very unkempt and dusty: first his hat, then his shoulders; as more hops were poured in he rose higher and higher. Cyril and I kept climbing down the ladder to see things from below. The sack shook and vibrated as Dan trod. It hung from the ceiling like a big cocoon. At last it was full, and Dan stepped out and shook himself. He was covered with bits of hop, but he didn't seem to mind. 'Bin' doin' it for twenty-five year,' said the man. 'Twenty-nine, come next pickin',' corrected Dan. When the pocket was full it was sewn up with a carpet needle. Then it was lifted off by a pulley, and was ready to go away to be made into beer.

We were covered with dust, and thoroughly grimy when we got back to the farm for dinner, and our throats tingled for days.

It was only a few days later that Father returned from London and reported that the mumps were over and that we must go home. I felt very sad at leaving the farm. I wandered round saying good-bye to the horses, and the little pigs, to Charlie and to Chance, and to the little lame hen. In the kitchen we all drank dandelion wine, and Mr Pollard was quite jovial. He was a silent man, as a general rule, whom we had hitherto seen only at a distance. We thanked Mrs Pollard, who asked us to come again, and said, if we liked, she could supply us with fresh eggs from the farm. Edith, behind the kitchen table, quite forgot to curtsey; she ran to the gate and stood there, a forlorn little figure, in tears, as the wagonette took us to the station.

On the whole it was nice to be back home again. Martha, all smiles, opened the front door. The fire was burning in the dining-room, and Lizzie had prepared a very particular tea with crumpets. Sambo joined us, purring and fussing round us all. Father and Mother had a lot of letters to read, and we children sat back feeling very comfortable and content. The trees outside were beginning to turn, and the old messenger man was sweeping up the leaves. Presently the lamplighter, with his staff, came along the Terrace, and one by one the lamps were lit. It really *was* rather nice to be home once more.

Chapter Seven

BELOW STAIRS

O<small>UR</small> kitchen was a comfortable place, especially on chill autumn afternoons. A large range occupied one end, with a coal fire burning cheerfully. There was a square deal table with Sambo's milk saucer beneath, and four or five windsor chairs grouped round it. On special occasions we children had tea in the kitchen with Lizzie and Martha. As we sat at the table, which was covered with a white cloth, we could look up and see outside the window the bottom of the area railings and the legs of the passers-by. When it was dark, the kitchen was lit by a gas bracket over the table.

'Always wore black kid gloves'

Every Thursday Lizzie's sisters, Esther and Mary Ann, came to tea. They both had fringes and wore black dresses, Esther's being the grander, with shiny black bugles down the front. She always wore black kid gloves, which made it awkward when eating hot buttered toast. When tea was over and the things cleared away, the black kid gloves would be carefully wiped.

Then would follow some family gossip between the sisters. Mary Ann had a piece of embroidery which seemed never-ending. She kept it in a duster, which she would spread on her knees. Once she showed us boys how to thread a needle without getting the cotton all black. She always bit off the ends of cotton on her stitchery, and this caused strong protests from Martha, who warned her of the fate which overtook a woman of whom her own mother had heard, who as a result of indulging in this practice, died suddenly in agonies. Post mortem examination showed that the ends of cotton had got wound round her heart and strangled her!

'The large tin roaster'

Now came the time for the fire to be made up in preparation for 'late dinner' upstairs. If it were to be a roast joint, the large tin roaster would be brought in from the scullery. This was a round tin box, standing on legs, with an open front, and a door at the back through which you could peep to see how the meat was roasting. There was a wind-up thing at the top which turned slowly round, with the joint on a hook. When loaded, it was pushed close to the front of the open kitchen range, and soon the fat began to sizzle and drip into the pan below, and smell good.

On the whole there was little conversation, except when Martha was there, and what with the tea and hot toast and all I was apt to get sleepy. But Martha did brighten things up, especially since she had been 'walking-out' with her 'young man', as she called him. She had known him for a long time, but, as he lived far away in the west of England, she only saw him when she went on holiday. That summer, when she returned, she told Mother, in some confusion, that they were engaged. She was so shy that all Mother could get out of her was: 'He is a very nice man. He is a guard on the line.'

This was of course great news for Cyril and me, for a guard ranked high with us, next after a soldier or a fireman, and we were very anxious to meet him. We could not understand why Martha

'A grand exhibition of how the points worked'

called him her 'Young Man', for in the photos she showed us he had a beard and did not look young. She told us that, when she got married, they were going to live near her mother's home in Gloucestershire. She also said that her 'intended' was going to receive a rise and work on the passenger trains. Thus he would be able to get a pass to London, and in fact was coming to see her soon. So it was arranged that he should be invited to tea.

He duly arrived, very shy, with Martha shyer still, and blushing a lot. But, alas! he was not in uniform. This might have spoilt the whole afternoon; but, after tea, when shyness had worn off, he was persuaded to talk about trains. He explained endless technical matters to do with signals and points and engines, and then gave a grand exhibition of how the points worked by emptying his match box on to the table and laying the matches out like lines. He asked Martha if he could smoke a pipe. 'Would the Missus mind if he did?' On being reassured, he lit up—a highly interesting and novel process for us, for neither Father nor any of our uncles smoked.

Altogether it was a most successful afternoon, hallowed by a vague hint that it might be possible to get the young gentlemen a ride on an engine if they came down West.

'Sitting in her easy chair'

Cyril and I liked to go down to the kitchen of an afternoon, when our parents were out and Martha had taken Ethel to her music lesson or to a rehearsal of the Toy Symphony, which was to be performed later at the Lloyds', along the Terrace. Lizzie would be sitting in her easy chair, and would tell us how she came to be Mother's nurse when she herself was only seventeen and Grandma no more than twenty-two. Grandma had married an artist named William Lee when she was sixteen. He was a water-colour painter, and much older than she was, and had died many years before this story begins.

Mother could only just remember him, but Lizzie would tell us about the house in Torrington Square, where Grandma lived and so many artists and actors forgathered.

Grandma had a very good voice and used to sing ballads, some-

132

times at the Crystal Palace, and she knew Arthur Sullivan, and Lizzie said, 'I always thought that Mr Sullivan was sweet on your Mamma.' Lizzie had always been fond of the theatre, and became a regular first-nighter. Father encouraged her to go, as, he said, she was the best critic he knew. She always spoke of Ellen Terry as 'Miss Ellen', for the actress had been a friend of Grandma's, and was often at the house. Then there was 'Young Mr Robertson' (Johnston Forbes-Robertson) who came too, rather stiff and shy, so Lizzie said.

I can remember one party that was given at Kent Terrace when I was very small. Cyril, Ethel and I had been sent to bed, but we crept downstairs in our nightclothes and looked through the banisters at the fun. It was a lively scene, with the ladies in their gay coloured evening dresses with neat little waists and bustles. Many of the men wore white gloves, and had flowers in their buttonholes. Mother worked hard to make the party a success and seemed to be everywhere at once. A white drugget had been laid over the drawing-room carpet which made the room look twice the size. It would have made a perfect subject for Tissot. There was no dancing, but Hayden Coffin sang, and a small woman tinkled on the guitar. Then Beerbohm Tree recited, but Cyril and I were much more interested in the pretty ladies. One had dark, almost black hair and a red velvet dress. She had lovely white shoulders. Looking up and seeing our faces through the banisters, she laughingly chided us. Then she came up and, sitting on the stairs beside me, said, 'Why, Ernest, you are half asleep!' Which I was, so I promptly cuddled up to her. I had to be carried up to bed, where she tucked me up and gave me such a comforting kiss.

There was more that Lizzie told us. She said that when Father and Mother were first married and lived in the little house in Boscobel Place, they were fond of having some of their closest friends in

to supper on Sunday evenings: Grandma was often there, and so
were the Dicksees. Polly, Minnie and Frank Dicksee had been friends
since childhood, so they were old friends of Lizzie's too. She told us
how, in the summer evenings, the guests would sit in the tiny garden
after supper while Mother played and sang. Sometimes Grandma sang

'Why, Ernest, you are half asleep!'

too. Aunt Fanny occasionally hazarded the journey from Gordon
Square (leaving Aunt Alicia in deep concern till she returned home).

When Mother's babies came and it was no longer easy for her
to entertain at home, she and Father more often went to the Sunday
evening gatherings at the Dicksees' large house in Fitzroy Square.
This had two studios, one for Minnie and one for her father Thomas
Dicksee, with a connecting corridor lined with classical statuary.

Frank had his studio in Campden Hill. As we children grew older, first Ethel, then Cyril and I, were invited too. We always enjoyed going; for one thing it was a treat to sit up to supper with the grown-ups, and then, most interesting people, musical and artistic, were frequently there. The Dicksees had a small niece, with the same name as my sister. Little Ethel sometimes stayed with them. She was younger than I was and though I did not see her often, we were great friends. I was more than ever delighted to go to Fitzroy Square when she was there.

She was very pretty, with dark brown hair and a dear little snub nose, and the most expressive eyes. We had plenty to talk about— our respective schools and the parties we had been to. We sat together on the sofa, or on little stools by the fire, with our arms round each other, and listened to the conversation among the grown- ups. Or perhaps it was stories about Uncle Remus and Brer Rabbit and Brer Fox, told to us by Florence Reason, an artist friend who was often there. She could always be persuaded to come to a quiet corner of the room and entertain us.

I was most interested when the conversation was about art or music. I remember old Signor Garcia telling us about his experiences as an opera singer at the time Queen Victoria came to the throne. He had sung at Covent Garden many times, and then turned his attention to teaching. Most of the famous singers of the time were taught by him. On one occasion Minnie Dicksee asked him if he had ever sung with Jenny Lind. He considered a moment. 'No,' he said. 'No, you see I left the operatic stage in eighteen forty.'

Quite a different type of visitor was old Dr Gregory. A confirmed bachelor, small, stout and quite bald, he reminded me of Mr Pick- wick. He always wore a well-cut frock coat made from the finest broadcloth, which, as the buttons failed to meet, was held together over his paunch by a cuff-link. He had a special frock coat for the cold weather lined with brown fur that smelt strongly of camphor. He had very short legs so that, sitting on a chair, his feet barely reached the ground. He wore elastic-sided boots with square toes, and was very proud of his small feet, which were certainly beautifully shod. He was a great character and very argumentative. The most harmless statement would be met with 'Well, I don't know ——' Then he would start off on a long list of reasons why this or that were not so, or were so. He was inclined to be censorious about people and places. For some reason he had a down on Stroud in Gloucestershire. 'Nothing good ever came from *that place*,' he would say. Even to mention it made him fume. He was great on hygiene, and had an abhorrence of long hair in men; he would refer to 'close-cropped men like myself' as being superior; there was not a hair on his head. His partiality for hygiene made him intolerant of anybody with a spotty face. 'No right to be like that,' he would say, and rumour had it that the one romance of his life was wrecked by the object of his affections sweating too freely.

If any subject to do with doctoring was raised he would give the company a full analysis of the causes and symptoms of each ailment. Little Ethel and I sat in fear and trembling and clutching each other even more tightly, as we thought of all the diseases we might have. With me the fear was not a possibility but became a certainty as I brooded over symptoms after going to bed. I would wake up with, perhaps, a pain in my leg. This meant that the limb would have to be cut off, a grim thought, and I wondered if little Ethel would like me any longer if I had to go about with a wooden leg. Finally, unable to bear the suspense any longer I confided my fears to Lizzie, who took a very practical view of things and assured me I was only suffering from 'Growing Pains'.

Lizzie was always most interested in our prattle about the people we had met at Fitzroy Square, and would remind us before we went there to give her best respects to Miss Polly and Miss Minnie. They remembered her at Christmas, sending her some gaily decorated calendar. She possessed a reproduction of one of Frank's pictures, in which he had painted Mother, hanging in the kitchen.

'Close-cropped men like myself'

Cyril and I helped in the decoration of the walls of the kitchen by cutting out pictures from the illustrated magazines and pinning them up, but we were not allowed to touch the dresser. This had shelves filled with plates and dishes, and there were cups hanging from hooks that were easily knocked off. Underneath there was a place for saucepans into which I had once climbed, several years before, and had been discovered dabbling among the saucepans.

Lizzie was very patient with our activities, and would go on with her preparations for the next meal regardless of us. When she pushed back the tablecloth and started to make a pudding on the clean wooden top, she knew that our interest in the proceedings would keep us quiet. It always did. I loved to see her making pastry, at which she excelled: to watch the way she rolled out the dough and fitted it on to the dish, decorating it with little fancy pieces. She had very definite ideas about food, and sometimes when Mother was ordering a meal would shake her head and say, 'Your Mother never had that.'

I always like to think that Lizzie had a happy old age. She was with us after we children had grown up, and then one day she announced that she and her sisters were going to set up house together. It was a romantic story. It appears that a distant relative had left them a considerable sum of money, enough for them to buy a house and live in comfort. Lizzie had spoken once or twice of a mysterious relation who had been a foundling. He had been found on the steps of St Benetfink's Church in the city, and had been brought up and educated by a charitable society. He became quite an important person in the City and built up a big business with a store in Cheapside. He left the sisters this handsome sum of money, and they bought a house in Streatham. Ethel would often go there and play the piano for them.

To return to the kitchen. . . . There was a back kitchen, or scullery, with a stone floor. A door at the end of the passage led into the tiny garden, which was partly paved and had once been covered with a shed with a glass skylight. Father had used this as a studio, but the wet came in so badly that it had to be pulled down. The garden was chiefly the haunt of cats, Sambo and his friends; if the door was opened quickly two or three would be seen scattering over the wall. There was a door in the wall which opened with difficulty. It was possible to squeeze through this and emerge into the mews; that is, if Martha and Lizzie were not about.

The mews was a most interesting place with plenty going on —horses being groomed or harnessed, carriages washed and polished, the grooms hissing and whistling at their work. Strings of washing hung from upper windows, whence the womenfolk leaned out and chatted to the men below.

I knew that, by picking my way over the wet cobblestones, I could run along to the end and come out by the alley-way that led back to Kent Terrace. It was dank and smelly and not a place to go through after dark. Hurrying through the alley I could come out on Kent Terrace and nip along to our own front door or area steps before anyone had missed me.

'Squeeze through this and emerge into the mews'

Cyril and I always had a comfortable feeling of security in that kitchen—the street noises, the occasional cab whistles, and all the familiar everyday sounds seemed so remote. Late of an afternoon the man would come round selling evening papers—'*Sun, Star, Echo, Pall Mall, Globe, St James', Westminster*, or *Evening News*'—so many there were. We could hear him calling the news a long way off and then along the Terrace. He would stop by the area gate and

'Seen Mr Gladstone at a private view'

Lizzie would buy her paper, then settle down with her glasses. The news seemed to be all about politics and Home Rule and what Mr Gladstone said or did. I asked Lizzie what *was* Home Rule? Her answer was that she 'didn't hold with politics'. I had seen Mr Gladstone at a Private View of the Royal Academy the year before, and had not been at all impressed when he was pointed out to me, for I thought he looked rather a scruffy old gentleman, and I was disappointed in the size of his collar. From his portraits in *Punch* I had the impression that he wore enormous collars, whereas in real life the one he was wearing was hardly visible. Lizzie would sit reading and I would ponder on the affairs of this world and think what a lot of time was being wasted in arguments. My father and his friends would sit for hours in the drawing-room arguing and arguing and sometimes getting quite fierce till I feared they would come to blows. Then, when they had finished, they would all sit down and have a meal together as if nothing had happened. Grown-ups were all right up to a point, but it was difficult to get them to understand anything important—Mother, of course, was different.

Cyril took a more detached view of things and was generally buried in his stamp album. He received a number of South African stamps from time to time and spent hours arranging and rearranging them. The stamps were sent by his uncle in Natal; one in particular was of great interest—grey-blue and roughly printed, I think it came from Zululand or Basutoland. Our uncle had told Cyril to keep it carefully, as it would be valuable some day. (He was right.)

A letter had come to my father about the same time from my uncle, which Father handed to Cyril as he thought it might interest us. I had read this letter several times and worried at its contents. It gave an account of the war in South Africa against the Boers in 1880. My uncle had volunteered for service, had been drafted to Transport, and was put in charge of a bullock wagon. In the very early hours of one morning they were at the foot of a steep hill, Majuba Hill. The Infantry had orders to climb this and, led by their General, they did so before it was light. Their action surprised the Boers, who, however, reacted quickly and counter-attacked them. Creeping close under cover of the rocks, they picked off our men by their good

'Down the steep hill they came'

marksmanship. Finally only a few of our men were left and the order was given to retire. As they fell back, the men started to run. Down the steep hill they came, as fast as they could, many, including the General, being shot on the way. We pored over this letter with the deepest concern, as we could not bring ourselves to believe that English soldiers *ever* run away. I certainly did not believe it and would not admit of any doubts; after all I had the evidence of the stories I had read in the *Boys' Own Paper* or *Heroes of Britain* to support me. I asked Mother what was her opinion. She thought that what our uncle had written was right, but that he might have exaggerated.

Then, one evening when I was going to bed, I tackled Martha about it. Toothbrush in mouth, I put forward my views, but she, a staunch chapel-goer, had no sympathy with wars or with fighting in any form. I could get no answer from her; in fact she told me I was wicked to think about such things. This was to me a new and disturbing point of view, but I knew that Martha had very strict ideas of what was right and proper. Honest as the day, she entertained no compromise—things were right or wrong. A Primitive Methodist from the Welsh borders, she loved to talk of the chapel to us children, or to sing us the hymn tunes that she herself had learnt as a child. Sitting by the fire in the nursery, or later in the playroom, she would sing the simple Methodist hymns to us, while Cyril was poring over his beloved stamps and I, perhaps, was drawing in my copy-book. Ethel learnt to play some of these hymns on the piano; she was quick at picking up tunes, and our little piping voices would sing them together.

> *When He cometh, when He cometh*
> *To make up His jewels,*
> *All His jewels, precious jewels,*
> *Bright gems of His crown.*

Twenty-nine years later I was to hear the words of those hymn tunes again. They were sung by Welsh voices on a dusty shell-torn road in Picardy, as a battalion of Welch Fusiliers marched into battle. I was standing by the roadside, close to what had been Fricourt, when they passed. I was grateful for their song. It seemed as if the men were singing a requiem. For that day I had found my dear

'Sing the simple Methodist hymns to us'

brother's grave in Mansell Copse. The spot was marked by simple wooden crosses bearing the names of the Fallen roughly printed on them. It was, and is still, the resting place of over two hundred men of the Devons who fell that Saturday morning in July 1916.

'They will shine like the Morning'

Chapter Eight

CHRISTMAS HOLIDAYS

WE three children were looking forward to Mother's birthday, which was December 18th. December was 'our' birthday month, Cyril's on the 20th, mine on the 10th: but the 18th was by far the most important. With a view to deciding what was to be done, we gathered round the schoolroom

'Gathered round the schoolroom table'

table, each armed with a statement of his or her financial resources. My assets were contained in an old purse that I kept hidden in a corner of the writing desk. This I emptied on the table. The contents were: one silver sixpence, one silver threepenny bit, and an assortment of coppers—total one shilling and tenpence halfpenny. Cyril was not in a much stronger position, and it remained for Ethel to retrieve the situation, which, I have to admit, she did most nobly.

Lucky enough to have a godmother who sent her postal orders she was able to produce nearly ten shillings. Most magnanimously, she suggested that we pool our resources and give Mother one really nice present rather than three inferior ones. Cyril and I volunteered to draw and paint a birthday card between us, and we left it to Ethel to decide on the nature of the present.

It turned out to be a yellow tea-cosy, padded and quilted and embroidered, with braid round the edge, finished off with a curl at the top. Cyril and I considered it to be a dull gift, but Mother received it with joy. It appears that she really wanted a tea-cosy, a fact that Ethel had found out by some subtle means. Anyway it was a happy choice, and when it was presented to Mother on her birthday morning, after breakfast, she kissed us all round many times. A lot of cards and letters had come for her and some presents were set out on the sideboard in the dining-room, with our tea-cosy in the centre. I was not sure that I envied her when I thought of all the thank-you letters she would have to write. When I said so she laughingly said: 'Well, darling, you shall come and help me and we shall get it done in no time.'

'A yellow tea-cosy'

The birthday card we had drawn and coloured was there among the others. It was a strange effort, and hardly appropriate, but it had cost us some hours of toil and a small bottle of gold paint.

At eleven o'clock we got into our outdoor clothes, for Mother had promised to take us to the Christmas bazaar in Peter Robinson's shop. It was a cold day, but Cyril and I, well wrapped up, were allowed to climb on top of the bus. The bazaar had all sorts of new ideas. There was a man got up as Father Christmas, but we considered him a failure and unworthy of the part; we had seen a much better Father Christmas at a school party the year before. There was a Punch and Judy show, rather special with spangles on the front, and we waited hopefully for it to perform, but all we saw was Toby, in a frill, having his dinner.

There were large tubs, full of bran, and by paying threepence you could have a dip, but were not allowed to fumble too long. I got a very small paint box. It contained only six colours, and the hairs came out of the brush. Cyril got a hammer, but that came to grief next day when he hit something hard. Martha said it was because he had put his shoes on the table, but I could not see the connexion.

The bazaar was very crowded and rather hot, and it was difficult to get near the special attractions. One novelty was a pair of mechanical minstrels, got up like the Christy Minstrels with stiff collars and large bow ties. One had bones and the other a tambourine. About a foot high, they sat on stools on top of a musical box, and, as the music played, they jerked and twisted and opened and shut their mouths.

There was a fairy who presided over a bower of dolls. She was really worth looking at, but the place was crowded with little girls and we had to move on. Mother bought several Christmas presents. I think that some were secret, for she had them done up quickly. Then Ethel spent a long time over choosing a gift for a special friend of hers, and Cyril and I, wandering off, got separated, and became rather anxious till we saw the others. Laden with parcels, we made for home. It was colder in the afternoon, too cold to ride Septimus up and down the Terrace, so I spent the time in the schoolroom

'The place was crowded with little girls'

taking stock of my possessions. The purse was now quite empty, but my birthday had brought me several exciting presents.

First there was a box of sailors in white uniforms with straw hats and gaiters, all running; an officer in a blue frock coat and white helmet held his sword aloft. This was Mother's present. Father gave me a box of coloured pencils, a great acquisition. Aunt Alicia gave me a box of puzzles, which were very ingenious and kept me occupied for hours. A surprise came from Uncle Robert, the one who was at Lloyd's and whom we hardly ever saw; he gave me a book called *Snap*, which was the only time he ever remembered my existence. In addition I had some really useful but dull things. Cyril was eagerly speculating on his chances for the 20th, but his mind ran almost entirely on stamps. He already had a good collection.

Our bedroom had had to be changed. A leak had developed in the wall, and the paper and plaster were stained with the damp and were peeling off. An evil-smelling oil stove was put in the room to dry it out, but did not seem to have much effect. From where we now slept, I could no longer see the plaster lady on the house opposite, but I thought of her, standing there in the cold. The one advantage of our new room was that we could look out on the Terrace and see what was going on in the world outside.

Our drawing-room, with its two front windows, had a back room attached. There were two folding doors between, but these were never closed; instead heavy curtains hung on rings could be drawn across. The conservatory at the back, with ferns and a cork rockery, gave an air to the room, but reminded *me* of the dentist. I had better explain why. The dentist, Mr Stocken, lived in Euston Square. (He had a son who sometimes did our teeth, and whom Father christened 'the Sock'.) In front of the dreadful Chair there was a sort of grotto or small conservatory. It had a large glass tank with goldfish, and this was supposed to distract our attention from the business in hand. But it never did. It only served to create a

'Now, open, dear!'

prejudice against grottos and conservatories. Mr Stocken had a ghoulish smile and what was considered to be a soothing manner, but his 'Now, open, dear!' made the blood run cold. I was never brave, and usually made a great fuss. I envied my sister. Ethel always took the business in her stride, and had been known to go on with her piano practice till the moment came to face the executioner.

Father had suggested taking Mother to a theatre for her birthday treat, but she decided that she would rather spend a quiet evening with us, which seemed to me a strange choice at the time. So when it got dusk we children sat on the floor in front of a roaring fire. Mother sat on a low stool and I cuddled down beside her. She told us about the time when she was young and lived with Grandma in Torrington Square, and all about the people who came to the house. She could hardly remember her father, who had died when she was small. Grandma was barely eighteen when she had her first baby. He, a boy, went when he grew up to South Africa. It was he who sent Cyril stamps. I saw him once, when he came back to England for a short time, but did not remember him well. Grandma and

Mother were almost like sisters, and it was a great blow for Mother when Grandma died four years after I was born.

When Mother and Father were first married they lived in a tiny house in Boscobel Place. It had a small walled garden and was one of those little cottagy dwellings which can still be seen in St John's Wood. But Boscobel Place vanished many years ago when the Great Central Line was built.

They were very happy in their little house. Lizzie, who used to push her and her brother round Torrington Square in the large double pram, came to them as maid-of-all-work. The self-same pram came into use again for Cyril and me to squabble in, on our outings with Ellen. Mother told us how she first got to know Father. She would see him passing the end of Torrington Square from her bedroom window when he went to business in the mornings. Presently the time came when he visited the house and was allowed to take her out, something which the household at Gordon Square was not sure was right and decorous. It is quite certain that Father's stern Papa would have objected had he been alive, for he never allowed young men to come to his house, much less to take his daughters out. Then came the day when Father proposed and he and Mother became engaged, a great occasion clouded only by the knowledge that she would have to face a visit to her Mother-in-law-to-be and the daughters. Oh! how nervous she was at the prospect! How she kept putting it off! But when the time at last came, she put on her best frock and summoned up all her courage.

·That was thirteen years before, when the Aunts were that much younger and were still together with their mother at Gordon Square. The old lady, sitting in her easy chair, wearing a white cap and side ringlets, made Mother come and sit beside her. She took Mother's hand, and did not speak for a while; then she said: 'I'm glad my boy Harry will have such a pretty wife.'

Mother stopped and sat very quiet. I was close to her knee and looked up. I saw that she was crying.

Presently she got up and went to the piano and played and sang for us. There was one song which I liked to hear her sing more than any other: 'Robin, lend to me thy bow.' She sang it to us then. We had a very special tea, all cosy in front of the fire, with hot buttered toast and cake, and Mother was gay and laughing by the time we had finished.

Before Christmas Day there was a party at our school in Baker Street. It was for the kindergarten, and the High School for Girls had lent us their hall for the occasion. There was a conjuror, and as a number of the bigger girls were there it promised to be a good party. I was very pleased about this, as I always seemed to like bigger girls, and I boldly asked one or two to dance. I could not dance at all, but one of them, a very nice girl named Maud, took a lot of trouble to show me how, so that I felt quite grown-up, and I suppose this made me rather cocky. Then one of the boys started to chaff me about my lace collar, a thing I was sensitive about. He was in Scotch clothes and I didn't think much of *his* get-up either. Anyhow, his taunts were more than I could bear and I lashed out at him. He retaliated by kicking me. Stung to fury, I made a dive at him. We were close to a table which had a lot of glasses on it and over it went, glasses and all. For some reason, I got all the blame. As I tried to hide the tears of rage by picking up the broken glass, a stern-faced woman in an apron said I was a naughty little boy. Even Miss Turner, my favourite mistress, looked severe and said I ought to know better. Covered with shame, I retired to a corner and had the mortification of seeing Maud dancing with my late opponent. The evening was ruined, and I was glad when the time came to go home. Silent and crestfallen, I wrapped myself up, and Martha got no answer when she asked me how I had enjoyed myself.

Cyril was very sympathetic over this misfortune. Perhaps it was as well that he did not witness the incident, for he would most certainly have intervened on my behalf and then it would not have been fair, two to one, and even more glasses would have been broken. After some sleepless nights over Maud, I decided that she was not worth troubling about.

'I made a dive at him'

The anticipation of Christmas made forgetfulness the more easy.

Both Cyril and I suffered from having our birthdays too near Christmas Day. People were apt to make one present do for the two occasions, which we did not consider fair. Now Ethel, on the other hand, had her birthday in August, so that she was in a much stronger position, though she never bragged about it. However, Cyril did not do so badly on this occasion, and we had an unexpected present from Frank Dicksee. It was a great lump of modelling wax which, when warmed in the hands, became soft and pliant. It kept us quiet for days and we made all sorts of things, including a whole farmyard of animals—modelled on the lines of Pollards' of course! Cows, horses, pigs, cocks and hens, and even loaves of bread, almost came to life. Unfortunately, it was impossible to colour them, as watercolour paint made no impression on the wax. We had a small bottle of gold but, after a trial, we agreed that it added nothing to the scene.

After a while complaints began to come from Martha that bits of sticky stuff were appearing all over the house. Enquiries traced the stickiness to the soles of our shoes. Modelling activities had to stop and we wasted a lot of time helping to clear up.

Christmas Eve was a murky day and we spent most of it putting

'Kept us quiet for days'

the final touches to our decorations. We had no Christmas tree. In my short life I had only once seen a Christmas tree, and that was in the hall of our friends, the Milners', house. It was gaily decorated with paper flags and candles and led me to extract a promise from Mother that we should have one one day.

In the dining-room and drawing-room our decorations were confined to holly, but Cyril and I let ourselves go in the kitchen. We had bought at Cole's, for a few pence, coloured paper streamers that opened like a concertina. By joining several together these could be hung right across the kitchen ceiling. We dragged the kitchen table from side to side and climbed on it, fixing the streamers, rather precariously, with nails and pins. However, when we had finished, and were admiring the effect, Lizzie reluctantly agreed that it did look gay. She was not much in sympathy with our activities, and wanted to know who was going to clear up the mess we had made.

After tea we children sallied forth with Martha to do some final shopping. Park Road was very much alive. All the shops were open, and the little stationer's had a show of cards in the window, tinsel, snow and robins with appropriate mottoes. In front of the poulterer's shop a small crowd was gathered for the selling off, cheap, of the remaining turkeys. They were scraggy birds, quite unlike the fine plump fellows with coloured rosettes stuck on their breasts which had hung there a few days earlier.

Martha and Ethel went into Cole's, while Cyril and I gazed in the windows. Even White's the chemists had celebrated the occasion by having holly and white cotton wool amongst the medicine bottles. Martha told us that the shops would stay open quite late, and we were reluctant to go home. When we eventually got back we were in time to see a boy with a large basket by the area gate. It was the Turkey, a great big one, and Lizzie was saying 'It's bigger than was ordered, and I hope it will go in the oven.' Then Father came out and gave the boy a shilling.

I had sent off my Christmas cards: not many, but each of the Aunts had to have one; then of course Father and Mother (these were put by till tomorrow); and there were Gussie and Lizzie and her sisters. It was fortunate that I did not have to buy all these cards with my own meagre savings. Mother always kept such of last year's cards as had no writing on them, or only in pencil, and we were able to use these again. The pencil marks were erased, usually quite ineffectually, with a rather grubby piece of india-rubber, and a greeting written on top, heavily, and in ink, to help in the disguise. The procedure was fraught with dangers and I was only saved from disaster by Mother looking over my shoulder and saying, 'Darling, you *can't* send that one to Aunt Alicia. It's the one she sent me last year.'

As we were going to sit up for late dinner on Christmas night, we were packed off to bed early. I did not mind this, as it was good to lie in bed and contemplate the morrow. I could hear the sound of church bells and the distant shoutings of the poulterer as he sold off his turkeys. Cyril and I had hung our stockings at the foot of the bed, and I tried to keep awake to see what happened in the night, but my effort was of no avail.

Waking up on Christmas morning in childhood is something that can never be forgotten. First I was conscious of something different about the day, then I remembered, and crawled to the bottom of the bed. It was all right! The stocking was full! I fumbled in the dark and turned out one thing after another. Some were done up in paper. There were crackers and an orange, and an exciting hard box which promised chocolates. I called to Cyril and found he too was exploring in the dark. Then he boldly got out of bed and lit the gas, standing on a chair. This was not allowed, but we felt that on Christmas morning it was different. We laid all our gifts on the bed and opened the chocolates.

Presently we heard the sound of movement downstairs, and Martha came in. We shouted 'Happy Christmas' but she was shocked at the gas, and said, 'You know what your Father told you!' We tried to pacify her with chocolates, but the only result was for her to tell us to put them away, else we'd make ourselves sick. We got into our dressing-gowns and went down to Ethel's room. She was sitting up in bed and feeling as excited over her stocking as we were over ours.

Then we remembered about singing, and went and stood outside Mother's room and sang her a Christmas carol. She came to the door and we all hugged her and wished her a happy Christmas. After we were dressed, Cyril and I hurried downstairs to arrange our cards and little gifts on Mother's and Father's plates, and to gaze in anticipation at the sideboard piled high with parcels. Then we went to the kitchen to greet Lizzie and to tie a ribbon on Sambo; we did not stay long, for Lizzie was already busy making preparations for Christmas Dinner.

After breakfast we all opened our parcels. There were no really exciting ones for Cyril and me, as we had only just had our birthdays, but I got half a crown from Father. Then we wrapped ourselves up, for it was a foggy morning, with white hoar-frost on the trees and railings, and walked to Marylebone Church for morning Service. The beadle there had a beard rather like the pictures of Abraham Lincoln, and was wearing a smart new cocked hat.

Cyril and I spent the rest of the morning being a nuisance to Lizzie and her sisters, who were preparing the dinner for which we children were to sit up. We kept running down to the kitchen to see how things were getting on, until finally we were sent upstairs to get ready for luncheon. In the afternoon we had to lie down. For tea we had a Christmas cake with sugar icing on it.

The lamplighter came along quite early to light up the street lamps. This took him some time, as he knocked on every door and stood there smiling rather sheepishly, in the fog, to wish 'The Compliments of the Season'. Having been duly rewarded with a Christmas box, he went on with his lamplighting. All the tradespeople seemed much in evidence on this and on Boxing Day, and Father complained that he was running short of silver.

Cyril and I were eagerly looking forward to our dinner. We hoped all would be well, without a repetition of what had happened the year before, when the kitchen range had gone wrong. On that

'The kitchen chimney is afire'

sad occasion the turkey had been carved and eaten and there had come the pause while the pudding was being lit up outside. We heard a noise as of something being dropped, and then in rushed Martha. 'Please, sir, Lizzie says as how the kitchen chimney is afire!' Father dashed from the room. We children sat, rigid with terror, expecting flames to burst through the floor. Nothing happened, and Mother reassured us. 'Now don't worry. Father will see to it.' And see to it he did, but he came upstairs with a very dirty shirt-front. 'I've thrown a lot of salt on it,' he said. Then, feeling the wall, 'It's quite hot,' he remarked. This was not comforting, and did not add to the enjoyment of the pudding. My faint hope that a fire engine might come was not realized. It was only the plumbers who came a few days later and said it was the sweep's fault.

However, we had no trouble on *this* Christmas night, and I begged to be allowed to sit up after dinner in the drawing-room while Mother played the piano and sang to us. So, in my nightshirt and dressing-gown and wrapped in a shawl, I squatted on the floor with Cyril before the fire. Ethel, who was making such good progress on the piano, also played. She could read music well, a thing I always found very hard. We could hear sounds of festivity from below, where Lizzie and her sisters and Martha were 'having company'.

A few days after Christmas we were invited to a children's party at a house along the Terrace. We did not know the family well. There was one child, a small girl about Cyril's age, named Muriel. I had taken a dislike to her ever since she had made sneering remarks about my beloved Septimus. Though she was rather pretty, she had a nasty assertive manner and, as we were taking off our coats and mufflers in the hall, started to hector us. Her father and mother had no control over her and spoilt her completely; in return, she was rude to them both, particularly her father.

There was to be a magic lantern show and the archway between the front and back drawing-room had been filled in with a sheet, behind which the apparatus had been fixed up. We had to sit in chairs while Muriel fussed about, ordering us this way and that. The lantern, a Christmas present, was hers, and she didn't let anyone forget it. Her father, behind the scenes, was in charge, as far as he was able, and we had to sit and listen to her telling him how the apparatus should be worked. Finally the lamps were turned out and

'Continually interrupted the performance'

all was ready. A faint circle of light appeared to one side of the sheet, which slowly and jerkily moved towards the middle. 'That's not bright enough,' shouted Muriel. The circle of light grew brighter and then disappeared. The audience waited expectantly. Then the light reappeared showing a small picture which looked like animals, but it was upside down. Muriel rushed behind the sheet, and we heard her bullying the unfortunate operator. When the picture appeared again, the right way up, it showed two cats in boxing gloves. This was greeted with faint applause, which grew louder when, accompanied by a slight clicking noise, the cats began to box. At this point a voice at the back was heard to wail: 'I can't see!' So the owner of the voice, a very small boy, was brought to the front. When the audience had settled down again, we had a series of highly coloured views of Swiss scenes. Muriel continually interrupted the performance by giving directions and orders to 'Make it clearer' or 'Turn up the light'.

Then she demanded some funny pictures and, after a pause, up came one with a dog beating a big drum. There was the same clicking sound as the dog's arm went up and down. This was greeted with mild laughter, but Muriel insisted on having it brighter. A muffled voice said: 'There, that's as high as it will go.' By this time there was a strong smell of hot metal and signs of agitation behind the sheet. A moment later a bright and unmistakable glow showed itself, accompanied by exclamations of dismay. The sheet was dragged aside to disclose the apparatus in flames, and Muriel's father with a jug of water trying to cope with it. Muriel herself was inarticulate with rage and started to howl, which for Cyril and me was the last straw. In any case the party was spoiled and even a fairly good supper, with meringues, failed to save the evening, and we were glad to go home.

A very different kind of party, to which we were invited the following week, was given by the Cohens, who lived on the opposite side of the Park. They had arranged some theatricals and Ethel had been given the part of Red Riding Hood's Mother. I was filled with envious admiration for the way in which she mastered her words and did not appear to be at all nervous.

The Cohens possessed a very large double room and had built up a proper stage, with footlights, curtains and all. There were several scenes, painted specially, and proper costumes. The music had been cribbed from Gilbert and Sullivan and the words had been written by an uncle. The part of Red Riding Hood was played by Mamie Cohen, her brother Maurice was the woodcutter-prince, and her younger brother Jeff was a forester. I had a crush on Mamie at that time, which got worse when she appeared, made up and looking quite bewitching, on the stage.

The play opened in her mother's cottage with Ethel, in a mob cap and apron, to speak the opening lines. The story was not in accordance with the usual version, for the wolf repented before he

'Too shy to kiss her'

had gobbled up Grandma, and became a friend of the family. Moreover the wood-cutter turned out to be a prince and was happily united with Red Riding Hood. It all went off swimmingly, and the audience was delighted. My cup of happiness brimmed over when Mamie chose me to take her in to supper and the red paint on her mouth got all smudged with trifle. My only regret is that I was too shy to kiss her.

Some days later a repeat performance of the play was given on a real stage at some Orphanage. On this occasion Cyril was roped in to play the part of the Prince, for Maurice had suddenly developed a bad cold. Cyril was coached in his part by Ethel, and though he was extremely nervous he did it well. I was just as nervous as he was and felt all hot and cold when he came on the stage in Maurice's rather-too-large green tights. I went into the actors' dressing-room after the show. The boys were in various stages of undress when, to our horror, the door was flung open and all the orphans came in 'to see the actors'. These heroes promptly disappeared under the table and refused to come out.

It was just about the New Year that the Toy Symphony, so often postponed, was performed. There were one or two final rehearsals at the Lloyds' house along the Terrace. Eirene Lloyd played first fiddle and Ethel second fiddle. Eirene's brother Picco, a great tall fellow, played the drums. I think that he may have been the cause of the postponements, as he was learning to be a soldier and was studying somewhere and had to be away a lot. I had a sneaking hope that there might be a war and he would have to go away and fight,

The Toy Symphony

for that would mean that I might be allowed to play the drum. But it was not to be: the triangle was my lot.

Mrs Lloyd presided at rehearsals in a cap and paisley shawl and she was quick to detect any shortcomings. I found the music difficult to follow and dreaded losing my place. The sharp voice, 'Now, Ernest, the triangle!' would jerk me into activity. 'Ping, ping, ping.' 'Stop! that's enough!' I could never get it quite right except at the end, when, triumphant, all the instruments scraped, banged, rattled and pinged together in a glorious crescendo, with Cyril's warbler gone silent owing to all the water having been blown out of it.

Chapter Nine

ANTICLIMAX

ETHEL had written a play. We had hoped to produce it in the Christmas holidays, but what with the parties, the Toy Symphony and other private theatricals, our home effort was almost lost sight of. It was only when things began to quieten down after the New Year that we were able to consider seriously ways and means of production.

The story revolved round two young lovers, one a Prince, the other, Margaret, a damsel. These two suffered much from the persecution of a Demon (myself), who made frequent and untimely intrusions into their personal affairs. Scenery was lacking, as we had no means of providing it, but an elaborate programme was devised, with an ornamental cover, which would leave the audience in no doubt as to where the action was taking place. Thus, 'The King's Palace', 'The Demon's Lair' figured among the scenes. There were several additional characters, and these also presented some problems because the shortage of actors prevented their appearing in person. Ethel solved the difficulty by quoting them as saying this and that. The general inference was that 'the King' (on paper only) was opposed to the union of the two young lovers (flesh and blood). It had been intended that a Lord Chancellor, or some such dignitary, should appear, in person, to preach evil counsels to the King and support his objections to the union. As no one else was available and I refused to forgo my part of Demon for the sake of a part so dull as that of a mere Chancellor, this character had to join those on the paper list.

I was glad to be able to devote all my talents to the portrayal of the evil spirit. We had been given some green grease-paint by a misguided friend of Father's who dabbled in theatricals, and I lost no opportunity of rehearsing my part fully made up. As we had permission to raid Mother's wardrobe, Cyril's get-up was quite magnificent. An old hat of hers was furbished up and decked with ostrich feathers, some long stockings provided tights, and a velveteen antimacassar with a fringe made a cloak. A sword was no trouble, for we boys had a small armoury between us, and I insisted that the Demon should be allowed to carry a pistol to fire real caps. This suggested a scene which I am proud to claim as my own idea. At a critical moment in the wood, when the young lovers were plighting their troth (as they did at intervals during the play) the Demon was to rush in and, gibbering and uttering strange cries, shoot Margaret, who would then swoon in the arms of her Prince (*Curtain*). I cannot help thinking that Ethel must have been reading *Lorna Doone* that she should so readily have accepted my idea. This, however, was not to be the end of the play.

On the day of the production we spent some time before the guests arrived in arranging the auditorium. We placed the smaller chairs in a semicircle in front. Then the large basket chair that creaked was put at the back and the india-rubber plant was moved on to the stage to give a touch of colour to the woodland scene. The blue glass globe on the gas bracket was adjusted for the moonlight effect and the doors of the conservatory at the back were opened, with a curtain draped across as a background, for 'The Palace' scene. A cork rockery flower stand was brought forward and made ready, with a night-light inside, to figure in 'The Demon's Cave'. It was unfortunate that when the audience arrived they should move our carefully arranged seating and dispose themselves to gossip round the fire. We found it a matter of some difficulty to rivet their attention on the performance and to keep them from resuming general conversation during the progress of the play. This was hardly surprising

'A jewel springs through the air'

as there were many gaps while the scenery was being shifted or costumes were being changed. Our back drawing-room, with the conservatory at the back and the blue lamp-shade, made a good setting for the woodland scene and, inspired by this, Ethel really let herself go. Besides writing a song, which was unfortunately a failure owing to there being no piano accompaniment forthcoming, she became all flowery over the stage directions. Thus at the point where the Prince was hiding behind the india-rubber plant, waiting for his Margaret, and she entered, sighing, the directions read: 'A jewel springs through the air.' (A jewel was at this point to be thrown by the Prince and fall at Margaret's feet.) She stoops. 'What is this?' She sighs. 'Can it be he?' She sighs again. 'Alas, I would it were my lover. . . .' The lover was not far off, and presently appeared in

'The fatal shot was duly fired'

person to take Margaret in his arms and await the moment of the shot.

There was some delay here owing to the Demon having trouble with the caps for his pistol, but the fatal shot was duly fired, Margaret fell, the Prince registered dismay, and the audience, applauding loudly, made to leave! Father intervened when we explained there was more to come and said it was too late and long past the Demon's bedtime. However, he agreed to let us sing the concluding chorus, which I had to admit bore little relation to the rest of the play.

Prince and Margaret together:
> *The war is over*
> *The battle's won,*
> *The Prince to his Margaret,*
> *Because the foeman's flown.*

The Demon (solo):
> *The Demon Lucifer runs about*
> *Through the palace in and out*

Curtain (pulled very promptly by Martha).

The audience was very generous in its applause but no encores were asked for.

Among the guests were our old friends, the Milners. We had lived next door to them in Springfield Road before we came to

'Ghosts!'

Kent Terrace. There were three daughters, Mary, Bessie, and Edith. Mary was grown up and engaged to be married. Bessie and Edith were more our own age and were the greatest fun. Mr and Mrs Milner were the most considerate of parents, for they would shut themselves up in the drawing-room when we were spending the afternoon at their house, and, when it got dark, give us the full run of the place. The great game was 'Ghosts'. Theirs was a grand house for the purpose, for there were two staircases. All lights were turned out, and Bessie, covered with a white sheet, would lurk in the darkest corners, from which she would spring out and chase a covey of shrieking children fleeing for safety to 'Home'. 'Home' was the dining-room, and the dilemma created by the two staircases was that one never knew which way the ghost was coming.

Cyril and Edith were particular friends. They would sit with their arms round each other. One evening Mrs Milner, to her great amusement, found them under the table, their retreat being given away by the sound of loud smacking kisses.

'Showed Cyril and me how to bowl over-arm'

The summer before last both our families had been to St Margaret's Bay where we had had lodgings in adjacent houses on top of the cliff. Mary was there, and her fiancé, a young journalist named Alfred Harmsworth, came to stay. Alfred played cricket with us in the field near our lodgings and showed Cyril and me how to bowl over-arm.

He started a paper called *Answers* and, with two other young men, made a lot of money.

During that holiday we all went to Dover for the day, taking the train from Martin Mill station and then climbing the hill to the castle. We were shown all over it by an elderly soldier, who evidently made it his job, for he had all the dates and facts by heart, but if we interrupted to ask questions he had to go back all the way to the beginning, after saying, 'Now, wer woz I?' He showed us the Armoury, containing goodness knows how many Martini rifles, all beautifully cleaned and polished, in long racks, with bayonets and models of guns. Also a small model of a capstan which revolved and pulled a rope. Then there were little service tents and a

'Shown all over it by an elderly soldier'

mast and yard with real signal flags. He showed us the well, so deep that if you dropped a stone you couldn't hear it strike bottom. (But I think that well must be getting full by now if every visitor in some sixty years has dropped a stone.) We were shown the great gun, a beautifully decorated casting, known as Queen Elizabeth's pocket pistol, standing on a stone pedestal and pointed across the channel.

Our guide said it could fire a shot into Calais, but I have no doubt that he was an optimist.

On leaving the castle we went down to the harbour and saw some German ships unloading timber. I stood watching one called the *Berlin* for a while; I particularly remembered her because later she was wrecked in the Baltic, so Father told us, having seen a report in the newspaper. Beyond the Lord Warden Hotel, where we had dinner, we saw a strange-looking cross-channel boat moored to the quay-side. She was a queer experiment in ship design, a sort of Siamese twin of a ship; two complete hulls joined together in the middle. She had two sets of engines and two funnels, one on each ship, and two huge paddle boxes. She was not only very ugly but very difficult to navigate, a sailor told us, and just as 'lively' in a Channel sea as any other boat, so that the claim made for her that she was the steadiest and safest ship hardly applied. She did not last long and no more ships were built like her. I believe she was called *The Calais Douvres*.

There was a fort near the shore with fat Armstrong guns, and I was able to explain to Mother how they were fired and how the heavy screw breech rotated. I always remembered everything about guns and would study the *Illustrated London News* or even an encyclopaedia in my thirst for knowledge on the subject. Father was in sympathy with me in this, having spent a short time as a volunteer in an artillery regiment; but the only 'active' service he had seen had been on a field day in Surrey, when he had been kicked by a horse and had had to spend the rest of the day riding on a limber.

Ethel was bridesmaid at Mary Milner's wedding in Hampstead the following spring. She and Edith Milner were dressed alike for the occasion—blue frocks and big Leghorn straw hats. On the morning of the wedding a cab fetched Ethel, all dressed up, while Cyril and I followed with Mother by train. We went from St John's Wood to Finchley Road by Underground, then walked up the hill. There were few houses on the right-hand side, so we could see Hampstead across the fields and, by following a footpath, climb up to the church. It was a gay wedding and Mary looked very charming. We all came back with pieces of wedding cake to put under our pillows.

We made the return journey by bus, passing Swiss Cottage and Eyre Arms, where we changed, and I watched the horses being watered at the trough in front of the old public house. During the hot weather an extra horse was stationed there to help with the pull up the hill; it was hitched on in front and the ostler who saw to it mixed oatmeal with the horses' drinking water in the pails.

I liked going up the Finchley Road. Beyond Acacia Road was the house called Moore Lodge, which belonged to 'Pony' Moore. It stood back from the road with a curved drive in front and the drive was adorned with stone pedestals topped with urns. In each urn was a fascinating large lustre glass ball, brightly coloured. I always wondered what manner of man was 'Pony' Moore. His real name, I believe, was George Washington Moore. He was said to have been born on the anniversary of George Washington's birthday and, needless to say, he came from the United States. He was the founder of the Moore and Burgess Minstrels, and I could only visualize him with a black face like the rest of the fraternity . . . Eugene Stratton or that robust comedian, Johnnie Danvers, and the many others who later figured so largely on the Music Hall stage. I had once been taken to see the Minstrels at the height of their fame in the small St James' Hall and I seem to remember a feeling of disappointment at having to listen to a black-faced man singing 'Close the shutters, Willie's dead'.

'Close the shutters, Willie's dead'

Before we went back to school there was still one treat in store for us. It was our annual visit to our favourite uncle's house in West Kensington. Uncle had a daughter and four sons. They were much older than we were, in fact almost grown-up. One of the sons, Frank, was going to be an artist and had been a student in Paris. We were invited every year to supper and a visit to Olympia. The house stood where Olympia Annexe now stands in Kensington High Road, close to Addison Road Station. From the back windows you could see Olympia all lit up and getting ready for the show. After supper Uncle Willie would take us children to his study and present each of us with two shining new half-crowns—untold wealth in those days. Then we would all troop along the terrace and, at the corner, turn to the brightly lit entrance to Olympia. Was it 'Venice in London' or 'Constantinople'? Anyhow, there was water and a ride in a gondola through exciting little canals and under arched bridges, with grilled windows above, all very realistic.

In the great arena with its huge stage we watched historic scenes being re-enacted, and as a Grand Finale there was a line of girls stretching the whole width of the stage, kicking up their legs in unison. Meanwhile the Stage Manager, Imre Kiralfy, ran around in his dressing-gown to see that all went smoothly. It was all very dazzling. I did enjoy seeing all those girls, and looked forward to the next time.

Uncle Willie was a master at St Paul's School as well as being a

'Present each of us with two shining new half-crowns'

parson. As a boy he had been a pupil at the old school in St Paul's Churchyard before it moved to Hammersmith, and he told us stories of the hazards of getting to school in the City from a house in Tavistock Square. He remembered seeing a man being hanged outside Newgate prison one morning and said that people seemed to be making a picnic of it, many sitting on the curb with baskets of food and drink. He said, laughingly, that he hoped we boys would not have the same unpleasant experience when *we* went to St Paul's.

Then he told us that he and Father had discussed the possibility of our going to the big School when we grew older. This was great news for us and it made us proud to think that, one day, we might go to a real Public School; it helped to reconcile us to the prospect of *ever* going back to school. The Christmas holidays were nearly over and our return to work at the Kindergarten loomed unpleasantly near.

Chapter Ten

GRAND CHRISTMAS PANTOMIME

Back at school again after the Christmas holidays, Cyril and I found it hard to settle down to work. Ethel, on the other hand, liked her studies and seemed glad to get back to them. Even homework she found attractive. Though I was not burdened with much 'prep', I always put off what I had to do for as long as possible, and the cry of 'Ernest, *have* you done your homework?' constantly rang in my ears.

We did not go to school on Saturdays; we had the mornings to ourselves. If the weather was favourable, I could have a good long spell with Septimus. I was not supposed to go beyond the corner of the Terrace, but I broke the rule on certain occasions and tried to race the cabs trotting along Park Road by pedalling on the pavement as fast as I could. This was great fun. The more sporting of the cabmen would enter into the spirit of the game and whip up their horses into a hand-gallop and give 'View Halloos!' I stood a fairly even chance with four-wheelers, but hansoms always beat me. One day I almost got into trouble when an elderly fare popped his head out of the cab window and threatened to summons the cabby for furious driving, and I too did not escape a few uncomplimentary remarks.

There was a dreary prospect ahead, with short and foggy days. If only the weather would turn really cold there might be snow-balling or sliding on the ice. I could remember my first experience of winter games when, two or three years before, we had a prolonged

'Tried to race the cabs'

frost, but this year there was little snow and the ice of Regent's Park lake was never thick enough to be safe.

It was the following year that the great freeze-up occurred and there was skating and sliding for six weeks. Then we spent whole days on the ice in the Park, while Father and Mother skated. Booths were erected with hot drinks, baked potatoes and hot chestnuts, and the men with skates for hire did a roaring trade. One day Father took us into Town to see the ice on the Thames. We stood on Hungerford

Bridge and saw the floes drifting down and piling up above Water-loo Bridge and were told that some men had crossed from the south side to the Embankment on the ice. Many water pipes were frozen, even some of the mains were affected, and stand pipes were put up in the streets where water could be drawn in cans and buckets. When

'Stand pipes were put up in the streets'

the taps froze up they had to be thawed by braziers of burning coke or by pouring kettlefuls of hot water on them.

There was generally a small group of children warming them-selves at the brazier. We all worked, carrying out our cans and pails and emptying them into the bath upstairs. This acted as a sort of reservoir and meant that we were not able to wash properly. Not that this worried Cyril or me.

We had no such fun in the winter of which I am writing. Cyril and I spent much time in the playroom, reviewing our armies of toy soldiers and fighting pitched battles on the floor. Father had made us a 'river' for our pontoon train; it was of painted cardboard with two 'banks' of green baize and was most realistic. Slots were cut for the little boats to sit in, so that we could build a complete bridge across. Our little blue-uniformed soldiers with the spiked helmets made light work of storming across, regardless of the hail of rifle fire from the opposite bank. Disputes always arose as to the number of casualties incurred, and I fear that we never solved any tactical problems. Always it happened that either a meal was announced or it was time to go to bed—and a very good way of settling a war too!

We unearthed Ethel's doll's house from the loft. This had once been a source of great joy to us. We had helped Ethel to arrange and re-arrange the furniture and to see to the comfort of the inhabitants. But this was before the advent of the toy soldier age. We now carried the house downstairs and set it up on the playroom table. Then we proceeded to take stock. It had been put away for some years so that things were in disorder, but Cyril and I got busy and did some extensive repair work. We made quite a number of useful additions, and, by using the forbidden modelling wax discreetly, we found that things could be kept in place: the members of the family in residence, for example, could be fixed to their chairs with dollops of wax on the seats, and thus the wretched creatures (a few china dolls) were condemned to sit at rigid attention instead of sliding off on to the floor. We tried to make a table-lamp with a real night-light inside, but the result was too big to go on the table and it fell off, setting

alight some lace curtains. The doll's house was then banished back
to the loft.

There were a lot of fogs that year, which made the winter worse.
Then Cyril started a snuffly cold and had to stay indoors for two
days, though it soon cleared up. He was going to leave the Kindergarten school at the end of the Easter Term and go to a day school
in Acacia Road. 'Olivers' we called it. This was a great adventure
for him, and I do not think he was looking forward to it—and with
reason, for it proved to be a tough place where the smaller boys were
bullied and some of them had a miserable time. I was to find this out
when I myself went there two years later.

Near the end of January, on one particularly murky morning
when it was dark enough to have the gas light in the schoolroom, I
was glooming over my work in class when I was called out by Miss
Gardner. She told me that we had been sent for. I hurried out to
find Martha waiting below. Cyril came out from his classroom, and
Martha told us that we were to go home at once on account of something important. While we scrambled into our coats and mufflers
we tried to get Martha to tell us what it was. All she would say was:
'You must wait till we get Miss Ethel from the High School.' When
we were all gathered together she told us that we were to go to
Drury Lane Pantomime that *very* afternoon!

It is difficult to describe the state this put us in. Cyril and I shouted
and sang all the way along Park Road and the fishmonger wanted to
know what it was all about. When we arrived home Mother was
waiting. She told us that Mr Olivier, who had the theatre agency in
Bond Street, had lent us his box for the afternoon performance at
Drury Lane. Cyril and I, overcome with joy, turned somersaults
round the dining-room table and were then packed off to lie down—
Lie down, mind!'—and told that we would have a light lunch and

then go by cab to Drury Lane. Though we obediently lay down, neither Cyril nor I could sleep; we just lay there exchanging speculations on the glories to come. We had never been to a pantomime before. We had seen Hengler's Circus the previous year and also the Minstrels, but this was far, far more thrilling.

'Turned somersaults round the dining-room table'

At midday we were told to get up and put on our best velvet suits. This usually irksome task, normally done under protest, was performed with quite unheard-of speed and we were soon ready to sit down at table. Appetite seemed to have deserted me; I was much too excited; but I was made to eat something. Lizzie was shaking her head over our chances of ever reaching the theatre. She recalled how once, years before, in just such a fog, Grandma had failed to arrive at a concert at which she was to sing. We were glad when Father came home from the office. He was just as pleased as we were, though

'Made our way up the steps'

he said we must allow plenty of time, for the fog was even thicker down in the West End. The old messenger man was summoned from his seat at the end of the Terrace and sent to find a four-wheeler. It was agony waiting while he was gone, but he came back seated inside and the horse all steaming in the cold foggy air. We started off, our progress getting slower and slower as the fog grew thicker. It was worse by the time we reached Marylebone Road, and along Tottenham Court Road gas flares were burning and the traffic moving at a snail's pace. Two or three times we nearly mounted the curb and it seemed as if we should never get to the theatre. Boys with flaring torches were guiding people along the streets. Oh, dear! suppose we should be too late! At last we reached Long Acre and, turning into Drury Lane, came in sight of the gas torches burning under the great portico of the theatre. There were crowds of carriages and cabs in the street, with touts running among them to guide people and earn a few pence. We left our cab and, struggling through the press of people and clinging to each other, made our way up the steps.

Two Grenadier sentries in overcoats and busbies were standing at attention, a strange contrast to the heaving crowd. Dodging among the people were boys dressed as pages, in bright blue suits with buttons and pill-box caps, giving away little bottles of scent. I grabbed one of these, but after the first whiff it began to smell very nasty and I threw it away. Waiting while Father fumbled for the tickets was misery. . . . Suppose he had lost them! Or suppose they were for the wrong day! But all was well, and we crowded inside and along the passage, where a woman in an apron opened a small door and we were shown into our box. There the full glory of the place burst upon us. I stood looking at the auditorium, fast filling up, trying to take it all in. There were pegs at the back of the box and the woman helped us hang up our coats and mufflers. The box contained only four chairs but that didn't matter as I was far too excited to sit and kept hopping up and down. Somebody brought a programme and the orchestra began to tune up. Then the great big circle of gas in the roof was turned up and the limelights in the wings began to fizz. A general hush descended on the audience. Threading his way among the orchestra came the conductor.

At this point Cyril was sick. He generally was when he got overexcited and it always happened at an inconvenient moment. However, the woman in the apron was

'Trying to take it all in'

most sympathetic and tidied everything up. My chief concern was that Cyril might miss something, but, having done his bit, he seemed to be all right. Then the curtain rose and I became lost to all around me, translated to another land, borne aloft on magic wings into another world.

The story must have been *The Babes in the Wood*, for otherwise why should Harry Nicholls and Herbert Campbell, both outsize Babes, have appeared seated side by side in an enormous double perambulator and proceeded to sing a duet?

Two bandits, though hired for the purpose of making away with this innocent pair, spent most of their energies in knockabout comedy. Can they have been the Griffiths brothers, the famous inventors of Pogo the horse? The scene in the kitchen of the wicked Baron's house was a riot below stairs, with a cat who jumped over a large kitchen table, all laid ready for a meal; he jumped like a real animal and landed on his forelegs, a thing no one but Charles Laurie could do. This was before Dan Leno's day; he did not come to Drury Lane till a year or two later. But I remember a gay young woman with prominent teeth and a flaxen wig who sang and danced bewitchingly. She could only have been Marie Lloyd, the unforgettable, aged seventeen and in her first Pantomime at 'the Lane'. In the Harlequinade the clown was an old favourite, Harry Payne, so Father told us, who had been clowning for years and was shortly to give place to another famous clown, Whimsical Walker.

It was all such a feast of colour, music, and fun, and it would be quite impossible to express all the emotions that were aroused in a small boy's breast. I know that I stood gripping the velvet-covered front of the box, lost in a wonderful dream, and that when the curtain fell at the end of the first act and the lights in the auditorium went up, I sat back on Mother's lap with a sigh. I could not speak when she asked me if I was enjoying the show. I could only nod my head. I did not think it possible that such feminine charms existed as were displayed by the Principal Boy. Ample-bosomed, small-waisted and with thighs—oh, such thighs!—thighs that shone and glittered in the different coloured silk tights in which she continually appeared. How she strode about the stage, proud and dominant, smacking those rounded limbs with a riding crop! At every smack, a fresh dart was shot into the heart of at least one young adorer. I had a grand feeling that it was all being done for my especial benefit: the whole performance was for *me*; the cast had all been told that they were to do their best because *I* was there. Nobody else, not even Mother, could feel exactly the same as I did.

I had one dreadful moment when I happened to look round

while the adored one was singing one of her songs. . . . Father, at the back of the box, was reading a newspaper. I could hardly believe my eyes. Could it be that he was so overcome that he was trying to conceal his emotion by this show of indifference? Yes, no doubt that was it; but I have since wondered if I was right.

The spectacle reached a climax with the transformation scene. Glittering vistas appeared one behind the other, sparkling lace-like canopies spread overhead, a real fountain poured forth in the background. On either side golden brackets swung out from the wings, each with its reclining nymph, solid and spangled and in a graceful attitude. Flying fairies, poised but swaying gently, filled the air and formed a sort of triumphal archway, below which the performers gathered. The Good Fairy, stepping forward, invoked in rhymed couplets the Spirit of Pantomime, and out from the wings burst Joey the clown, Pantaloon, Columbine, and Harlequin to complete the tableau. Not quite, for, led by the Principal Boy, there came Augustus Harris himself, immaculate in evening dress with white waistcoat, to receive the plaudits of a delighted audience.

There was still the Harlequinade to come. The red-hot poker (that kept hot for a remarkably long time), the strings of sausages, the stolen goose, the Pantaloon always in difficulties, the Policeman, blown up and put together again. Oh, how I longed for it to go on for ever! Then Harlequin, with a wave of his wand, brought on his Columbine, so fair and dainty, but not so lovely as to steal one's heart, though she helped Joey to rob the shopman. On came the tall thin man who sang and sang the while he was belaboured by Joey and Pantaloon. And then—the end!

It was really over at last. No use to gaze at the dropped curtain, the dimming lights or the emptying theatre. I was speechless as we muffled up for the journey home. Speechless as we sat in the cab and

'Augustus Harris himself'

crawled slowly through the same fog which seemed so much blacker than it was before. Speechless as I tried to eat the unwanted supper, while the others prattled of all the lovely things they had seen. 'Do you remember when the cat . . .?' and 'Did you see those two men fight and their swords come to pieces . . .?' I could only see one vision: *she* floated before me, superb and feminine.

My tongue was loosed when Mother came up to kiss me good night. 'Darling,' she said, 'did you really enjoy it?'

'Yes, oh yes!' Then, rather breathlessly, 'Wasn't she lovely!'

I did not want Mother to go, so I took her hand as she sat beside me on the bed. I asked her if she had been to a pantomime when she was a little girl. 'There were very few pantomimes when I was your age,' she replied, 'and none anything like so grand as this one. I remember a clown and a harlequin, but all the girls wore skirts to their knees' (this with a smile at me). Then she said: 'I must have been twelve years old before Grandma took me to one, but not in a box, we had quite humble seats.'

I thought about this for a moment or two and then said: 'Do you think we shall be able to go to one again next Christmas?'

She laughed and replied: 'Why, that *is* a long way off, but perhaps we may be able to.' Then she kissed me good night and went downstairs.

I lay back in bed and made up my mind that I would draw all I had seen, using my new coloured chalks, red, blue, and yellow for the clown and pantaloon, the choice sky-blue tint for the spangled corsage of my beloved's costume which she wore when she came on at the end. Yes, and primrose yellow for her little short cloak and those shining legs. The hat, bedecked with ostrich feathers, should be pink. But oh! could I ever draw her as she really was? Sleepily, with my head on the pillow, I thought all this over and tried to decide where I should begin. Overcome with drowsiness, I lay there watching the faint light from the gas lamp on the stairs. The door was open and I could hear the cistern making its usual dripping noise. Then Mother's voice came to me from below. She was singing in the drawing-room, 'Robin, lend to me they bow'. I think she knew it was my favourite song.

Drawn from Life

TO MY DAUGHTER MARY

PREFACE

I WROTE *Drawn from Memory* because I had always promised my children that I would one day write down the memories of my childhood which I had been in the habit of telling them verbally. The writing, and the drawing of the accompanying illustrations, afforded me much private pleasure; but when the result was published I did not expect to receive encouragement to embark upon the description of a further stage of my life. But encouragement was what I received in good measure; and, fortified thus by the good wishes of friends and the blessing of my publisher, I have tried my hand again.

The first book covered roughly a year of my boyhood. It was an important year outside the Shepard family circle – 1887, the year of Queen Victoria's Golden Jubilee. Within my family it was a period of peace before a storm. We were living in our house by Regent's Park, and I see myself riding my tricycle horse up and down the terrace pavement in untroubled bliss.

The second book begins with the illness and death of my mother in 1890, when I was ten years old, a bereavement which entirely altered our family life. It covers the period of my adolescence and early manhood up to my marriage in 1904. Some of the friendships I made in those years have endured to the present day, and, to my surprise, I have found that some of the letters I wrote then have survived. I am particularly grateful to Chattie Salaman for lending me some letters which include drawings that I have reproduced. I am also indebted to Alan White for his help and advice in arranging my book, and above all I am deeply grateful to Norah for her unfailing help and encouragement.

PREFACE

It may surprise some of my readers to hear that when I married, my wife and I were able to live perfectly comfortably on twenty-one shillings a week, of which only 2*s.* 3½*d.* went on the rent of our cottage in Surrey. But such facts, which contrast so sharply with conditions at the present time, seem to me some justification in themselves for presenting this account of one kind of life at the turn of the century.

E. H. S.

Chapter One

LIFE WITH THE AUNTS

IN the middle of April 1890 we three children – my sister Ethel, my brother Cyril and myself – were se . away from our home in Kent Terrace. We did not know why; still less did we guess that we were never to go back. My mother, lying in bed, said goodbye quite cheerfully, as though we were leaving for a short visit, and we detected nothing in her appearance to tell us that we should not see her again. She had been ill for over a year and it had become part of our daily life to carry her meals upstairs to her bedroom and to push her wheel-chair on our walks round the park. We would sit round her bed in the evening and tell her of our day's adventures, and Ethel would sometimes write a letter for her. We did not know that her illness had recently taken a turn for the worse and that Father had been warned that she had not long to live. The decision to send us away must have been a hard one for him to take, but it was a wise one, for it spared both Mother and us the sorrow of parting. He knew we should be well cared for at our Aunts' and that we should not be far away.

We had a warm welcome at the house in Gordon Square. Even Aunt Annie, the invalid, brightened up and invited us to sit on her couch while we prattled away. The house was just the same as it had been three years before when we had stayed there for a fortnight in the Easter holidays. The imposing hat-stand in the hall was adorned with more of Father's cast-off hats; the Albatross head hanging on the wall was perhaps a trifle more moth-eaten; the hand-bell, brightly polished and ready to announce the advent of a meal, was still on its stand; and last but by no means least, there was the ever-present smell of dinner. One addition to the dining-room was a 'Fernery' of solid iron construction with a domed top reminiscent

of the Crystal Palace. It was not unlike a tea-trolley on wheels surmounted by a glass conservatory filled with ferns. The ferns were diligently tended by Aunt Fanny and Aunt Emily, who had collected them on their visits to the country. Aunt Emily's plants never seemed to thrive; I suspect they received too inquisitive attention from her, for she was constantly disturbing them to see if they were 'making root'. Moreover, there were frequent disagreements between the Aunts as to the wisdom of opening or shutting a ventilator in the roof. The glass top of the fernery was always steamed over, so that it was not easy to see what botanical developments were taking place inside.

Of my two other aunts the eldest, Alicia, spent most of her time in an unequal battle with the weekly accounts, while Aunt Annie, a trifle paler and more wan, lay on her couch all day.

The maids, five in number, were the same as before – Edlin the cook, Jane the parlourmaid, Alice and Mary the housemaids, and the little one at the end whose name I could never remember and whom I had no means of identifying. The erstwhile charwoman had left under a cloud with a few pounds of butter smuggled in her basket, and Henry the odd man was odder than ever. The maids trooped into morning prayers at ten o'clock; evening prayers were at nine in the drawing-room, and I was now deemed old enough to attend the ceremony and afterward to carry my candle upstairs to my bedroom on the top floor, a long journey in semi-darkness. There I was condemned to sleep alone, for Cyril had been given a small room on the floor below.

Soon after our arrival we were told that Mother was worse. We were troubled, but even so did not realize the seriousness of her condition. I never dreamed that she *could* die. A few days later Aunt Alicia called us together in her study and told us that Mother had died early that morning. It must have been an ordeal for my aunts to have three heart-broken and bewildered children in their care, and their kindness was beyond words. In three days Father joined us, and it was a consolation to us to have him, as I am sure it was also for him to be with us.

When the pain of our grief lessened, Cyril and I would spend hours talking over what was ahead of us. We solemnly agreed that we would cry no more, as we knew Mother would not have liked it. And we would not complain about the black clothes and ties we were required to wear. I found an Eton collar particularly irksome after the freedom of my open-necked sailor tunics. We were glad when the blinds were raised and the sunlight streamed in on our darkened lives.

The shock of Mother's death went much deeper than I realized at the time. By temperament I was a resiliently happy child, but this event left a scar for years. I was my mother's youngest child and circumstances drew us very close together. While Cyril and Ethel were at school, I would 'help' her about the house, which of course generally meant getting in her way. She would take me shopping with her and sometimes she would tell me her worries. I enjoyed the outings. We always had fun, and the expeditions frequently ended in the sharing of an ice-cream at Elphinstone's. Elphinstone's sixpenny strawberry ice was so generous as to be almost too large for one small boy, and Mother would take a spoon and raid mine. Our laughter and scrambles were not, however, considered proper by some of the elderly customers; to behave like a schoolgirl was not thought decorous even in a mother as young as she.

I had, I am afraid, a hot temper and often distressed Mother by my outbursts. Afterwards I would creep downstairs, ashamed, to sit beside her, and she would hold my hand and bathe my forehead with eau-de-Cologne and dab my eyes. Then I would sit quietly and listen while she told me about her life as a girl and of the actors and singers who were often at the house in Torrington Square. Her father, William Lee, the water-colour painter, had died when she was a child. He had known a number of artists, and these visited my grandmother (she was only seventeen years older than Mother), so that the house had a Bohemian air. I loved hearing all this, for it was such a contrast to the conventional atmosphere of my father's home.

Mother always encouraged my drawing and, though she had little talent herself, would show me how to use my paints. We made plans together for when I grew up and became an artist myself. She, almost more than Father, inspired me to persevere. After her death I missed her companionship terribly and determined to justify her faith in my talent. So I was particularly glad when Father told me he had taken a studio and that I should be able to practise in it.

He was an architect and adviser to University College Hospital, and for convenience he rented the studio in Gower Street. It was on the first floor, over an artists' colourman's shop, where the students from the Slade School came to buy their paints. I made a habit of going there to do my lessons. Carrying my drawing-book, I would spend hours at work there. Father had a plaster cast of the Venus of Milo: the sketches I made of this cast from every angle were my first attempts at drawing from the antique.

Cyril and I had left the elementary school in Baker Street six months previously, and he had gone as a day boy to St John's Wood Preparatory School in Acacia Road. I was to join him later. I was not looking forward to it, for Cyril's description of life there was, to say the least of it, harrowing. I was glad when Father decided that I should have lessons in his studio until after the summer holidays.

Ethel was able to continue her music at Gordon Square. There was a piano in the back drawing-room, a large room with three windows and a stone balcony overlooking Tavistock Place. She

could practise on the piano while I scraped away on my fiddle. Ethel and I started violin lessons with a Herr Kartenhausen in St John's Wood. He was tall and very fat with a beard so thick that he had difficulty in stowing it away when he played his violin. He had a large family; I never knew just how many children he had, for every time we visited his house a few fresh ones would appear. Frau Kartenhausen spent her time nursing babies. On the whole it was a jolly household, though rather noisy, and music lessons were constantly interrupted. That, however, did not matter, for the 'Herr Doktor', as he called himself, did not teach us much and we soon left. Ethel and I had tea with them one afternoon; for me the meal was spoilt by the detestable presence of caraway seeds in all the cakes and even in the bread. The eldest daughter, a complete *Hausfrau* in miniature, kept order at the table, admonishing the younger children with 'Attention! Now, Elsa and Walther, do not wr-r-r-angle!' while the Herr Doktor drank coffee from a cup fitted with a device to prevent his moustache from getting wet. I had been promoted to a full-sized violin by this time. The instrument was a gift from my godfather and the fingering was far from easy for my small hands. I had to continue my lessons the following autumn at the London Academy of Music in Mortimer Street.

We lived with the Aunts for almost a year. They did all in their power to console us for our loss and make us happy, but though we had the morning-room for our own use, life was not the same as it had been at home. For one thing, we had to tidy up every night and put things away in a cupboard. And then for me there was the bitterness of having to part with Septimus, my beloved tricycle-horse. It was true that he had lost his tail, and in any case I had grown too big for him, but it was nevertheless an agony to see him packed off to a children's hospital. Ethel endured the corresponding sadness of seeing her doll's-house and all its inhabitants dispatched to the same destination. It seemed that all that was left to us were our toy soldiers, but our attempts to parade them on the morning-room floor were not a success, for on the thick carpet they would not stand upright.

As the summer drew near plans were made for the holidays, which we were to spend with our aunts. As neither my godmother, Aunt Alicia, nor Aunt Annie, the invalid, could bear travelling by train, it was their practice to rent a house in the country within easy driving distance of London. This year they chose Wimbledon, then quite a rural place. I remembered my father's description of the Aunts' journey to Highgate three years before, when the 'bus came to a stop on Highgate Hill; and I had hopes of some like adventure on this occasion. The drive, however, was uneventful.

When the 'bus came to Gordon Square to fetch the party, boxes of stores and baskets of linen were stowed on top, Aunts and cages of canaries were packed inside, while Cyril and I were allowed to ride on the box. With the horses trotting in front, this was as good as being on the Atlas 'bus. We crossed Putney Bridge and ascended the hill to a common beyond. This had a windmill standing alone and the driver told us it was Wimbledon Common. The house we were going to was down a side-road off the Ridgeway. It looked fairly new, with large casement windows and virginia creeper on the walls.

Some of the maids must have arrived before we did, for in the drawing-room, which had a grand piano and was crowded with furniture, afternoon tea was already laid. The garden was disappointing – full of shrubs and with no tennis court.

We had not been many days in Wimbledon when, about six o'clock one evening, we heard shouting at the top of our road. Cyril and I rushed out to investigate and found that a haystack on the common was on fire. We joined a small crowd that had gathered to watch, dodging the hot sparks and white smoke that drifted across the road. Someone said that the local volunteer fire brigade had been called. It was a long time in coming, but eventually the engine arrived, pulled by two ill-assorted horses, with the firemen in their

workaday clothes and only brass helmets to identify them. Having witnessed Whiteley's great fire three years before, I was inclined to be critical of their appearance and performance. The manual engine was prepared and pump-handles unstrapped. Then a search for water was made. A pond near by provided it, and volunteers were called for to man the pumps. I tried to join them, but was told that my arms were too short, so I had to stand by and watch. Encouraged by the bystanders, the pumpers got to work. 'Up! Down! Up! Down!' A jet of water shot from the nozzle. Meanwhile some firemen were pulling the rick to pieces with pitchforks. We could not wait to see the end of it all, for Father appeared to call us in to high tea, which we were accustomed to take at seven o'clock while the grown-ups had their late dinner.

From the upper windows of our house we could see miles of open country lying below, with fields and a few straggling houses. One large meadow was fenced in to mark the bounds of the local cricket club. During our stay one match of some importance took place there. Whether or not it was for charity I do not know, but several tents and a large marquee were put up and the field was made gay with flags. They charged a shilling to go in, children half-price. Father took us boys and we sat on the grass and watched what was my first cricket match. Among the players were the redoubtable Dr W. G. and the Read brothers, W. W. and Maurice. It was pleasant sitting on the grass and watching the game, but I nearly went to sleep.

The thing that I enjoyed most at Wimbledon was walking across the Common to the rifle-butts. On a Saturday afternoon, when the red flag was hoisted, I would watch the shooting, sneaking up as close as I dared to the firing-point. Some of the riflemen wore Volunteer uniforms and were using Martini-Henry rifles. (Readers of *Drawn*

from Memory will remember that I knew quite a lot about guns.) It was fun to listen for the bullet hitting the iron target – 'Whang!' On off days I could explore the butts and inspect the dents on the targets and perhaps pick up a flattened leaden bullet or even a brass cartridge-case.

Once a week our household trooped to the bottom of the garden after the evening meal. The Aunts were muffled up and we waited in the growing darkness for the firework display at the Crystal Palace. Though we had only a distant view, it was an impressive sight, for which I was given a special dispensation to stay up late.

I did not go back to London with the others at the end of August. I had been invited to stay with Father's cousins in Guildford. Great-Uncle Richard had built a house on Guildown, and his daughter, my cousin Marion, lived there with her aunt. This aunt, Georgina Warren by name, was a great character of unknown antiquity, for she was always at pains to keep her age secret. When the time for

the census came along she would pack herself off for the night to a friend of presumably the same age as herself; this friend alone knew the truth. Great-Aunt Georgina was in charge of the livestock at Guildown, but never would admit that chickens grew up. She kept a large square basket with a trap-door at the side for them to roost in. As they regarded this as their home from an early age they would go in there to roost when almost fully grown. The gardener tried to point out that this meant overcrowding, but Aunt Georgie was adamant. 'They have always been there,' she argued. Finally the lid of the basket was unfastened in her presence, and layers of chickens were disclosed, the luckless ones at the bottom nearly suffocated.

Then there was the matter of wine. The old lady said that she could not bear the taste of it, but always seemed willing to make quite sure by trial. She would shake her head and say 'No! You know I don't like it.' Then: 'Well, perhaps I'll have just a taste.' The glass would be poured out and she would take a sip. Another shake of the head and 'No, I don't like it.' After a pause it would be noticed that the glass was empty. Then: 'Try a little more, Aunt Georgy,' and a little more would be tried.

She was an indefatigable gardener, and I spent a large part of my time following her round and learning the names of the flowers and when seeds should, or should not, be sown. She had a cat called Agnes and in the evening after dinner Aunt Georgie would sit on her special chair with Agnes on her lap; half-asleep, she would clean the cat's ears with a hairpin.

The thought of going to school at 'Oliver's', as St John's Wood Preparatory School was called, bore heavily upon me as the end of the summer holidays approached. I felt self-conscious in my black clothes, which did not fit at all well. The knickerbockers were too long and became known at school as 'Shepard Secundus's three-quarter bags'. I was also ashamed of my hat, a horrid round thing with a small peak. When the dread day arrived Cyril and I trotted off to Gower Street Station on the Underground and changed trains at Baker Street. From the platform I cast longing eyes upwards to the walls of the primary school where I had spent four happy years.

Chapter Two

OLIVER'S

OLIVER'S was halfway along Acacia Road on the north side. Two stone gateposts gave on to a weedy drive, which in turn led to a gravelled playground. Across the corner stood the school house, square and forbidding. It might well have been a prison; all it lacked was a notice over the door: 'Abandon hope, all ye that enter here'. This academy for young gentlemen was run by

two 'Heads': Mr Oliver, with a mortar-board tilted forward on his forehead and an ever-present cane, and Mr Jones, a quiet bearded fellow who sometimes took the top class. There were two assistant masters: one, Tucker by name, was known as 'Tommy', a kindly man and a contrast to the other, Payne, a young man with a personality far from being calculated to inspire confidence in the young.

Our days were spent in trying to avoid punishment. If this did not come from Oliver or Payne, then it was dealt out in full measure in the playground, where it was the custom for small fry to be chased around, herded together, and then made to run the gauntlet of the bigger boys' lethal weapons made from elastic and called 'Tollywags'. Sometimes catapults were aimed at us, and on occasion even an airgun fired at our legs. The journey home had its perils too. For there was perpetual warfare between the school and the local errand boys. It became usual for us to proceed as far as we were able in convoy. Woe betide the youngster caught alone! He was pelted with stones or mud, and after defending himself as best he could with his school satchel, often had to take refuge in a shop in the High Street.

I do not remember learning anything at Oliver's beyond an apprenticeship in self-preservation. It happened in the playground one day after some unusually savage bullying that a small boy named Puente, who was half Spanish, became slightly hysterical. I think this rather frightened the offenders, for they melted away. I got very worked up, for Puente was a friend of mine, and I made up my mind that something must be done. Hardly aware of what I was doing, I cornered one of the bullies, and, tears streaming down my face, poured forth a torrent of protest. He looked very surprised and wanted to know what it was all about. He was really a decent chap and didn't smack my head and tell me to mind my own business, but listened patiently while I became more coherent in my plea for the underdog. 'What's your name?' he asked. I told him. Then to my surprise he said: 'You kids should show fight. Use your fists. Look here, I'll show you how.' There and then he gave me a lesson in boxing, telling me how to keep my thumbs tucked in. I promptly passed this on, rather cockily, to my fellow sufferers. I should like to be able to say that from that day all bullying ceased, but it would hardly be a statement of fact.

I do not know when the school building was erected or for what purpose. There was an old white house alongside, where the Head resided, and the house must at one time have been a home with a drive and extensive grounds. The school hall was a big room with a great iron stove and windows high up which rumour said had once been a chapel. There was a platform at the far end backed by a wooden partition and the walls were matchboarding below with white-wash above. Lockers ran along one side. Junior classes were held at each end of this hall, while Mr Oliver took a senior class in a smaller room at the back. I remained among the small fry all the time I was there, thus achieving the ambition of every boy to be as inconspicuous as possible. There was a football team, and I believe it occasionally played a match, but as our ground was gravelled, very little could be done there and games were usually played out at Neasden. It was not till I went to St Paul's that I began to take an interest in football.

That Autumn term seemed endless, but towards the end things brightened up when it was announced that the school was to produce the trial scene from 'Pickwick' before the Christmas holidays. Rehearsing for this meant a busy time for the elder boys who had parts. I had faint hopes that I might get slipped in amongst the jurymen, but I was too small. Cyril, however, was luckier, and I always wanted to stay behind with him to watch the rehearsals. This had the added advantage of avoiding going home alone. Though I do not suppose that any boys in the school were over

fourteen, they seemed to an undersized creature like myself very big and imposing when they stood up and declaimed their lines. The boy who played Winkle was a huge success. He had a natural stammer combined with a vacant expression, and his genuine efforts to give his name in court, 'W-W-W-Winkle', brought the house down. There was no scenery, nor were there any costumes, which I considered rather spoilt the effect.

We did much better in that respect at home in Gordon Square, when we produced a composite pantomime introducing Cinderella and other well-known characters. The whole was written and directed by Ethel, who had a genius for both writing and story-telling. Our cousins, Violet and Stanley, and two or three younger children were roped in, and though there was little chance of rehearsing, for they lived far away in Kensington, the parts were written out, and it was hoped that they might be learnt. In the event the script was brought on to the stage and constantly referred to. We were allowed to improvise some scenery in the back drawing-room with screens and curtains. The lighting left much to be desired, with a gas chandelier hanging from the ceiling in the centre. Also there was no curtain, the large double doors having to serve the purpose. As it was winter, we could not open the sash-window on to the balcony and so give an excuse for a woodland scene, but we achieved a most convincing firelight effect with a large lamp fitted with a red glass shade like a glorified strawberry.

Seated before this, Cinderella, in scene two, was discovered pining for the ball. Cyril was the Prince and I played several parts, but most of my time was spent in changing costumes and fixing up the 'scenery'. Ethel alone knew her words; in fact, she knew all our words too and was able to prompt. As we all dried up sooner or later she had to fill in a good many blanks. Violet, as the Fairy Godmother, suffered from stage fright, and after her opening sentence, 'Why are you crying, Cinderella?' incontinently fled behind a screen without waiting for the answer. The audience was composed of our Aunts, our cousin from Guildford, who was staying in the house, and, seated on high chairs at the back, the maids. Father, having had some experience of our theatricals, had provided himself with an evening paper. However, we children all enjoyed it immensely and had a grand supper afterwards down in the dining-room.

Cyril and I each had a birthday in December – too near Christmas for our liking, as one present often did duty for both festivals. 'With love from . . . for birthday and Christmas' was, we considered, not playing the game. But we did not do at all badly, for no Aunt could overlook the two anniversaries while we were living in their house. My Godmother, Aunt Alicia, gave me a conjuring set for my birthday, a real slap-up affair with some very ingenious tricks in it, and we felt that this called for a special performance. The set contained instructions on how to arrange a show with an accomplice hidden from the audience. We borrowed a small table such as a conjuror would use and draped it with a gay tablecloth. In this

confined space I, being the
smallest, hid myself, and
there I had to remain
concealed till the double
doors closed upon the
scene. Ethel acted as conjuror with wand (pro-
vided with the set) and
top-hat (provided by
Father). She placed the
hat on the table brim
downwards, having first
shown it to be empty.
Then, 'Hey, presto!' a
wave of the wand, the
hat was lifted, and there
lay a silver watch (bor-

rowed from Aunt Annie's nurse). Ethel was adept at distracting
the attention of the audience while my small fumbling hands reached
up from behind and placed the object under the hat. I had a small
collection of articles down there in the dark – a coin, a playing-card,
an old snuff-box – and all Ethel had to do was to say: 'And what
shall we find now? I think it will be a coin of the realm,' and lo
and behold it was! With Cyril, she essayed a thought-reading act,
but this had to be carefully rehearsed and was quite beyond me.

We looked forward to Christmas with mixed feelings. It would
be the first we had spent without Mother, but Father and our aunts
did their utmost to make it as happy a time as possible. Aunt Fanny
took us shopping at Shoolbred's in the Tottenham Court Road, and
we bought cards at the stationers in Torrington Place. Then there

were the barrows in the back streets where we bought holly and mistletoe. I had saved up nearly ten shillings and decided that I would buy Father a really good present. I spent hours debating what it should be and pestering Ethel and Cyril for advice on the subject. What I finally bought was a silver toothpick, price four and sixpence. It was a dainty little thing that slid in and out like a pencil-holder, but I do not think it was much good to Father, for I never saw him use it.

Christmas Day brought excitement and the opening of presents. We all went to St Pancras Church in the morning and were allowed to sit up for late dinner. This was a grand feast, with crackers and crystallized fruits, almonds and raisins. There was an enormous turkey which Father carved, and a blazing plum pudding; moreover, the pudding had new sixpenny-pieces in it and each child somehow found one in his or her helping. Before dinner we sat in the back drawing-room and sang carols to Ethel's accompaniment. The only blot on the day was that such a rich dinner called

for a dose. At bedtime I had to sit up while Aunt Fanny handed me two small pills. I made a great show of swallowing them, but I am afraid they were slipped under the bed while her back was turned. Consulting Cyril next day, I found that he too had taken evasive action. Neither of us was any the worse.

A few days before we went back to school Father told us that he had decided that we must have a home of our own. He had been looking for a house, something that he could afford to rent, and had found one in Hammersmith. It seemed a very remote place to me, but it had the attraction of being on the river, which meant that it would be near the University Boat Race. What he did not tell us then was the fact that he had been consulting our Uncle Willie, who was his elder brother and a master at St Paul's, as to our becoming pupils there. There had been some talk of this before, but with all the changes in our lives we had given up hope of its ever happening.

We were delighted at the thought of once again having our own home and eagerly asked Father to let us see the house. So one afternoon we all set forth by train to Hammersmith, boarded a horse-tram at the Broadway, and alighted at Ravenscourt Park.

Theresa Terrace stood on the opposite side of the road to the Park and next to Beavor

Lane. It was a terrace of Georgian houses, built, in pairs, of London Stock bricks about a hundred and sixty years ago. There was a narrow strip of green in front surrounded by posts and chains, much in the style that can still be seen in Chiswick and

the Mall. The house, No. 2, had three stories and a basement with area railings. There was a portico over the front door topped by a balcony with iron railings. The front door, wide and square, had a fanlight over it. Inside was a stone-flagged hall. It was a most attractive house, as indeed were all the houses on that terrace, and Father told us that there was a nice garden at the back with a studio. Moreover, the rent was only fifty pounds a year, an important point, since Father's finances were in a bad way. The tenants were an old artist and his wife, who showed us over the house. I think they were sad at leaving the place, as it had been their home for many years. The artist told us that his next-door neighbour was Stacpoole, the engraver, while farther up the Terrace had been the home of George Mason, the painter, and at the end lived Gleason White. Only a short distance away was Beavor Lodge, the home of W. B. Richmond, the Royal Academician.

The view from the upper rooms of our house was quite countrified. Adjoining Ravenscourt Park were the grounds of Hamlet House, and acres of market gardens filled with fruit trees stretched all the way to Young's corner and beyond.

Father told us that it would be some time before we could move into the house, for even when the artist and his wife had vacated it there would be much work for the builders and decorators. He planned to add on a bathroom and small bedroom at the side, and all the rooms needed repapering and the woodwork painting. He was particularly pleased with a fireplace in the drawing-room, though it had a dreadful overmantel with wooden shelves. The mantelpiece itself and the sides were fluted white marble. A medallion at each corner had a lotus pattern in the centre. He said it was a fine example of late Georgian work. Another thing that pleased him was a pair of tall mahogany bookcases built into recesses flanking the fireplace. Being an architect, Father naturally valued such things. It was a great many years before I learned to appreciate them too. These bookcases, saved from the house-breakers when the house was demolished, now ornament my own drawing-room.

The Aunts were very distressed at the thought of our going so far away, but they realized what it meant to us to have a home of our own and did all they could to help. They had been told of the plan for Cyril and me to go to St Paul's School, and they appreciated that we should benefit by being near the School. Meanwhile, we were still in the dark about all this and could only look forward to more dreary terms at 'Oliver's'. Relief, however, was to come sooner than we expected.

Chapter Three

THERESA TERRACE

PERHAPS because Cyril and I had become used to the life, the Easter term at Oliver's did not seem so bad. The thought of moving to a house of our own, with a garden, gave us a lot to talk about and we made all sorts of plans. What pleased us as much as anything was the knowledge that we were to sleep together in the upstairs bedroom, whence we could look out on to the high road and see the horse-trams going by. Cyril was now nearly a head taller than I and was no longer an object for bullying. I benefited from this, for I could always rely upon his intervening on my behalf. We boasted the titles of 'Shepard Primus' and 'Shepard Secundus' and trouble stopped when Primus came to the aid of Secundus.

It was Aunt Emily who let the cat out of the bag about our going to St Paul's. One Sunday, Uncle Willie came to tea at Gordon Square, and Aunt Emily in spite of nudges from her sisters asked him at the tea-table whether we should be in his class. Father saved the situation by saying: 'There, boys, it's out. Are you glad?' To judge by our expressions no answer was required, but it was not until we were alone in the study that we gave full vent to our feelings. Uncle Willie came in to us before he left and told us something about the school, warning us that we should have to spend several terms at the St Paul's preparatory school, Colet Court, before moving up to the big school. This did not, however, damp our spirits. In the light of my subsequent knowledge of Father's financial state at the time,

I am quite sure that Uncle Willie had arranged for us to be taken at reduced fees, otherwise Father could not have afforded it. Nothing mattered now; we were going to be real Public School boys, and didn't we let them know it at Oliver's! We became the envy of the smaller boys and were dubbed 'lucky young swine' by the elder ones.

I don't know how long Oliver's continued after we left. To me it soon became no more than an unpleasant memory. But, years afterwards, when I was a student at the Royal Academy Schools, the student at the next easel was Denis Eden, who had been at Oliver's with me, and we some-times talked of the school. He turned to me one day and said in a low voice, 'Shepard, do you ever wake up in the morning with a feeling you have to go back to that place?' I am sure it had a blighting effect on both our young lives.

It was a great relief to us, as I am sure it must have been to the grown-ups, to be able to talk openly about the future. I felt that I ought to go into long trousers, as Cyril had already done; my 'threequarter bags'

were a continuous source of shame; but relief was denied me and I had to wear the wretched things for several more terms.

Our greatest treat at this time was to be taken to Hammersmith by Father to see how the builders were getting on at Theresa Terrace. There was a pile of slates stacked outside and the hall was full of timber. Upstairs the walls were being stripped and the wood-work painted. Cyril and I clattered up and down the stairs into every room and down to the basement, where the scullery floor was being relaid. The garden was rather a wilderness, but we all got to work on the weeds, and rescued clumps of flags and other plants. There was a grape-vine on the house wall, and a lovely Morello cherry-tree coming into bloom at the end. The studio had been a stable. It had been properly floored and a north light added. A door at the back gave on to a lane, and an old stove was being replaced by an anthracite burner from Pither's in Mortimer Street. We were allowed to choose the wallpaper for our own bedrooms. Ethel chose blue, and we boys took a long time to make up our minds, finally settling for a spotted paper that I was never quite sure about. The work seemed to progress with agonizing slowness, but it was finished at last, and in the Easter holidays we were able to take our two younger Aunts to see our new home. Aunt Fanny, ever practical, closely inspected the kitchen fireplace, and was not very com-plimentary about our choice of bedroom wallpaper. Aunt Emily complained that the stairs were steep; in fact, she was breathless when she got to the top and quite failed to see that the view from our window was enhanced by the horse-trams. However, it was a fine day, the sun was shining and the Morello cherry was in full bloom, and that, they agreed, was a very lovely sight.

The great day came when the furniture arrived. It had been stored in a depository and was very dusty. We all helped to carry

The Morello cherry was in full bloom

in the smaller things, Father giving us directions as to where to put them. I do not know how they managed to get the piano up the narrow stairs, but somehow it reached the drawing-room, after the carpet had been laid. We spent the first night camping on mattresses after having a picnic supper of bread and jam and cocoa. The next day, to our great joy, our dear Lizzie arrived in a four-wheeler. She had been with us ever since I could remember, and before that too, for she had been Mother's nurse, and when Father and Mother were married came to them as cook. She brought her cat in a basket and he had to be kept in for several days to get used to the place. She promptly took us out to find the most promising local tradesmen. There was plenty of choice in the High Road. It was exciting to see the postman arrive with letters, including one from the Aunts with love and good wishes for happiness in our new home.

Cyril and I had one more term at Oliver's, but the end was in sight. We knew that we were to go to Colet Court in September. For the summer holidays we did not feel we wanted to go anywhere, but the Aunts had taken a house at St Leonards and wanted us to join them, and Father said that they would be very disappointed if we did not go. So it was arranged we should spend four weeks with them. Father, meanwhile, was to go to Normandy for a painting trip. He had always made a hobby of painting in water-colours, and would settle down with his easel and white umbrella to paint what he called 'A nice little bit'. This usually consisted of a church or some picturesque cottage. So we saw him off armed with his traps.

The house at St Leonards was called Rosemount and stood above the Archery Gardens. Cyril and I found plenty to amuse us down on the beach. We were now old enough to go out alone, and sometimes we forgot the passage of time, and arrived home late for midday dinner. We were not allowed to bathe alone. Bathing was rather a formal proceeding. Aunt Fanny or Aunt Emily would accompany us, carrying their voluminous bathing-dresses strapped in a towel. They would choose a machine, which they would share with Ethel, while Cyril and I scrambled into another. We could not swim, but were taken to the sea-water baths on Hastings Front and given lessons. The instructor fastened a rope round our middles and then made us jump from the diving-board. Ethel made light of this, but I would stand shivering on the board, urged on by cries of encouragement from aunts and instructor, till finally a tightening of the rope forced me in. Coming to the surface, I floundered frantically to the steps, deaf to the shouts of 'Take it slowly!'

Father was in Normandy for a fortnight, and he brought back sketches of Lisieux, Honfleur and Rouen. He told us about the cathedral there and the lovely Normandy churches, and how he had spent two nights at a little *auberge* with sanded floors where wine

Stand shivering on the board

was less than one franc a bottle. One day when he could afford it, he promised, we should all go there.

Ethel was now a pupil at Queen's College, Harley Street, and was miles ahead of us boys in learning. She was reading Ruskin and we got rather tired of hearing him quoted on all occasions. She was having piano lessons at the London Academy, where I went with my violin once a week. I had to stand up and play before Herr Politzer and was then handed over to Miss Salmond, very patient and, what was more important to me, very good looking. I studied there for three years, but I never found time for practising and made little progress. Before I left St Paul's I gave up music for good.

There was plenty to do in our new home, but Cyril and I found time to go exploring round the neighbourhood. We would slip out of the back studio door into the lane. It was unmetalled and very muddy and we had to pick our way past the high walls of Beavor Lodge. There was a factory at the bottom of the lane by the river. Here we could turn either to the right or to the left; we preferred the right as it led towards Chiswick and the barges, their red sails furled, lying on the mud opposite the Eyot. We liked studying the old houses, Walpole House in particular, and would then go as far

We speculated on the size of her guns

as Chiswick Old Church, with the little inn alongside and Thorney-croft's the shipbuilders. A new type of torpedo-boat called a Destroyer had just been built and was being fitted out in the river. We speculated on the size of her guns and came to the conclusion that the one to be placed on the fo'c'sle would be a twelve-pounder. A waterman told us that she could steam at nearly twenty knots. Later we were to see the 'Speedy', a torpedo-gunboat, quite a large vessel for the river.

Every Sunday Father took us to church at Chiswick. I went very willingly as I knew I should see something of interest lying off

Thorneycroft's. After church we would walk back with the Calthrops, who were old friends of Father's. Claude Calthrop, an outstanding painter who had barely reached middle age, had died recently, leaving a widow and two children, Everard and Hope.

Everard was several years older than us. He had been to St Paul's, but had left before we entered the school. He was at that time a cadet at Woolwich, learning to be a Gunner at the 'Shop'. He was a very clever draughtsman and would certainly have made his name as an artist. He had a brilliant career in the Artillery, where he made a special study of Eastern warfare, learned Chinese and Japanese and became Military Attaché at Tokyo. The Calthrops' house was on the Mall, close to Hammersmith Bridge; it was a charming old house with a glass-covered verandah on the first floor. It was from here that in the following year I was to see my first Boat Race. We had a struggle to reach the house, for the crowd was thick by the Bridge and the public house close by was overflowing. Among the throng were men selling favours, light or dark blue, some made of paper and others of dyed straw costing a penny. More expensive ones were fashioned like birds. Everyone seemed to be wearing his or her fancied colour. When the race started the sound of cheering could be heard along the banks, gradually coming nearer until the boats shot under Hammersmith Bridge and came in sight. On this occasion, to my joy, it was a Dark Blue boat that appeared first.

Dion Clayton Calthrop was Everard's cousin and was often at

their house. He was a son of John Clayton, the actor, and Nina
Boucicault. He, too, had been at St Paul's and was now studying at
St John's Wood Art School. He asked me if I wanted to be an artist.
When I said yes, he told me that it was a precarious life and badly
paid, but all the same, he was going in for it and it was jolly well
worth while.

We often went to see the Calthrops, and when Everard was there
he would talk to me about art and artists. He had been studying the
French Impressionists. Now, I had heard about these fellows from
some of Father's artist friends, those who painted in water-colour and
would sit round and condemn what they called 'slipshod work'.
The pains they themselves took to produce, year after year, the same
kind of subject with the same dull colouring were rewarded by a
ready sale. The galleries were filled, and on the opening day dealers
would compete and sometimes buy up a whole wall of pictures,
taking the bad with the good.

I listened to such remarks as 'Might as well paint a pair of old
boots' or 'The fellow paints a field of mustard – *mustard!* – and has
the cheek to call it a picture.' I just listened and wondered. Father's
great friend Frank Dicksee, with all his academic training and in spite
of his being a Royal Academician, never spoke in such terms and was
far more catholic in his tastes. It was years before I was to make
acquaintance with the Impressionists, years spent in painstaking study
of the antique, a cautious introduction to painting. Frank encouraged
me in this by allowing me to try my hand with oils. I sat for him on
several occasions at his studio in Peel Street, and, the sitting over, he
would give me a palette and brushes and set up a vase or some
bottles. Working on a piece of canvas board, I would quickly get
into trouble, but dabbled on quite content and feeling I was being a
real artist. We often spent Sunday afternoon and evening with the

Dicksees in their house in Fitzroy Square. Frank's sister Margaret, whom we all called Minnie, was also an artist, and an illustrator too. She had a studio on the first floor in their house. Their father, Thomas Dicksee, had recently died, and they were looking out for a new home farther out of London. Now that I was old enough to stay on for supper, it was a great treat to meet so many musical and artistic people and to hear what was happening in the great world.

On one side of Fitzroy Square was the headquarters of a Volunteer Fusilier regiment. From the Dicksees' window on a Sunday afternoon we could watch the men mustering, streaming out of the building, adjusting busbies and accoutrements. Then the band would appear and strike up, and off they would all march, followed by a crowd of sightseers, the music gradually dying away in the distance. I decided that if I could not be a soldier, I might at least be a Volunteer.

We travelled home by train from Portland Road to Hammer-smith. Walking along King Street on a Sunday or Saturday night was not a pleasant experience; there were too many 'drunks' about. The public-houses were open till midnight and each was filled with a noisy crowd which overflowed on to the pavement. It was a pathetic sight to see a woman, often with a baby in her arms, patiently waiting outside to guide her man home. Fights were not infrequent, and we had to take side-turnings to avoid them. Sunday was a dreary day in London. It was no wonder so many people found solace in the pubs. Saturday night was quite a different matter; then the shops were open until very late and did a roaring trade. Jim Burrows, 'the Butcher King' as he called himself, stood outside his shop selling off his meat. He had a stentorian voice and a ready wit and kept up a running commentary on the choiceness of his wares. There was a rival shop opposite and prices were cut first by one and then by the other, with the crowds dodging backwards and forwards to get the best bargains.

It was some time later that I learned that the astute Mr Burrows owned both shops and staged this mock rivalry for his own advantage.

Jim Burrows, the Butcher King

Chapter Four

BEWSHER'S

IN a state of intense excitement Cyril and I set off for our first day at Colet Court. We walked all the way: along King Street, the Broadway, then past the hospital, to come in sight of the big red school standing back from the road. Its gold-faced clock would tell us if we had plenty of time or must hurry. 'Bewsher's', as Colet Court was called, stood opposite, red like its big brother but not so imposing. Along with other new boys we were lined up and inspected by 'Jimmy' Bewsher, the Head Master. We were allotted to classes and were told to go to the office 'in the break' to be fitted with our school caps. There was no school uniform, but we were warned that gay ties must not be worn. I felt very small and followed the excellent principle of making myself as inconspicuous as possible. In the break we got our caps, dark blue with a white Maltese Cross, and found ourselves the object of the interest of some of the older boys. 'What's your name?' 'How old are you?' 'What's your father?' 'Where have you been to school?' No one seemed to have heard of Oliver's. There was no suspicion

233

of bullying and the masters were quite a different type from what we had been used to.

After school we walked home with a boy called Broad. He had been at Bewsher's several terms and was rather condescending, but he gave us a lot of useful advice. He lived at Stamford Brook, and later I got to know him well. The eldest of a large family of brothers and sisters, his parents had a comfortable white house called Stamford Brook Lodge with a garden facing the Green. He was the same age as myself but nearly as big as Cyril and told me that I ought to be in long trousers, which to me was like rubbing salt into an open wound.

I was terribly ashamed of my Christian name and had blurted it out under questioning. This, he said, was a cardinal error, and laid me open to any amount of chaff. ' "*Ernest*"! Fancy being called that!' followed by loud laughter. How I wished that I were George or William, or just John as he was.

Lizzie had tea ready for us when we reached home and was eager to know how we liked our new school. We were able to tell her that it promised well and had a nice big playground. I drew a map of this for her, showing where the wash-houses were and the asphalt piece at the end with the giant stride in the middle. I told her how relieved I was to find several other boys in knickerbockers. We showed her our school caps and told her which classes we had been put into. We had taken sandwiches for our lunch, and when Father came in he asked us if we would mind doing this every day, as having our meal in the dining-hall at school would come expensive.

School began with Morning Prayers and a Hymn in the Big Hall, and as I had a good treble voice it was not long before I found myself in the school choir. The winter game was Soccer and I became quite keen on this, kicking a ball about with other small

234

Meet in the Broads' summer-house

boys in the luncheon hour. I did not find the work too hard at
first, but could never get ahead with Latin or Greek, which was a

handicap when, later on, I got into the higher forms. Drawing classes were dull; we were given cubes and cylinders to draw and shade; and it was not till I moved on to the Big School that I was able to let myself go in the drawing school.

We had not been at Bewsher's long before Broad invited us to tea on a half-holiday. With his large garden and several brothers and sisters this promised good fun. We started a sort of club, chiefly devoted to eating. We would spend our pocket-money on any delicacies we fancied, and then meet in the Broads' summer-house, pool our supplies, and make a feast of it. This was all very well, but it did not always come off. Funds were sometimes low, and then the younger Broads would raid their mother's store cupboard, and this led to trouble with the cook. On one occasion we found a shop in King Street selling off a job lot of sardines; we bought a dozen tins for two shillings and opened them in the summer-house. We thought they tasted a bit odd, and sure enough we had stomach-aches all round, and Mrs Broad dosed us with purgatives. We were always getting into trouble with the gardener, and I am not surprised, for we had no respect for the beds and would build huts among the shrubs, raiding the tool-shed to find any likely pieces of timber. The stable and coach-house had a loft above in which apples were stored. One of the younger boys found the key, but kept the fact dark until his elder brother caught him pocketing the apples. He was then arraigned as a traitor, the key was confiscated, and we older boys used it for our own satisfaction.

With a friend of the Broads, a little girl named Eva, I fell deeply in love. She lived in Sinclair Road and had two younger sisters. They were often at the Broads' house and we all played together in the garden. She was about my own age and John and I were rivals for her affections. I regret to say that he always cut me out.

It was the urge of love that led me to ask Father to let us join a dancing-class. This was held at a Dr Pope's near by, and once a week Ethel, Cyril and I would go there, carrying our dancing-shoes and, as far as I was concerned, cleaned up and dressed with the greatest care. Our teacher was a Miss Thompson, very small and dainty but wrinkled. She used a scent that I did not like, but it was a treat to

dance with her. She would call, 'Take your partners for the Barn Dance, please,' and a rush would be made for Eva. It was not often that I got there first, and when disappointed had to content myself with another, less attractive, partner. A young man played the piano: 'Tumptity-tumpity tum!' He had a wonderful head of hair, curled and pomaded. The class over, we would walk to the tram with the girls and their governess. When we parted I would live for next week. I chose a Christmas card for Eva with the greatest care. It was embellished with the most amorous verses, but it did not have any effect. The fact was that I was not a good dancer, and though I felt safe with a polka or barn dance, it took me a long time to master the waltz.

In November preparations were made for a big firework display in the school grounds and we were asked to bring along our own fireworks to augment it. Posts and wooden frameworks were erected and we all hoped for a fine night, but we were disappointed as it poured with rain and the display had to be put off. When it did take place a few nights later, the night was damp and foggy, and all our own fireworks had been expended. The display was not a success.

The Broads had grand parties at Stamford Brook Lodge at Christmas time. We were given the free run of the house, and their cousin, who was a professional entertainer, amused us for hours. He had one pet song:

> *Oh, Susannah! Don't you cry for me!*
> *I come from Alabama with me banjo on me knee.*

Our favourite verse finished like this:

> *A piece of cake was in her eye,*
> *A tear was in her mouth,*
> *And Oh, Susannah! Don't you cry!*
> *For I'm coming from de South.*

There was plenty of snow that winter and we had properly organized snowball-fights, 'Oxford' versus 'Cambridge', led by two masters named Sankey and Brownjohn (Sankey afterwards became Lord Chancellor). I won my first prize ever at the end of that term. It was, of course, for drawing, for in nothing else did I shine. The prize was *Tom Brown's Schooldays* with the original illustrations. I read it with joy and have done so frequently since. Soon after that a move brought me into Skinner's form, Lower Ist A. We earned distinction at football by winning the class 'sixes', the games being played with six a side. The final, with Lower Ist B, was a hard-fought battle. Skinner and MacDougal, the Form Masters, were as excited as any one. We just got home by a goal. Bridges, our goal-keeper, was one of the heroes of the match. He was a dour stopper. I played back with Douglas Home. Skinner let us off all homework for three days.

I had two terms in Skinner's and then, to my surprise, was moved to the top class, the Upper First. My time there was a happy one. We had a master called Botting who, besides being a good teacher, was a cheerful nice fellow. My particular friend in Upper First was William Temple: 'Fatty' we called him. He and I were always at different ends of the class in weekly lists, and I need not say which end I occupied, though on one occasion I did soar above him, much to his surprise. His father, then Bishop of London, had confirmed me. Temple left Bewsher's at the same time as I did, to go to Rugby. I wished at the time that he could have gone to St Paul's with me, but it would have made little difference if he had, for he was on the

239

Classical side while I was on the Science. I think he was always keen to follow his father into the Church. As a boy of thirteen he had a most forthright character and a grand sense of humour. He was, I believe, a few months younger than I.

With the coming of summer our aunts invited us to spend part of our holidays with them at the seaside. This year it was to be Eastbourne, where they had taken a house in Enys Road; we joined them for three weeks in August. What I remember best about that visit is being taken to see the All-England Lawn Tennis Tournament in Devonshire Park. The play was something quite different from what I was accustomed to see on the lawns of our friends. Though the ladies' dresses were equally conventional, their standard of play was, to me, astonishingly higher. I saw Renshaw win the men's singles, and the Baddeley brothers knock everyone out in the doubles. The ladies served underarm, and though handicapped by long skirts, tight waists and high-necked blouses, managed to skip about the court exceedingly nimbly. The mixed doubles was won by Mrs and Mr Hillyard – I put them in that order for it was evident that she was the senior partner; any mishit by Mr Hillyard was the subject of muttered abuse from Mrs Hillyard; I sat quite near and heard it all. I had not realized before this that lawn tennis could provoke such strong feelings.

Some days later we went fishing with Father's boatman-friend of a previous year. On that earlier occasion the party had narrowly escaped destruction at the hands of the Sussex Volunteer Artillery engaged in target practice at a buoy out at sea. On this occasion our only danger was when Aunt Emily caught her first fish and nearly upset the boat in her excitement.

My brother Cyril left Bewsher's a year or so before I did, and although we continued to make the morning journey together, the big school finished an hour later than Bewsher's. In the evening we did our homework together in the back study overlooking the garden, helped by our tame magpie. He lived in a cage, but as the door was never shut he was always hopping in and out and would peck about on the table and pick up any small object. This bird loved hiding things, and once he upset the inkpot over my prep. In the warm weather we would carry his cage into the garden and there he ruled supreme. Though we kept his wings clipped, he would chase all the birds, and woe betide any cat that ventured over the wall. He was after it in no time, chattering and flapping his stumpy wings. The only cat he did not chase was Lizzie's, between whom and himself there seemed to be an armed truce.

Christmas was like old times. The buying and sending of Christmas cards and such small presents as we could afford with our very limited pocket money added to the enjoyment of our holiday. We paid our annual visit to Uncle Willie at his home in Kensington and came home the richer by five shillings apiece (two shining new half-crowns). After supper we were taken to Olympia to see a stirring military display called 'Chitral', with plenty of red-coated infantry storming cardboard heights. This was followed by a very realistic 'Derby Day'. The arena was filled with vehicles of all sorts from four-in-hands to donkey-carts. Finally we had a real race with jockeys, race-horses, bookies and all – not forgetting the welsher bookie who made off and was chased by the crowd.

A few days before Christmas we went shopping in King Street. I thought the lighted shops and the kerb lined with barrows wonderful. These barrows were lit by naphtha flares, dangerous-looking things which frequently went wrong and belched black smoke. All sorts of fruit could be bought, apples, oranges, pineapples and grapes. Roast chestnuts, hot potatoes and pomegranates were a penny each. Oyster barrows, lit by candles stuck in inverted bottles, were very popular. A man in dirty pink tights did a juggling act, helped by a small boy whom he balanced on his shoulders while tossing up shiny balls which the child caught. This all finished with a posture and a smirk. The boy then went round with a hat. I did not envy him; he must have been very cold in his little tights.

Farther up King Street the 'Butcher King' was in full blast, his shop-front hung with turkeys of all sizes. We watched these being sold off, competition with the shop opposite being as lively as ever.

It was long past my bedtime when we arrived home and Cyril and I stood looking out of our top-floor window. The trams had stopped, but in the faint light of the gas-lamps we could see the carts carrying fruit and vegetables from the market-gardens at Acton to Covent Garden. The horses plodded slowly along; they knew their way blindfold, which was just as well, for the drivers, wrapped in sacks, would certainly be asleep. The glow over King Street died down, but the voice of Jim Burrows could still be heard in the distance and somewhere a barrel-organ ground out the notes of 'The Lost Chord'.

The Aunts had given us a turkey and boxes of crystallized fruits, figs and dates. We peeled almonds, and on Christmas afternoon arranged the fruit with crackers around. Lizzie cooked a glorious pudding, and we all helped to lay the table and carry the dishes up from the kitchen. Esther and Mary Ann, Lizzie's two sisters, were below to keep her company and help with the disposal of a bottle of port wine that Father provided for them – Esther correct as ever in her black kid gloves which she never seemed to remove. After dinner Father read to us. He was a very good reader and had taken us through most of Dickens and some Walter Scott, but on this occasion I found myself dropping off to sleep.

Chapter Five

A COLD WINTER

IT turned very cold after Christmas and I suffered accordingly. Wearing knickerbockers, as I did, with rather rough worsted stockings, the icy winds chapped my ankles and knees, and as I never could find my gloves, my hands suffered also. I must have had a sensitive skin, for neither Ethel nor Cyril seemed to experience the same trouble. I had been set some form of holiday task and the best place to do it was in the kitchen, where it was always warm and cosy. In the back study where we usually worked there was only a small fire and we had to crouch over it to keep warm. After supper there was a much larger fire in the drawing-room, and we sat in front of this as long as we could. Father dozed in his chair and did not mark the passage of time. Suddenly he would wake up, look at his watch and exclaim: 'Look at the time, boys! You ought to have been in bed an hour ago! Off you go at once and no talking!' It did not take us long to undress and tumble shivering into our cold beds.

To add to our troubles this year our pipes froze, even the main pipe in the terrace. The Water Works man who came to see to things said that the main was too near the surface and he put up a stand-pipe for us. We endured the same discomforts we had experienced four years earlier at Kent Terrace, when we had to fill the bath with water carried in cans and jugs from outside. Our bedroom was always cold. The water in the washstand jug generally froze in the night, so that getting up in the morning by gas-light was a penance. Repeated shouts from below failed to move us until Lizzie rang the breakfast-bell. The poor horses pulling the trams had a bad time. They could not start until sand had been thrown down, and even then they would snort and steam in the cold air.

We had one great treat during the holidays. Father took us to a Christmas pantomime at the Crystal Palace. We travelled by train and arrived before midday to have dinner in a restaurant where we were served by a waiter in a very grubby white shirt. The dinner was a grand one—grilled chops, nice big ones, washed down with glasses of cider. The pantomime in the afternoon was not so elaborate as the one I had seen at Drury Lane three years before, but for me was nevertheless unforgettable on account of Cissy Loftus, who played the Principal Boy's part. Not only could she mimic and sing to perfection, she was so gay, and no male boy ever had such lovely legs! Father bought us a pictorial programme with a photograph of her. I cut it out and kept it for years. Afterwards we saw a Panorama in a circular building in the grounds. It represented the siege of Paris in 1870, reconstructed by a famous French battle-painter. We entered a small tower in the centre and climbed up to a gallery and from there looked all round on the scene of battle in the suburbs of Paris during one of the sorties. It was so realistic I could almost

Drawn at the Crystal Palace

imagine it to be the real thing. I had seen a similar panorama of the battle of Waterloo at the Aquarium in Westminster a year or two before, but this one was far better.

About this time Father arranged to share his studio with an artist named E. F. Brewtnall. Mr Brewtnall lived in Bedford Park, and his easel and some of his paintings arrived in a barrow. He was a member of the Royal Society of Painters in Water Colour, but spent much of his time painting sunsets in oils. I do not think he found a ready sale for these, and he was, I believe, quite as hard up as Father, but he was a good tenant and a kindly man. He would arrive about half-past nine in the morning, and if our magpie was out it would accompany him down the garden, pecking his trousers on the way. Brewtnall was a fellow member of a society of artists called 'The Anonymous', the members of which met on Thursday evenings at Frank Dicksee's studio. Each week a paper was read on a subject of topical interest. As one or two of the members were strong radicals some very heated discussions took place, Father told us.

There was a lot of unemployment at the time and small groups of men paraded the streets, chanting:

We've got no work to do-o-o,
We've got no work to do.
We are poor hungry lab'ring men
And we've got no work to do.

Sometimes the traffic had to stop while a procession went by carrying banners. We heard that there were meetings in Trafalgar Square which were followed by rioting. Dramatic pictures of it all appeared in the illustrated papers. It was a good thing when the hard weather broke, for the unemployed must have had a bad time with no money to buy firing for their homes. We, too, were thankful to see the last of it, and Lizzie could light the kitchen range again, for she had found it difficult to cook on a gas-ring.

It was some time in March that we received an invitation from my Aunt Ellen to stay with her in Sussex. She had delicate health and London did not agree with her, so she had decided, many years before, to leave her sisters in Gordon Square and, much against their advice, to live by herself in the country. It had turned out well, for she had found a Scots maid who became devoted to her and remained with her till her death thirty-five years later. The maid, Ganson, came from the Shetland Islands. She had strong views on religion and the evils of tobacco. The two lived at Steyning, and it was arranged that we were to go there in the Easter holidays. The house was one of a pair on the Bramber Road. It had a fine view of the Downs from the back, but was badly built of brick and flint and most unattractive to look at. It still stands, as ugly as ever. Aunt Ellen was very deaf and used an ear-trumpet, but as this was generally mislaid in the folds of her dress it was difficult to pitch one's voice so as to avoid startling her. There were two dogs, Dick and Jip, of indeterminate breed and growing fat from lack of exercise. There was also a strange pet, a young lamb, that lived in the garden. The little thing had been given by the next-door neighbour, an eccentric doctor called Clouting. For me, it was a most enchanting household, with the dogs and the lamb – all, I may say, on the best of terms – and Ganson ever solicitous for our welfare and providing the most delectable meals.

In the morning the lamb would greet us. It had a shed at the end of the garden, and when we called would come bounding towards us. We made it a little collar and took it out on the end of a rope, but Dr Clouting warned us to keep off the road because of stray dogs which might not be as friendly as Dick and Jip. We climbed through the fence at the top of the garden on to the Downs, where the lamb would skip about on the end of his long rope, and the dogs, glad to be out for a run, would hunt for rabbits in the hedges.

We found the Doctor most entertaining. He took us for walks and told us about the countryside. He had a bearded friend who sometimes joined us, a naturalist. He certainly knew all about birds, and was very quick at spotting them, but he carried a walking-stick gun and shot those with the brightest colouring, slipping them into a capacious inside pocket. I cannot help thinking it was the bright feathers he was after; there was a big demand for them at the time for the adornment of ladies' hats.

Father joined us for the week-end, and I realized how fortunate it was that he did not smoke, for Aunt Ellen, as well as Ganson, had a horror of it. The doctor next door was a confirmed pipe-smoker and my aunt complained to Father that the pernicious fumes from his pipe even penetrated into her house. Father, with his experience as an architect, started to investigate, and soon found the explanation. There was a wide crack in the brickwork between the two houses in one of the upstairs rooms. Ganson and Kate the maid soon got to work with strips of paper and glue to try to seal it off.

The station at Steyning was about a mile from our house. It was on a branch of the Brighton Line and had a goods yard. Cyril and I often went there to watch the little tank engine sorting out the trucks. She was painted mustard yellow with L.B. & S.C.R. on her side and a bright copper band round the top of her funnel. I was beginning to take a great interest in engines, and could classify them – 2-4-0, 4-4-2, and so on – according to the arrangement of their wheels. One day we saw a real tender engine standing in a siding, a 2-4-2 passenger locomotive. We climbed the fence and had a good look at her. The fireman was polishing her with an oily rag and we sidled close up to him. He turned and said, 'Fond of engines, eh?' 'Oh yes!' I replied. Then boldly I asked: 'Could we please have a look in the cab?' The fireman called: 'Tom, 'ere's a couple wants to look in your cab.' A head peered over the side, then a voice said: 'Come up, but mind the oil!' Cyril and I scrambled up, not minding the oil, and there we were on the footplate of a real engine. Tom then explained what all the taps and handles and gauges meant and how the reversing gear worked. Everything was polished and shining and he was rightly proud of his engine. 'How does she start?' I asked breathlessly. 'Hold tight and I'll show you,' Tom answered. 'Stand clear, Dave!' and he pulled a handle. We moved steadily forward to the stop block, stopped, and reversed. One of my life's ambitions had been achieved and I could hardly find voice to thank him. 'That's all right, son,' he said. 'Perhaps you'll drive an engine yourself one day.' Aunt Ellen was rather horrified when she heard of our exploit, but reassured when we told her we had not travelled far.

We were sorry when the time came for us to leave, but as we said goodbye our aunt said she would ask us again. 'If I'm spared!' she added. We were able to visit her almost every year, and long after I was married my wife and I often took the children to stay at her house. She never got over her abhorrence of tobacco, so when I wanted to smoke I had to take my pipe into the garden. She would watch me from the sitting-room window, smiling and shaking her head, rather as if I were a naughty schoolboy.

There were a few days to go before the end of the holidays and I spent them trying to catch up on my holiday task.

Lizzie had told us on our return that she had seen a paragraph in the paper saying that Frank Dicksee had been injured. It seemed that he had stopped a runaway horse. 'A brave act,' the paper said. We promptly went to Fitzroy Square to inquire after him, and found him in bed with a large cage covering his legs. His sister told us that he had arrived home in a cab with torn trousers and a battered top hat, and it was not until he had undressed that he realized the state of his leg, which had a wound from knee to ankle. The doctor, after dressing it, packed him off to bed, and there he had to stay for a fortnight. Frank told us it was a carriage and pair that caused the trouble. The horses took fright and bolted. He caught the flying reins but was knocked down and kicked. He was very modest about it all and joked about the colour of his other leg, which he said was pea green. He told us he had bought a house in St John's Wood, and that as soon as the necessary alterations had been made he and his two sisters and their aunt, Miss Alice Bernard, would be moving. The house, in Greville Place, was a late Regency building with a pleasant garden. A studio was to be built at the back, and Frank would then give up the studio in Peel Street.

After they had moved, and before the studio was finished, we often went to see them on Sunday. Their niece, little Ethel Dicksee, was sometimes there and it was fun playing in the new building. Little Ethel and her Aunt Dolly Burroughes, who was only two years her senior, Cyril and I would clamber and chase about and get our clothes in a nice mess.

Among the musicians we met at the Dicksees' was a **Dr Arm-**bruster. Besides being a conductor, he was a very good pianist. He was also a great Baconian, and he told us that he had proved that Bacon wrote all Shakespeare's plays. He then proceeded to claim that Bacon was a German. With Teutonic thoroughness he had marshalled his 'facts' and it was useless to argue with him.

Father was rather concerned about the work that Lizzie had to do, and he consulted Polly Dicksee about it. She promised to find a girl to help with the housework. Soon she wrote to say that she had heard of a young relative of their cook whom she thought would be suitable. The girl, who had only just left school and was very small and shy, came with her mother, and it was all arranged. Her name was Virtuella. She was very willing, and Lizzie, though not without misgivings, said she would 'do'. Though Virtuella did her best she was not adept at answering the door.

On the principle that all visitors must be made welcome, the gas man was shown into the drawing-room. It was pointed out that some discrimination should be exercised with strangers. We had finished supper one night and were sitting in the drawing-room when there was a knock at the door and an agitated Virtuella put her head into the room and quavered, 'Please, sir! There's a rough man outside!' Father went down to investigate and found the front door on the chain. He opened it cautiously. Outside was a figure in a wideawake hat and heavy cape. It was Mr Stacpoole, the artist from next door, come to call.

Chapter Six

ST PAUL'S

I RARELY saw my uncle at school as his classroom was among the high-ups on the top floor. Occasionally I caught sight of him descending the stairs in his mortar-board and gown, or passing to the Masters' Common Room. He was very near-sighted and I never did anything to attract his attention, except once when Father had given me a note to deliver to him and I tried to catch him during Break. He was deep in conversation with another master, and I had to wait until after school hours, when I boldly braved the sanctity of the top corridor and waylaid him as he left his classroom. He looked surprised at being accosted by a small boy and peered at me curiously through his glasses.

'Please, sir,' I stammered, 'I have a letter for you from my father.'

'Oh!' he said. 'Your father, eh!' It was clear he did not recognize me.

I handed him the note. He removed his glasses and put on another pair. Then I said, 'Please, sir, I am your nephew Ernest.'

A smile lit up his face. 'Dear me! Why yes, of course, of course. How stupid of me not to recognize you, but I am near-sighted, you know. Well, and how do you like being at St Paul's?'

'I like it very much, thank you, Uncle Willie,' I replied.

He stood smiling at me and then said: 'Oh yes, the note! Let us see what your father has to say.' Having read the letter he asked: 'And how do you like your new home?'

'Very much thank you, sir – Uncle Willie.'

'Well, tell your father I will write to him.'

'Thank you, s – Uncle Willie.' And I bolted.

It was different with the High Master – the 'Old Man' as we called him. We saw him all too often. The worst punishment that could be inflicted upon any boy was to be sent from the classroom to wait outside until recalled. The Old Man had a habit of going the rounds and descending on a classroom without

258

warning. He would sail majestically down the corridor, and it was useless for any boy doing penance outside a door to try and hide behind the lockers. He was spotted from afar and the enemy bore down on him. With a growl he was asked what he was doing there. A stammering explanation was sure to be cut short with 'Speak up'. Then, 'What's your name?' The door was flung open and he was sent to his place. I think most of the masters dreaded these visitations as much as we did. If the Old Man was heard approaching it was the signal for all to assume an air of intense industry and lamb-like innocence. Each junior master was provided with a cane, though I do not think the weapons were often used. Only once was I caned, and I have no doubt that I had earned the punishment. It was dealt out by Mr Wainwright, and Broad suffered at the same time. It was not laid on heavily, but my behind was tender for days. The worst crimes were 'tried' by the High Master, and if the deed were proved it meant a 'portering', a chastisement administered by the head porter, a great bearded fellow. Rumour said that this really hurt.

Wainwright's formroom was on the top floor, with a fine view over south London towards Earls Court. We could see the Exhibition buildings going up and the Great Wheel in the process of construction. My desk was luckily placed near the window, and I could watch the structure gradually rising above the surrounding buildings. First the supporting arms: then the great round hub, 150 feet above ground-level: then the steel spokes. When finished it looked very much like a gigantic bicycle wheel with railway carriages hung round the tyre. But the wheel was not a great success; it stuck on several occasions and unfortunate passengers were marooned for hours in the sky. One advantage of being in 'Wainwright's' was that the Old Man rarely penetrated as far as our corridor on the top floor. It was the abode of the science forms and included the laboratory.

Broad and I were moved to 'Chater's' after two terms, with a class-room on the ground floor, where we were never safe from surprise visitations. On the whole, however, we liked 'Chater's', though our form master was apt to be sarcastic, a trait hated by schoolboys. We learnt history and English and did readings from *Twelfth Night*. So far I had done no science; that was to come later when I was moved up to Thomas's form, where the work was really interesting, for we were given periods of practical science and physiology and it became the fashion to write long essays on these subjects for homework. We vied with each other to produce the longest essay. Thomas would look over the closely written foolscap sheets, tugging at his moustache, then throw them on his desk saying, 'It may amuse you, but it bores me – take the rotten stuff away.' For physiology we went to Dr Watt's classroom. We liked him. He was a thin, active little man, and he really taught me a lot. As there was another master named Holmes it was only natural for us to couple them together – Trevelyan Holmes and his friend Dr Watts is how we referred to them, and it was rumoured they went crime-hunting together. One day a week we listened to Watkins talking on physics. He pumped air out of bottles to create vacua and drew diagrams on the black-board. We were supposed to take notes, but mine were very sketchy. Part of our time was spent in the laboratory. We were nominally in charge of Mr Wright, known as 'Bottlewasher'. He had no sense of authority and we practically did as we liked, spending much time in unauthorized and risky experiments. Lined up at the benches with a bunsen burner and blower, we would try to produce a coloured bead from certain white powders, or start dissolving things in nitric acid. Once there was a loud explosion, which sent Bottlewasher rushing to the corner where a boy had burnt his hands badly. The sulphuretted hydrogen was kept in a glass cupboard, and whenever

we had occasion to go there we
made a point of leaving the door
open so that the smell gradually
spread across the laboratory until
it reached Bottlewasher. We
would all start coughing and
making as much fuss as possible
while he hurried to the cupboard
and threatened to report us all. We
would quench our thirst by con-
cocting lemonade. We made it
from bicarbonate of soda, citric
and tartaric acids. I do not think
it can have been good for us, for
we had no idea of the right proportions, but it fizzed and was quite
refreshing.

Two mornings a week we worked in the drawing school. This
was a great change from Bewsher's. It was well provided with casts
from the antique and the walls were hung with drawings by Old
Paulines. Among these was one by Everard Calthrop, a charcoal
study of Hammersmith Bridge. What pleased me most was the
encouragement I was given to put my own visual thoughts on paper.
I drew every sort of subject, with a preference for battle scenes, and
I usually produced one or two by way of homework. The art school
was the place where the great and the small came in contact. It
was there that I saw G. K. Chesterton and Compton Mackenzie (he
was 'Compton' then).

We were taught by Mr Harris. He would often cry: 'If yer do
it again I'll cane yer,' but I never knew him do so. Then there were
the two assistant masters, 'Foxy' Holden and his younger brother

A preference for battle scenes. Age 14

'Baby'. They seemed to be able to tackle any form of art, including theoretical perspective, which I never succeeded in mastering.

I was soon promoted to a drawing-board and a stool to make studies from the antique. There were one or two lucky fellows who spent most of their time in the art school, and later on, in my last two terms, I was to join them in what was called 'the Special Drawing Class'.

The High Master had raised the standard of work in the school so much that St Paul's had won the highest number of scholarships at the universities of any of the public schools. The Old Man was a keen scholarship-hunter, and when he learned that I was going to make Art my profession, he made it clear to me that I was expected to secure a scholarship to the Royal Academy Schools. He became quite affable to me when he visited the Art School. Indeed, it was almost embarrassing to have a heavy hand laid on my shoulder and to hear a gruff voice saying: 'And how is our young artist getting on?'

Working in the Art Class I got to know two older boys who were, I think, in the Army Class, Ritchie and Collison Morley. Collison Morley was as keen on soldiering as I was and he showed me drawings he had made while following the army manœuvres the previous autumn. On leaving school he joined the Territorials and rose to command a London battalion. He was killed at the battle of Loos in September 1915. Ritchie passed into the Regular Army and was given a commission in the Scottish Rifles. At the battle of Givenchy in the spring of 1915 the Scottish Rifles were cut to pieces, losing most of their officers. Ritchie and Watkiss Lloyd, who was a friend of my early childhood in Kent Terrace, were both killed. How glad they would have been to know that, fifty years later, plans for the greatest military operation of all time were to be made by an Old Pauline in this same building.

The winter I was moved from Bewsher's to St Paul's was a memorable one for the big school, which that year had one of the finest rugger sides in its history. In the team were Clementi Smith, Bailey, 'Milky' Stedman and Ricketts, the last a brilliant full back who helped to win all their matches save one – either Tonbridge or Bedford. How we stood behind the ropes and cheered 'P-A-U-L-S'! It could be heard all down the Hammersmith Road, fathers, mothers and sisters joining in. I enjoyed playing rugger in 'Little Side'. Being small and quick I played at half-back. Cyril was big enough to be a forward and was put on Middle Side. He did well enough to be moved up to Big Side and then got his third fifteen colours. He left school at seventeen so he had no chance of rising higher.

At cricket at that time the school shone less brightly. But in athletics there were two good runners in Francis Williams and

St Clair Smith, both of whom broke school records, Williams for the mile and 'Tommy' Smith the hundred yards. Lacrosse was played in the Easter term, but I do not think it was very popular: it was almost impossible to get match fixtures, for no other schools played the game, and though there were a few club opponents they were far away and in any case greatly outclassed the school.

Then of course there was the Cadet Corps. In spite of my keenness on soldiering I could not summon up enough enthusiasm to ask Father if I could join it. It was not exciting to parade on the gravel at the back, slope arms and form fours, march and counter-march, in recreation time. In any case I was too small to join the ranks. This was before the days of properly organized camps when all the schools went to Salisbury Plain at the beginning of the summer holidays and were given regular field days and sham fights.

The year after I started at St Paul's the Aunts took their summer holidays at Shalford, near Guildford. They rented the Vicarage and, in accordance with the now-established custom (which continued for three more years), we were invited to stay with them. We had a grand holiday. Our cousins from Kensington had taken a house on Guildown which could be reached easily by ferry across the river at St Catherine's, and we were always in and out of one another's houses. The cousins were a large family, five girls and two boys. Douglas, the youngest, was several years our junior, but a most sporting boy and a great acrobat. He distinguished himself later by entering the Café Royal walking on his hands with his feet in the air.

We had picnic parties together, and were fond of sitting on the railway bank between the two tunnels by St Catherine's and watching the trains steam by. The grown-ups had solemn croquet parties on the Vicarage lawn. To one of these the local curate and his wife were invited. During the game Aunt Emily made one mighty swipe and we watched, horrified, as the ball bounded across the lawn straight for the legs of the curate, who was deep in conversation with his back turned to the game. The ball caught him fair and square, and with a loud squawk he leapt in the air. Poor Aunt Emily was never allowed to forget this sad affair.

The Vicarage garden ran alongside the main road and had a stream at the bottom. On the other side of this was a potting-shed and the tool-house. Cyril and I soon discovered that the gardener kept an old tricycle in the shed and that the door was unlocked. The man only worked three days a week, so on his off days we would trundle the machine out and ride it round the garden. We pushed it up the slope and then had a fine down-hill run to the stream. Alas! the brakes were not to be relied on and the inevitable happened.

We were both on the machine when it got out of hand and we
landed in the stream. We did our best to clean it up, but it still
bore traces of mud when the gardener came again, and we were
severely reprimanded. The shed was henceforth locked, and that
was the end of that little game.

During our stay at Shalford we took some picnics on the river.
Boats could be hired at The Jolly Farmer, and though we were not
supposed to go on the water without a grown-up in charge, we
managed occasionally to get a punt and go off on our own. I expect
the man in charge of the boats knew that it was almost impossible
to upset a punt.

It was the best summer holiday we had had for years and I was
sorry when September came and we had to go back to school.
Father must have been better off at this time, for we were allowed
more pocket-money, and Cyril and I made the most of it. We would
save up and then have an evening at the Lyric Opera House. I do
not know why it was called 'Opera House', for I never heard of an

opera being performed there. It was not until Nigel Playfair took it over and produced *The Beggar's Opera* that this happened; then it was renamed 'The Lyric Theatre'. In the nineties it was the home of melodrama. There were frequent changes of programme and a seat in the pit could be had for ninepence. We would scan the posters and lay out our limited funds on something really spicy,

Secured some luggage and made for a barn

such as *East Lynne* or *The Still Alarm*. The latter involved the presence of a real steam fire-engine at work on the stage. We also saw a drama about an innocent man wrongly convicted. His escape from Dartmoor in broad-arrow clothes, with the old lag (comic relief) and a young boy, was sensational. The boy was played by a buxom girl with a fair wig. How one of such tender years came to be 'doing time' in the prison was difficult to understand. Anyway, they escaped and, profiting by a most realistic railway accident, for which the villain was responsible, they secured some luggage and made for a barn. Climbing up the ladder to the hayloft was too much for the 'boy's' breeches; they split at the back and the curtain came down amid tumultuous applause.

Almost our favourite was *For the Honour of the House*. This was high melodrama if you like! The villain, hissed by the whole house whenever he appeared, was foiled in the end, though it was a near thing. He had lured the heroine to a lonely part of the Alps and left her there, bound and helpless, to die in the stage snow. The audience waited, tensely anxious. Would the hero arrive in time? Distant shouts were heard! The heroine raised her voice in a despairing cry, and on to the stage lumbered a full-grown St Bernard dog, ploughing his way through the 'snow'. This, of course, brought down the house, and I doubt if there was a dry eye among the audience.

Lower down King Street was another playhouse, the Hammersmith Palace of Varieties. 'The Temple', as it was called, produced shows of a not very high standard but perfectly respectable and usually rather dull. A seat in the gallery cost fourpence, and one sat in extreme discomfort with the knees pressed against the back of the seat in front. The floor of the auditorium sloped very steeply and gave the feeling that a false step would mean landing in the pit. Any unpopular turn was continually interrupted by loud comments from the audience.

We did not tell Father that we went there, for we knew that he had a prejudice against music-halls. I don't think he had ever been to one himself; he regarded all music-halls as haunts of vice. No doubt this was due to his upbringing, for my grandfather's views on all things theatrical, even the legitimate drama, were extreme, and my aunts were never allowed to go to a theatre. I know Father often went to the theatre with his friends, and after his engagement he used to take Mother, who had many friends in the profession, among them Ellen Terry.

Additional pocket-money enabled Cyril and me to break out in other ways than the theatre. We tried smoking. 'Woodbines' were five a penny, and we would indulge in a packet and smoke them on the sly, either in the summer-house in Broad's garden or, if we knew Father would be out for the evening, in our own bedroom at home. One afternoon Broad and I bought a packet of Woodbines after school. Crossing Hammersmith Bridge and turning down to the tow-path we found a dark corner and lit up. It was quite secluded under the bridge, so we thought we were safe and were pulling away when to our horror we saw Wainwright approaching. We had taken the precaution of hiding our school caps in our pockets. We dived behind a pier and cowered there while he passed quite close to us. I do not think he even noticed us, but for days I was in terror, expecting to be hauled up before the 'Old Man'.

Chapter Seven

TO BE AN ARTIST

I T was during my last year at St Paul's that I began to take a real interest in music. Ethel, by now an accomplished pianist, would play Bach to me by the hour. I did not understand it, and the variations seemed, to my uninformed mind, monotonous. I would complain: 'But, Ethel, there are no tunes.' She would painstakingly try to explain how fugues did not depend on tunes, but it was many years before I understood what she meant, and I was always relieved when she turned to Chopin. Ethel had an excellent musical memory, besides being able to read music at sight, and when asked to play at the Dicksees' or at other friends' homes would sit down and play without music.

I had one friend at the school who was keen on music. His name was Peyton; we called him Pen. I sometimes went to his home in Holland Road and listened to him playing the piano. He told me that his family had a young friend with a beautiful singing voice, and he invited me to come and hear her sing one evening. I was astonished to find she possessed a long fair pigtail. Her name was Muriel George, and she can only have been about fifteen years old, but her voice was mature and perfectly trained. She sang to us all the evening. I had never heard anything like it and was quite overcome. She told us that she was going to make singing her profession. After school broke up in July the Peytons took a house at Dachet, and asked Cyril and me to spend the day with them. Muriel was

271

there, and after an early supper we all went on the river. While we drifted slowly along she sang to us. Passing boats stopped, and people came out of house-boats to listen, and though I have often heard her voice since then it is that evening that stays in my memory.

By now I had quite definitely settled that I would be an

272

artist. This pleased Father and he gave me every encouragement. 'Heatherley's' was chosen from among the many art schools, because Father had once attended evening classes there. I was, of course, eager to start, but I was only fifteen, and was told that I must have at least another year at St Paul's. I did not consider what effect

Drawn for my homework, age 15

leaving school so early would have on my general education, and I have often thought that another two years would have given me a better start in life. However, there it was; I was earmarked by the High Master for a scholarship and was put into the 'Special Drawing Class'. Needless to say, I enjoyed it, and in spite of my fondness for music, violin-playing ceased to interest me.

273

As the only member of the Special Drawing Class I had a very independent time. I could choose the particular cast I wanted to draw. Homework was no longer labour, for I was always drawing at home, anyway, and therefore had plenty of sketches to show each day. Nominally in Thomas's form I had only to do French or Mathematics twice a week.

That summer term Cyril left St Paul's. It was sad for him, as it meant that he would have to work in an office in the City, and, instead of five weeks in the summer, with Christmas and Easter as well, his holidays would be limited to a fortnight. He went as clerk to a firm of underwriters at Lloyd's. However, this had the compensation of placing him in the proud position of earning a salary and of being a 'City Gent', on the strength of which he bought himself a bowler hat.

I spent my holiday with the Aunts. They had taken a house at Eastbourne, a girls' school, in Selwyn Road. There were far too many bedrooms and most of the top floor was shut up. The greatest asset of the building, in my opinion, was a fully equipped gymnasium where I spent hours climbing ropes and swinging on rings. There was companionship in the person of a young man called Charlie, who came every day to chop wood or carry coals and to attend to the fat, round and docile pony which was needed to pull the chaise. Once it had been established that the pony was quiet and the chaise safe, Aunt Alicia ventured out in it, Charlie driving her round the links. Even the invalid Aunt Annie was persuaded to embark. The chaise was the shape of a huge Bath chair on four wheels and so close to the ground it could not possibly turn over. It was very much the same as the one Queen Victoria is pictured as driving in the grounds of Balmoral.

In the gymnasium Charlie gave me lessons in climbing, and before long I could get to the top of the rope and slap the rafter. It was much more difficult to climb the pole, and it was some weeks before I accomplished it.

There was a large garden with a tennis court, but it was not well kept and we hardly played at all; in fact, it was not until Cyril arrived for his two weeks' holiday that I made great efforts to cut the grass properly, and to mark it out. Cyril came down one Saturday evening and said he was very lucky to get his holiday in August; it had only been possible because one of the other clerks had switched his holiday at the last minute.

With the tennis court and the gymnasium we had plenty to amuse us, and we also took long walks over the Downs. Sometimes Father and Ethel would accompany us, and we would all go off for the day, getting a sandwich or bread-and-cheese lunch at a public house (Ethel and I had to sit outside). We walked for miles, to Birling Gap, Friston, East Dean and then to Alfriston. Father always made a bee-line for a church and generally found something interesting. His great find was at Alfriston. While we were looking round the church he was exploring a jungle of weeds and bushes close by where there was a tumbledown building. We heard him call out:

275

'I say, boys, I've found something.' We joined him at once. He was almost dancing with excitement. 'I believe this is an old clergy house,' he said, and dived in through the broken doorway. 'Yes, look! There are the rafters of the roof, and this is a little chamber alongside.' The floor was roughly paved, but matted with weeds. The walls were of stone and fairly sound, but the roof was half gone and the whole place covered with bird-droppings. We spent a long time there while Father paced it out and made notes in his pocketbook. Outside, the weeds and shrubs were so thick we could hardly get through, and in some places they had grown into the walls. It was late before Father could tear himself away. 'I wonder,' he said, 'if the Vicar knows what this really is. It is unique, quite unique!' When we reached home Father wrote a letter to the authorities and, I have no doubt, to the Vicar as well, telling them what he considered should be done to save the building. It is now, of course, well known and, having been restored, is one of the ecclesiastical gems of Sussex.

It seemed a very short fortnight for Cyril, but we found time to go down to the front and listen to 'Dan Randall' and his troupe. Dan was a long way behind the great Harry Randall of the 'Halls', but he made us laugh. It was not a good summer for bathing; too many cold winds and boisterous seas. One morning Charlie came with the news that a vessel had been driven ashore and was lying on the beach. We were off in no time, and found a crowd gathered to watch a coasting ketch being smashed to pieces in the breakers. The crew of three had struggled ashore; a narrow escape for them, for the mast had come down and the vessel had broken her back. She carried a cargo of cement and the bags were stacked inside, setting in the wet, with the ship's timbers falling away. I had never seen a shipwreck before, and it struck me as a very melancholy sight. A bystander told me that the ship had sprung a leak off Beachy Head and the skipper realized their only chance was to run her ashore.

In Selwyn Road there was a house that stood below ours: it had a garden separated from us by a low brick wall, and one day, to my surprise, I saw a fellow Pauline in the garden. He was a foreigner named Camacho and he told me that his father was the Brazilian Consul in London. They had taken the house for the summer. He went to fetch his sisters and we all talked over the garden wall. The sisters were most attractive little girls with long black pigtails, and

277

we would often meet by the garden wall. They told us they would be having a garden party soon and that if we looked over the wall we would see it all. When the day came Cyril and I watched all the preparations: a marquee was erected, coloured flags hung up, and when the guests came we had a grandstand view of the proceedings. There was a band playing, and presently the girls came running up in smart white frocks to ask us if we would like some ices. Needless to say we said 'Yes, please,' whereupon they darted off and came back with a tray full of ices into which we all tucked away until the girls were called. 'Now we have to dance,' they told us; 'but wait here and we'll be back.' We watched the dance: a group of little girls prancing around. Then they came flying back with more ices.

On Cyril's last morning we got up early and tried to play a last game of tennis, but the dew on the grass made the balls too wet. As a result we had to run nearly all the way to the station. After his departure I missed him terribly. The Aunts did not seem to understand that we needed companionship of our own age.

A few days later there was a terrific thunderstorm at night. I was lying awake in bed watching the lightning when an agitated Aunt Emily appeared. She was collecting the fire-irons from each room and putting them under the beds. It appeared some friend had told her that fire-irons attracted the lightning down the chimney. When she had gone I crept out of bed and went to Ethel's room. She too had had a visit from Aunt Emily, and we had a good laugh about it all.

The winter that year was long and bitterly cold, with the usual accompaniment of burst pipes. We went skating in Richmond Park, and both the Serpentine and the Long Water in Kensington Gardens were frozen over and safe enough to bear crowds of skaters. After Christmas, with the Pantomime season in full swing, Cyril and I saved up our pocket-money and went to the half-crown pit at Drury Lane. It was not my first visit to the Lane, for I had been to Pantomime before, and on one unforgettable occasion spent the evening in a box. This time it was the pit with a two-hour wait outside the heavy double doors, which looked like the entrance to a prison. Itinerant musicians helped to pass the time. When the opening time arrived, muffled footsteps sounded within, then the rattle of bolts being withdrawn – and the crowd did the rest. There was a stampede, the opener running as if for his life. Once inside, the young and agile, able to jump over the back seats and seize places in the front row, scored heavily. It was a happy sensation to settle down in the hard-won seat and watch the house light up, the audience arrive and the orchestra file in, all too slowly. Finally, to a round of applause, Dan Godfrey took his place on the conductor's stand. All this for a carefully hoarded half-crown. I cannot remember what the pantomime was about but I know we had Dan Leno and Herbert Campbell – an immortal combination – Fred Emney the Elder, with Laurie and Zanfretta. Nor do I know who played the principal boy, though I am sure she was quite as ravishing as the 'Boy' I had seen seven years before. I did not suffer the pangs of unrequited love on this occasion; surely a warning sign of advancing age. I was beginning to grow up and I knew that I was about to enter on my last term at St Paul's.

Chapter Eight

HEATHERLEY'S

ALTHOUGH technically still a schoolboy I felt I had one foot in the great world when Father arranged for me to spend Saturdays working at Heatherley's. I felt very small, as indeed I was at sixteen, when I took my place in the Art Class among the free and easy students, some of them grown men with beards, to draw from the living model. I found drawing from life very different from the casts I had been used to.

The principal of Heatherley's was John Crompton, an imposing presence. He wore a beige frock-coat and a flowing salmon-pink tie. He was a small man, but his carriage lent him height so that he seemed to tower above me. To be addressed as Mister Shepard was startling. His criticisms were conducted in the plural. Standing before my drawing he would say: 'If we look at our legs, Mister Shepard, I think we shall find them a trifle on the heavy side.' Nothing seemed to put him out and he never forgot his dignity. It was a rare thing to see him smile.

Heatherley's had an interesting history. It had been established for many years and was the original of Thackeray's 'Gandishes' in the *Newcomes*. It certainly preserved its old-world atmosphere. The house in Newman Street had been converted to serve the purpose of an art school. Passing through the house one descended three steps to the Antique School, crowded with plaster statues. Beyond this was the Costume Studio, with benches and 'donkeys' disposed

Never forgot his dignity

round the model's throne. A large choice of costumes was available, and these were sometimes arranged to suit the convenience of what might be called the permanent students. I hesitate to use the word 'student' for elderly ladies, but I feel the atmosphere at Heatherley's at that time was regulated by their presence. Many would-be Academy pictures were painted within its sacred walls, when cavaliers and pirates were the vogue for subject pictures.

With so much to look forward to, my last term at St Paul's was quite a pleasant one. In July, Father told me that the Aunts were renting a house in Hampshire for the summer. This pleased me immensely, for if we stayed with them, as we usually did, I should have the chance to see the army at work. So it happened. After school broke up we received the expected invitation, and in due time Ethel and I found ourselves in the train for Bentley, near Farnham.

Aunt Fanny met us, wearing a shady straw hat and, with her skirts girded up, looking very summery. A pleasant walk across fields brought us to the 'Welches'. The house, attractive and roomy, looks much the same today. It had large grounds, a paddock, a tennis court, and a fine kitchen garden surrounded by an old red-brick wall. On this wall were peach, nectarine and plum trees, a delectable sight. There were stables and outhouses at the back, where a man was grooming a very fine horse which he said was a thoroughbred. We had a warm welcome from the Aunts, and from the maids as well. It was the first time that I had stayed in such a mansion, and I very much enjoyed the novelty, especially as having the run of such a well-stocked garden meant a lot to a boy of my age.

On making inquiries about the military I was told by Mary the maid that there were a lot of soldiers about. I was glad when Father arrived from London on his bicycle the next day, for I was itching to borrow it and set off on the Aldershot road. The next morning I was up early, and walking towards Farnham I came on some engineers with a wagon fixing up wires on a pole. Then some helmeted cavalry trotted by. 'Dragoons,' I thought. Things were warming up. I ran home and swallowed some breakfast, then borrowed Father's cycle and set off. I had no difficulty in picking up the trail of the troops, for the roadside was littered with empty 'Woodbine' packets. Presently I overtook the tail end of the column –

camp cookers and ration carts. It was getting very hot, and the cooks had unbuttoned their tunics and some had dock leaves stuck under their helmets. Farther along I came upon a lot of infantry halted by the roadside, and sheltering from the sun under the hedges; marching in the heat of the day in red tunics with helmets and pipeclayed belts can have been no fun. By now I was feeling like a real war correspondent and went ahead in search of adventure. I came upon it at a cross-roads, where an infantry outpost was disputing the advance of a cavalry patrol. The Hussars in full uniform dismounted and, creeping up, started taking pot-shots with their carbines at the redcoats. It was a mild form of warfare, and presently both sides settled down to an exchange of highly coloured badinage. I left them to go in search of something to eat, and found a small pub where I had bread and cheese and ginger-beer. In the afternoon I was in luck, for I saw a full-scale battle with a horse-drawn maxim gun chattering away and kilted and trousered infantry storming up-hill in close order, in the Inkerman style. I got into trouble when I reached home at nearly dinner-time, for I had caused grave anxiety among the Aunts by being out all day.

Father and I spent several days at Odiham, walking over there and carrying our sketching materials. It was my first experience of painting out of doors and my efforts were not a success. We had a festive time at Bentley, where we made several friends and were asked out to tennis parties. There was also a cricket match at which I distinguished myself by bowling our opponents' star batsman. I must confess that the condition of the pitch favoured me; whether the ball broke either way had nothing to do with my delivery. Cyril came down for his fortnight's holiday towards the end of our stay. He and I got up very early one cold and misty morning and went cubbing. The arrival of the hop-pickers in the neighbourhood gave the gardener and his boy plenty to worry about, though their vigilance was rewarded and only a few apples were lost. It was mid-September when we went home.

When I began regular work at Heatherley's most of my time was taken up with drawing from the antique. I was not encouraged to do any painting, and never learned anything of construction or design. The tuition was not good and I often think I should have done better to have gone to the Slade where, under Tonks, more attention was paid to good drawing and less to stippled finish. However, with the Scholarship to the Royal Academy Schools in view I had to stick to the prescribed course, and was much helped by seeing some drawings done the previous year by a student, George Stampa, who had been successful in winning the same scholarship for which I was trying. I looked at his drawings with awe and wondered if I could ever rise to such heights. George himself was, however, most reassuring.

I soon made friends with a boy of my own age, fresh from Haileybury, Arthur Connor. The son of a doctor, he lived with his parents at a house overlooking Clapham Junction Station. We had much in common and both of us felt strange in our new surroundings. I often went to tea at his home, where I met his sister Dot, a gay and charming schoolgirl of fourteen, and we all became great friends. I had acquired a nickname by this time, 'Kipper'. I think I earned it by somewhat gay and irresponsible behaviour, the expression 'Giddy Kipper' being a music-hall catch-phrase at that time. Anyway, it has stuck to me ever since, though usually shortened to 'Kip'.

It was later in the autumn when Chattie Wake appeared at Heatherley's. She came in one morning like a being from another world. With her copper-coloured hair she looked like a bacchante. Four or five of the younger students soon became a 'set' and livened the place up. Besides Chattie and Arthur Connor, there were Colyn Thompson, and Bartington, a young bearded American with a soft southern accent. We lunched together at 'Buck's' restaurant, next door to Heath's the hatters in Oxford Street. Our lunches were very frugal as we had little money. Arthur, who always had a good appetite, complained bitterly when funds were low. I managed better, for I soon found I could last all day on very little, knowing that Lizzie would have a good meal ready for me when I arrived home in the evening. In the afternoon, when the old trouts had packed up work for the day, we played hockey amongst the casts in the antique school with a rolled-up paint rag for a ball, until the noise brought Crompton downstairs to register a dignified protest.

When I could borrow Father's bicycle I rode to work. I enjoyed this, for riding in the slow-moving traffic of those days had no terrors. I could cycle back with Chattie to her home in Cliveden Place, where she lived with her mother and sisters, wave goodbye to her there and pedal home to Hammersmith. Those happy months at Heatherley's were all too short. Our little 'Club' broke up early next year: Chattie to study at Rolshoven's in the Brompton Road, Colyn Thompson to study at the Slade, and 'Barty' to return to America. Had I not had to settle down to a hard grind on my Scholarship drawings, I should have missed them more even than I did.

Chapter Nine

DIAMOND JUBILEE

L ONDON was full of exciting sights in the spring of 1897, the year of Queen Victoria's Diamond Jubilee. I borrowed Father's bicycle as often as I could so that, after work at Heatherley's, I could ride round the streets of the West End. Great stands were being erected in the streets, and in the parks camps were being made ready to receive troops from all parts of the Empire. London was very full; great numbers of people had come up from the provinces to see the preparations.

Soon after Easter Father was asked to play Malvolio in *Twelfth Night*, which was to be performed in the open air during the summer. The producer was Charles Fry. Malvolio was a part Father knew well, having played it several times with the Irving Club, an amateur dramatic society in which Henry Irving took a great interest and which had been the nursery of several distinguished actors. On one occasion Irving had lent the society the Lyceum Theatre for a production of *Henry IV*, and had been so impressed by Father's acting that he had offered him a place in his company. Father, however, knowing the hazards of an actor's life, wisely refused.

The outdoor performance of *Twelfth Night* was given in the grounds of a big house at Richmond, where there was a natural stage of smooth green turf with a fountain playing in front and a background of rhododendron bushes. It is strange, but no one gave a thought to the weather. There had been so many sunny days in June that no arrangements were made to provide for a break in the fine spell. Happily the day turned out blazingly hot, almost too hot for comfort in Elizabethan clothes and grease-paint. Cyril and I played minor roles and thoroughly enjoyed them. Indeed Cyril was bitten with a desire to go on the stage.

In spite of all the excitement I managed to get on with my drawing at Heatherley's. It was early in June when Chattie Wake asked me to a garden-party. She was living in rooms in Kensington, in a house overlooking one of the small squares, and the party took place in the square. I had the thrill of my young life when Chattie introduced me to Baden-Powell. He was then a Major, just back from Matabeleland. Dressed as he was in conventional frock-coat and top hat, his very bronzed features did not look at ease. Chattie introduced me with 'This young artist is very keen on soldiers'. I was quite tongue-tied, but Baden-Powell smiled broadly and told me that he also was a bit of an artist. At length I plucked up the courage to ask him about Matabeleland. He said the great advantage of working with light horse was that one could be independent. Scouting over country day and night, camping rough and cooking when one could, was altogether a great life. One could learn a lot by keeping one's eyes open all the time. Spellbound, I said it must be wonderful. 'Yes,' he answered, 'it is a great game . . . a great game.' I cannot help wondering if he was not already thinking of his Boy Scouts.

The time for the Diamond Jubilee was now very near. Although I had seen something of Queen Victoria's Golden Jubilee in 1887 when I was a small boy and lived near Regent's Park, we children had not seen the procession itself. Now, this year, we were to join with our friends the Dicksees in hiring a room somewhere on the route. By answering an advertisement a room was found over a butcher's shop in the Westminster Bridge Road which the procession would pass on its tour of south London after the Thanksgiving Service in St Paul's Cathedral. Through the early summer the weather, though fine, had been cool, and the soldiers from Africa and the Indies must have found it trying in their canvas camps in the Park. The London populace, however, was in high spirits, and sure it would be 'Queen's Weather' on the day. They were right. June 22nd turned out to be one of the hottest days of the year.

We were up by five o'clock. Too excited to eat much breakfast, we waited for the carriage to come that was to drive us to our butcher's shop. The early morning was grey with a cool white mist, and we did not feel very hopeful about the weather. Our packets of sandwiches were in our hands and we were beginning to worry about the carriage when it turned up, with Frank, Pollie and Minnie inside. Father and Ethel joined them while Cyril and I scrambled up beside the driver. He was a gloomy man and not encouraging about the weather, which, he said, *might* clear later. We drove through Fulham and Putney to avoid the crowds north of the river. As we reached Lambeth people were already lining the kerbs. Many of them had spent the night on the pavements and were having a picnic breakfast. We had to make a detour to reach our shop, and it took our flyman some time to pick his way through the alleys so as to arrive at the back entrance. We could hear the noise in the street in front as we climbed the staircase to our third-floor room. The place smelled strongly of meat, but this diminished as we rose.

A continuous muffled roar came from the crowd below, with occasional bursts of cheering as detachments of soldiers marched up to line the streets. We could see everything that went on, for our room, being so high up, gave us a good view down the Westminster Bridge Road. There were loud cheers for the municipal sand-cart as it passed throwing grit on the roads. The horse, plodding slowly along, was decorated with rosettes on his harness and ribbons on his tail. Presently a band arrived and marched up and down the street. But by far the best entertainment came from the other side of the road, for our room was exactly opposite the old Canterbury Music Hall. All its windows were occupied by music-hall stars and we were given the latest songs, the crowds joining in the choruses. One of the favourites was:

> *She was a dear little dicky bird,*
> *Cheep, cheep, cheep, she went.*
> *Sweetly she sang to me*
> *Till all my money was spent.*
> *The last time we met,*
> *We parted on fighting terms,*
> *For she was one of the early birds,*
> *And I was one of the worms.*

It was my first introduction to community singing. Shouts of 'Give us another one, Gus!' or 'Come on, Charlie!' quite drowned the band. By this time the sun was blazing down and the St John Ambulance men were busy.

The Thanksgiving Service in St Paul's was timed for midday, and presently the head of the procession came in sight. A strange hush fell upon the crowds. First rode a solitary officer in the uniform of the 2nd Life Guards, the tallest man in the British Army. It was so quiet as he passed that the sound of his horse's hooves could be heard

294

clip, clop, but from the distance came a muffled roar of cheering telling us that the Queen's carriage was drawing near. The waves of sound grew gradually louder until the State carriage, drawn by eight cream-coloured horses with purple trappings, and moving at a steady walk, came in sight. It was an open carriage on 'C-springs' and it seemed to rock slightly though the pace was slow and stately. The little old lady, a bonnet with a white osprey feather on her head and a black-and-white parasol in her hand, kept bowing to left and right. She looked pale. We learned afterwards that she was overcome more by the warmth of her reception south of the river than by the heat of the day. Indeed she nearly broke down, the tears streaming down her face. There could be no doubt what she meant to her people.

The carriage was followed by a glittering array of Emperors, Kings and Princes, Grand Dukes and Heads of State in uniforms of all colours. I was particularly impressed by a magnificent old Hussar, and also by a Guard Cuirassier from Germany. The Indian Princes who followed were splendidly mounted and their turbans and swords shone with precious stones.

The procession of troops from overseas followed. It was headed by Lord Roberts on a white horse, a famous animal wearing a service medal on his harness. Marching in small detachments and led by British officers, the men had a great reception. Brown, black or white – red coats, blue coats, khaki – turbans, helmets, fezzes – they were all loudly cheered. The naval contingent pulling their nine-pounder guns and wearing their summer straw hats were given a special cheer, as were the guns of the Royal Horse Artillery.

It was all over before two o'clock. The Queen must have arrived back at Buckingham Palace and had her luncheon by that time and was no doubt being called on by the crowds outside to appear on the balcony in her wheeled chair. It was much later when we were able to leave our room and make our way home. The streets were thronged with people. Indeed, this was the case for the rest of the day and most of the night. We were very tired by the time we reached our own house. Lizzie had prepared us a high tea, which was very welcome, and as Cyril and I were determined to go out again and see the illuminations, Father insisted, most wisely, that we went upstairs to lie down. I know that I slept soundly, and it was dusk when I woke.

King Street was doing its best with fairy-lights and gas signs, but we wanted to see the shops and clubs in the West End. We fought our way to the top of a bus on Broadway and payed double fare for our seats, and then were stopped and told no farther when we reached Piccadilly. Everyone seemed to be in the same situation, and we joined the crowds moving along by Green Park. The only wheeled traffic we saw in the main streets were a couple of Royal Carriages trotting up St James's. These produced some desultory cheers. Piccadilly Circus was very gay. Small groups of revellers were dancing, coster girls with their lads, to the music of a concertina. Family parties were struggling to keep together in the crush by holding tightly to their children. All were gazing upwards at the illuminations.

Cyril and I progressed slowly up Regent Street, where the shops made a brave show, and when we reached Oxford Circus turned left down Oxford Street. It was a hot night, and jostling with the closely packed crowds after being up at such an early hour was beginning to tell on me. By the time we reached Marble Arch both of us had had enough. The decision to go home was right enough, but we had to discover a way of getting there. We found places on the kerb and sat down for a rest and to think things over. Quite a number of people seemed to be of the same mind, for the kerb by the park was lined with tired family parties, the children fast asleep. Some of the small boys were making journeys to the drinking fountain near by and coming back with dripping handkerchiefs which were passed round and squeezed out. It was only with a great effort that we shook ourselves to life again; I was almost asleep when Cyril shouted in my ear. The thought of having to walk five miles or so back to Hammersmith was intolerable, but something had to be done. We decided to walk to Hyde Park Corner and try for a bus there. As we passed through the Park it seemed that many people were preparing to spend the night in the open.

We were lucky enough to find a bus, and, after a struggle, to board it. The journey to Hammersmith was very slow, for the bus was a 'pirate' and regulations about overloading did not seem to apply on Diamond Jubilee Day, nor regulations on fares. The conductor just charged everyone a shilling. In one case this nearly led to a free fight. King Street was still *en fête* as we crawled along it. When we reached home I was too tired to think of supper, and tumbled into bed as quickly as possible.

It was a few weeks later that a letter came from the Royal Academy telling me that I had been admitted on probation as a student, and that I was to attend with my drawing materials for a further examination to be held at the Schools. I think Father was as pleased as I was about this, for it meant that if I passed the further test, I should be given three years' free tuition. There were eight of us on probation, among them Cadogan Cowper, Gilbert Holiday and Fred Appleyard, and we worked together in the back school for a fortnight. I think we all passed the test. But I know that I gave a great sigh of relief when it was all over and I could look forward to a summer holiday before starting work at the Schools at the end of September.

On the evening of the first week of August Father came home in a state of great excitement. He had been spending the afternoon at 53 Gordon Square. Only two aunts, Alicia and Fanny, were living there now, for Aunt Emily, the youngest and the only stout one in the family, had passed away in the winter, and the invalid Aunt Annie had died the year before. Owing to these bereavements there was not to be the usual long summer holiday in a house rented in the country. My godmother knew we would be disappointed about this, so she suggested that Father should take us to France and they would help to pay our fares. When Father broke this news to us Cyril and I nearly stood on our heads with joy. To be going *abroad* seemed too good to be true. The first thing to do was to write letters of thanks, not such an irksome task as it had been three years before. Ethel made a special journey to Gordon Square to render her thanks in person.

Going abroad was a relatively simple undertaking in those days. No passports were required, and there were no currency regulations. An English golden sovereign was welcomed at any hotel or restaurant, and would fetch 25 francs or more. Cyril's holiday fell at the end of August, so our plans were made for then.

I cannot remember a greater thrill in my life than I felt on the morning we started off with our bags for Victoria Station on our first journey abroad. We travelled to Newhaven, and as the train passed the level-crossing in the town I saw the Channel boat lying alongside the quay. She had two funnels and was flying the French flag, but was not as big as I had expected.

Passing through the Customs took no time and we climbed aboard the S.S. *Tamise*. The ship was crowded and we piled our luggage in a corner where Ethel and Father found seats. Then Cyril and I started to look around. It was wonderful to be on board a real steamer and we explored her from stem to stern. When the time came for her to start there was very little fuss – a long blast on the hooter, the ropes were pulled in and we were off. It was a bright day with a fresh breeze, just how fresh we soon found when we left the shelter of Newhaven breakwater. *Tamise* began to pitch and to throw showers of spray over her bows. We ran in and out, dodging these, until stopped by a French sailor.

A great many people became sea-sick and the crew were kept busy handing round small basins. Some French nuns made particularly heavy weather of it. We went to see how Ethel and Father were getting on in their corner. Father looked rather green, but my sister was quite well and cheerfully joined us in going aft, where we got as near the stern as we could and enjoyed plunging up and down and seeing our wake fade away in the distance. About halfway across the Channel we passed the packet going to Newhaven and exchanged signals. She was a paddle-boat, steadier than we were, and not so crowded. Then some French fishing boats sailed by, waving to us and holding up fish as they passed. Then the coast of France appeared. I had once seen this through a telescope at Dover, but now, watching it grow larger and larger as we approached, was much more exciting. The sea calmed as we neared Dieppe and I was interested to see how quickly our sea-sick passengers revived; the nuns particularly became quite lively and vociferous.

The breakwater at the harbour entrance was lined with people waving to us. I suppose that the arrival of the daily packet was an event in the lives of many people. Everything looked so refreshingly different from England and the novelty of it all made a strong appeal to me. We moved very slowly up the harbour as if we were going right into the town, then the ship made a complete turn. There did not seem to be any room to spare, but she was handled skilfully and fetched up gently alongside the quay. The

gangways were run out and immediately a throng of French por-
ters rushed on board. We had to cling tightly to our bags, for
they almost fought for our luggage. Once ashore, we were herded
into a wooden shed where perspiring Customs men tried to cope
with the influx. '*Thé? Tabac? Alumettes?*' We had none of these and
were passed through.

I was particularly impressed by the French gendarmes, who
looked so picturesque after our London policemen. There was one
outside the gates, talking to a little man in a peaked cap with a brown
corduroy jacket and gaiters. Near him was a chaise with a speckled
white pony. Father said, 'Now I wonder if that can be Monsieur
Hotot? I had a letter to say that he would meet us.' The little man
came forward and handed Father a small card. 'Bonjour, M'sieu','
he said. Sure enough it was Monsieur Hotot. He introduced us to
the chaise and to a dog which appeared from underneath it. 'Fiaton,'
he said, indicating the dog with his whip. I did not know what he
meant by the word, but it turned out to be the dog's name. After
crowding our luggage on to the chaise we climbed the hill from
Dieppe, the pony straining upward while we walked beside. Our destination was Varengeville, about four miles away. Once on the level
we rattled along the *pavé*, with Fiaton running ahead. Father tried to
carry on a conversation with our host, but was not very successful.
Then Ethel, whose French was better, acted as interpreter. We pulled
up outside our *pension*, a small *estaminet* in the main village street.
Madame Hotot, several sizes larger than her husband, met us at the
door and showed us a front room with tables and a sanded floor that
did duty as a bar, and a smaller back room, separated from the bar
by a glass-topped door, which was to be our dining-room.

I was much intrigued by the display of bottles of all colours on
the shelves of the bar, also by the advertisements on the walls for

Rattled along the pavé

'BYRRH' and 'MAGGI'. Cyril and I were to share a small bedroom
upstairs which looked over the main street to a butcher's shop labelled
'Boucherie, Charcuterie'. I was really very hungry, and when we
had carried our traps upstairs I sat by the window, looking at the
butcher's shop, waiting for tea. But time passed and nothing
happened, so I consulted Father, who said they never had tea in

France. However, he spoke to Madame Hotot, who kindly produced some kind of sweet biscuit that helped to stay the pangs.

We had a happy five days at Varengeville. Father spent a lot of his time painting, carrying his camp-stool and white umbrella and settling down for the day, while we explored.

There was a yard at the back with chickens and ducks and a couple of geese. Here Monsieur Hotot spent most of his time, carrying in hay for the pony or working in the garden beyond. There were two tortoiseshell cats, lean and shy animals, who bolted when Cyril and I tried to make friends. Monsieur Hotot did not help in the bar: that was Madame's province. She spent the mornings, between her journeys to the kitchen, polishing the tables and glasses. Everything in the inn was spotlessly clean. She was a friendly soul and I tried to converse with her, but we did not get very far for my French was, and still is, rudimentary. She did her best to help me along by pointing to various articles and naming them, then making me repeat the word until I pronounced it correctly. She told me the way to the sea-shore, passing the church and the little cemetery and then down the steep wooded slope. The beach was not exciting – rocky and covered in seaweed.

In the evening the bar-parlour filled up with blue-bloused labourers. We watched them through our glass door while we had supper. When it grew dark a smoky little oil lamp was lighted, but by this time I was usually so sleepy I was glad to go to bed. It took me some time to get used to the French breakfast of coffee and rolls, and I was always ready for *déjeuner* at 12.30. Madame cooked this herself, though she had a young girl called Denise to help her.

The day we were to leave, Monsieur Hotot brought the chaise round from the yard and we gathered in the bar to say goodbye. Madame produced a bottle and filled six small glasses with brandy.

303

It was my first experience of a *petit verre* and I tried to swallow it too quickly, with the result that I choked. Solemnly we drank to 'La Belle France'. We drove to Dieppe station, Fiaton bounding ahead again. Waiting for the train to start I had a good look at the engine. It

did not impress me. It was black and dirty and had too many pipes and bits of extraneous machinery for my taste, and it hissed steam from every joint. The carriages were very narrow, with hard wooden seats, and the low platforms were quite different from ours at home and I thought inferior.

The journey was not a long one. When we reached Rouen we found a yellow bus in the yard labelled 'Hôtel de la Poste'. We climbed in along with several other people. The Hotel was an old-fashioned place with a yard in front adorned with plants in tubs. A gateway and iron railings separated this from the road. It had the air of an old coaching inn. It must since have been entirely rebuilt, for it is now quite a grand hotel.

Rouen, with its many lovely buildings, including the famous clock – a favourite subject with the water-colour painters of that period – still had the air of an old provincial town. The shops seemed never to close, and there was a pleasant bustling air about the place, also a distinctive and rather pleasant smell. The very horses had a different look from what I was used to. But what particularly pleased me was the number of soldiers about: little infantrymen in long dark-blue coats reaching below their knees and red trousers. Some very smart ones had white gaiters.

Cyril and I shared a room high up and at the back of our hotel. The window looked out over the roofs to the Cathedral, whose ornate iron spire showed above the houses. The Cathedral was sur-rounded by narrow streets of half-timbered houses, closely packed and leaning at all angles. How I wish now that I had made better use of my time by drawing some of these houses. They were very lovely; and they were completely destroyed in 1944, when all that part of the city was bombed and burnt and the Cathedral itself narrowly escaped destruction.

Besides spending hours in the Cathedral, we went up the road to St Ouen and on Sunday afternoon climbed the hill to Bon Secours. This was a regular Sunday promenade for the townsfolk. There were family parties, nursemaids with children, and more soldiers – little cavalrymen in light-blue tunics and red breeches carrying their sabres in the crooks of their arms. The weapons looked much too big for them.

One evening we spent an hour sitting outside a café near the big clock, and Father told us how, twenty-seven years before, he had sat in almost the same spot talking to an English friend. They were both

A regular Sunday promenade

students and were in Rouen together studying architecture when the
crisis between France and Germany arose. It was July 1870, and the
streets were thronged with people and soldiers shouting 'A Berlin'.
Father's friend advised getting away as quickly as possible, and they
were lucky enough to reach home before the storm broke.

Over a week had passed since we left home, and our holiday was
more than half over, but we had one more treat in store. After four
days in Rouen we took the train again and arrived in the late afternoon at Les Andelys. This time there was no bus waiting at the little
station, but we found a porter with a barrow who took charge of our
luggage and promised to deliver it to the 'Grand Cerf'. Father had
been told of this inn by a fellow artist, who reckoned it to be one
of the best examples of the period. This naturally caught Father's
interest. The inn, a fine half-timbered building, was close to the
church. In the hall was a circular panelled 'tambour' containing a

Hotel du Grand Cerf at Les Andelys

Drawn in Normandy, 1897

stairway. Viollet le Duc mentioned the Grand Cerf as being one of the outstanding examples of woodwork of the period of Francis I. I speak of it in the past tense, for it too shared the fate of the houses in Rouen. When in 1947 I went to Grand Andelys hoping to see the place again, nothing remained of the town but a heap of rubble. Only the church still stood.

We spent nearly a week there, for there was plenty to see. We walked the half-mile to the little town by the Seine called Petit Andelys, and from the towpath watched the long barges going upstream to Paris. We climbed the hill to the Château Gaillard, a grand ruined fort with a tragic history. Cyril and I explored the old stones, and in the little valley below the walls, pictured ourselves among the starving crowd of non-combatants who, turned out of the fortress, were denied passage by the invaders – 'Les Bouches Inutiles'.

In the evening we gathered for table d'hôte in the dining room. The company, largely composed of commercial travellers, was most entertaining; many of the jokes were at the expense of our waiting woman, who was quite equal to the situation and gave as good as she got. The local notary in particular was a great wit. He looked like Don Quixote in pince-nez and the exchange of repartee between him and Marie provoked roars of laughter. I saw Father glancing rather nervously at Ethel, who understood French, on several occasions.

I was sad when our holiday came to an end and we had to leave the 'Grand Cerf'. On the last morning we drove to Gisors and had time to see something of the old town before catching the train to Dieppe. The night boat was lying alongside the quay and we put our luggage in charge of a porter while we had our evening meal in a restaurant facing the harbour. It was dark when we boarded the ship, which was an English paddle-boat named *Rouen*, more spacious than *Tamise* and certainly steadier. It was fine with a calm sea. Rather than spend a night in the stuffy cabin on hard narrow bunks, Cyril and I found a corner on deck. I made a pillow of my overcoat and lay on my back, watching the clouds drift across the moon, and reviewed all that had happened in the last few months. It had been a wonderful year for me, and I looked forward with enthusiasm to life as a student at the Royal Academy Schools.

Chapter Ten

THE ROYAL ACADEMY SCHOOLS

I KNEW that I should have a year's work in the Lower School before passing – I hoped! – into the Upper, and that, a certain standard having been reached, time would be allowed for painting from life and, in the case of male students, in attending life classes for drawing in the evenings. Men and women students did not work together in the painting schools and the women had no evening life class. We always understood the reason for this to be the objections of some of the more antiquated Royal Academicians, who considered that young lady students should never be called upon to behold the nude.

The Academy Schools possessed two curators, Herbert and Cauty. Cauty looked after us in the Lower School, and his slow and ponderous steps could be heard approaching down the corridor, warning us to get on with our work. Herbert, though somewhat more eccentric, was more popular.

The Keeper at that time was a man of Spanish origin named Calderon, a Royal Academician and an accomplished painter. He had a most aristocratic appearance. Given a ruff round his neck he would have made a perfect model for a Spanish Don.

We started work at ten o'clock and stopped at three. So long as my family lived at Hammersmith I usually cycled to the Schools, but early in the year we had been warned that Theresa Terrace was to be pulled down. It seemed that the whole property, a valuable one facing the main road, had been sold and that a row of shops was to be put up on the site. This distressed me greatly. I had grown fond of our home, and it was not likely we should find another house with a studio. Father, on the other hand, was not sorry to make a move. Hammersmith, he said, had never agreed with him. He suffered from rheumatism, and his doctor had ordered him to take a mineral water cure at a spa. Llandrindod Wells was suggested, and it was settled that we should all go there for our summer holiday.

I had never been in Wales, and was quite pleased at the prospect. For one thing I looked forward to trying my hand at landscape painting in oils. I intended to enter for an Academy Schools prize called the 'Creswick' of which the specified subject was 'A Bridge over a Trout

Herbert and Cauty, Curators at the Royal Academy Schools. Drawn in 1897

Stream', and Wales seemed just the place to find this. The size of the picture rather frightened me – about 4½ feet by 3; I did not see myself lugging a canvas of that size over the mountains. A fellow student put me up to having a folding canvas made, but while this reduced the size it increased the weight. When the time came for our holiday I was much concerned about the transport of my canvas and was not reassured when Father, Ethel and I arrived at Euston and saw the way it was being bundled into the van with all the other luggage.

Our destination was a private hotel called 'Ye Wells'. It had a most friendly atmosphere and stood facing a large stretch of common with hills beyond. The pump room where the waters were dispensed stood in the middle of the common, and every morning a procession of patients filed across to take their early libations of flat-iron water. Father joined them. I tasted the water once and found it most disagreeable.

The proprietress of our hotel, Mrs Smythe, had two daughters and a small son. With the younger daughter, Winnie, I soon struck up a friendship. She was sixteen, with a long, fair pigtail tied with a ribbon, and as tall as I was. When she could get away we stole out together for a walk on the common, which was more fun than playing parlour games with the other boarders.

For many days I was preoccupied with the hunt for a subject for my picture. There did not seem to be anything suitable in the immediate neighbourhood. One afternoon I joined in a picnic which involved driving several miles in a horse wagonette. This brought us to an old stone bridge over a tumbling stream. Just what I wanted! But the scene was much too far away for repeated visits, and I was obliged to recognize that I should have to do with something nearer at hand. In the end I settled for a cranky wooden bridge and a stream that was no more than a brook. Thereby I set myself a difficult task; but I really had no choice. Even this was two miles from our hotel, and lugging my canvas and traps to it was a tiring job. Fortunately I found a cottage near by where I could leave my picture from day to day. Very few people passed that way, and I was able to work undisturbed – except for the flies! They attacked me from every side. At intervals I would leap to my feet and run round the rocks, but the flies would return directly I settled to work again.

I had one visitor. I spotted him crossing the wooden bridge but ignored his proximity. Presently I became aware of him standing close behind me.

A voice said ' 'Obby?'

'I beg your parden,' I said. 'I . . .'

' 'Obby?' said the voice more loudly.

'Oh yes, it is, in a sort of way.' I turned my head and saw a small man smoking a curly briar pipe. He came nearer and regarded my canvas.

'Flies a bit troublesome, I expect,' he said, as a cloud of them scattered at the smell of his tobacco. 'You want to smoke a pipe on a job like that.' Then, 'What are you painting?'

'I'm trying to paint the bridge.'

'Oh! That! Don't call that a bridge.' After a pause he went on. 'My old father was a bit of an artis' – took to painting after he retired.' He said this as if art were the drink. ' 'E didn't do big 'uns, but he did 'em quick, real shiny slap-up pictures, nice bright colours, gold framed an' all.' ˙

I surveyed my own effort with loathing, and muttered acquiescence.

'Going to frame that one?'

'I can't say till it's finished.'

'Ah!' he said. 'Cost you a bit if you do.' And after a pause he said, 'You'd 'a' done better farther down. Much prettier and there's a stone bridge below the pool. Ah well, we all 'as our tastes. I must get along.' He left me to carry on my struggle with the despised bridge and the flies.

At length the time came when I could do no more. As I had to lug all my traps back to the hotel I chose a day when I knew the boarders would be out; I felt sure they would want to see my picture if they knew that I had brought it back. So I consulted Winnie, and we arranged that she should meet me at the back door and help me to hide it. We felt like two smugglers as we hid the picture in an empty room, where it remained till I went home ten days later. It was my first attempt at landscape painting in oils and I made the mistake of painting on the spot. Working on a large canvas in constantly changing light is always difficult, and I should have been wiser to have made a series of water-colour studies and then worked from these in the studio at home. However, the mischief was done, as I fully realized when we got home and I unpacked the thing. I was horrified at the mess I had made, and spent days trying to pull it together. When it was alongside the other 'Creswicks' at the exhibition of student's work in December, I felt acutely what a dismal failure it was, though it was not, I think, quite the worst entry.

Every half-year there was a scholarship examination at the Schools and a fresh influx of students. The newcomers were always objects of interest. I had observed this when I was a new boy myself, working on probation, and some of the older students had come to inspect us. I learned later that after one of these visitations a senior girl student had burst into her painting class protesting, 'Have you seen the new lot? There's a boy of twelve! What *is* the place coming to?' I am sure I was the boy in question, for though I was seventeen I was very small for my age, a fact which earned me the name of 'Little' Shepard.

It was while working in the back painting school that I first saw Florence Chaplin. I was copying the Philip of Spain by Velasquez when she came in with another girl and stood watching me at work. I had heard her spoken of as being one of the cleverest students, a distinction she shared with Flora Lion. Florence Chaplin's talent was inherited from her grandfather, Ebenezer Landells, the artist and engraver and one of the founders of *Punch*. I felt very conscious of my poor painting and turning to her said, 'I am afraid I am not making a very good job of it.' 'No. It is difficult,' she replied, 'but I think you're frightened of it. Try painting more thickly.' She went on: 'The drawing's all right but don't worry about going over the edges.' It was the only advice I had received so far, and I thanked her, explaining rather lamely that I had learned no oil painting and was trying to find a method. I always remembered what she told me. It cheered me up to be noticed and encouraged by her and sometimes to be greeted by a quick smile when I passed her in the corridor. It was nearly two years before I got to know her well, for the men and women did not work or lunch together as had happened at Heatherley's.

I had my own particular friends among the men. Philip Streatfeild was my own age, and altogether bigger. He was always cheerful, and being endowed with a good voice often led us in song while we were cleaning up in the wash-house after work. Our music was of quite a high order and sung in parts, with Gilbert Holiday, Denholm Davis and Stanley Young providing baritone and bass. The corridors rang with 'Holy, Holy, Holy' or 'The Song of Praise' most afternoons at 3.15. George Swaish, who entered the Schools the year after I did, came from the West Country. It was he who taught me how to fill my pipe. He was diffident and shy, and it was some time before I came to know him well. He was one of the most single-hearted men I have known, and of my friends the truest.

At the end of my first year I duly passed into the Upper School. There was no more drawing from the antique: it was painting, painting all the time, with a visiting Royal Academician to teach us. Some of this teaching was good and some quite the reverse. Marcus Stone, for instance, would lay down the law, discoursing on 'a sense of fatty sweetness' which was quite in keeping with the subjects of his pictures. G. H. Boughton, who favoured Dutch scenes of the seventeenth century – fancy-costumed figures skating – would seize my favourite brush and grind it on to the canvas so that it spread out fanwise, and then tell me to go ahead. We had Seymour Lucas and Arthur Hacker and several others. Solomon J. Solomon was an infrequent visitor, but he did teach us something.

It was quite different when Sargent was the visitor. He was dynamic. Bursting with energy and enthusiasm, he inspired us all. Everyone tried to paint as he did. On one occasion he seized palette and brushes from a student and got to work himself. The painting remained untouched after he had left and was taken home by the lucky student, though several of us tried to bribe him to part with it.

George Clausen was quite as popular as Sargent, though of a different temperament. A rather shy, quiet man, almost diffident in his criticisms, he was a most excellent teacher besides being a distinguished painter. I think he enjoyed being among students, for one day he joined us in the yard outside the Schools, where Arthur Connor took a photograph of us all.

The same autumn we heard that the fate of our home in Hammersmith had been finally decided. The whole of Theresa Terrace was to be pulled down forthwith. My secret hopes that the place might be saved were completely dashed and there was nothing to do but to make the best of it. Father and Ethel had been house-hunting for some time and the most favoured place was Blackheath, in south-east London. Father was attracted to Blackheath because he had been to school there before he went to Rugby; moreover, it was high and said to be bracing, which was considered good for rheumatic sufferers. It certainly was bracing, especially in winter, as we found out when crossing the heath with a north-east wind blowing. Cyril and I were not very enthusiastic about the choice; we thought it too far out of Town. However, Father told us one day that he had bought the lease of a house in Shooters Hill Road, and the following Saturday we made the journey to Blackheath to see it. The train from Charing Cross was slow but the walk across the heath was pleasant. No. 34 was a semi-detached house with a good garden, large enough, I was pleased to see, for a tennis court. The rooms were large and had a good basement. But there was no studio. I went to the top of the house, hoping to find a suitable room. Finally I decided that the spare room was the only possible place, though even this, cluttered up as it soon would be with a large double bed, a wardrobe and a washstand, did not seem very promising.

We took a lot of measurements, and found the ground-floor

rooms were high enough to take the Georgian mahogany bookcases which were a fitment in our house in Theresa Terrace and which Father was determined to save from the housebreakers. It was some compensation to find that we should have electric light instead of the oil lamps and gas we had been used to. The local builder met us at the house and arrangements were made to start redecoration.

Both Cyril and I were much concerned about our daily journey to Town, for the trains were not good, though he could get to Cannon Street more easily than I could to Charing Cross.

We also felt that the house was too far from the shops, which Lizzie would not like. I did not take as much interest in the redecoration as I had done in that of our old home; in fact, I did not visit it again until we moved in one cold day in late autumn. The vans arrived early in the morning at Theresa Terrace and the bookcases

were carefully and safely moved and packed in with our furniture. Then we took the train to Black-heath.

It was cold waiting about in an empty house for our furniture to arrive, and this added to the depression and unhappiness I already felt at leaving our old home. Darkness came on, and still we waited. Finally, overcome with hunger, we went in relays to the 'Sun in the Sands' to warm ourselves with hot supper. It was nine o'clock before the vans came, and nearly midnight before all was unloaded and stowed in the house. The local policeman showed great interest in these proceedings. I believe he thought we were trying to 'shoot the moon'. But he got a drink and a tip and all was well. Lizzie arrived next day without her beloved cat, which had died some weeks earlier . . . no doubt some instinct had warned it of the coming upheaval.

Our two bookcases were duly fixed up in the dining-room and Ethel began the work of sorting and arranging our books. She enjoyed doing this; she was studying literature at Queen's College and spent a lot of time in the library there. It was her third year at the College and she was making good progress, besides keeping up her piano playing. She told us that the College was holding a reunion of old girls, and that she was particularly anxious to go in the hope that she might meet some of Mother's old friends. When the day arrived Father went with her and they both returned in great excitement. They had met Gussie and Poppie Tucker, two of Mother's friends. Gussie, whose full name was Augustine Boucneau, had been at the College with Mother, and they had kept up the friendship until Mother's death. We remembered Gussie from our early childhood and the lovely presents she used to give us at Christmas and on our birthdays. We had not seen or heard of her for eight years. She was now married to Groby Rogers and lived at Kingswear in south Devon. A warm invitation had been given us to visit her in her new home in the following spring. I was particularly glad about this as I had never been to Devonshire, and, indeed, on only one occasion had I ever seen the country in the springtime.

Cyril and I bombarded Ethel with questions about Gussie and her husband. It seems that he was smaller than she, and having spent much of his life in South Africa was very bronzed. The other college friend of Mother's, Poppy Tucker, I remembered well. Poppy had grey eyes and a mop of red hair – most attractive in my eyes. She had very little use for the conventions, and used to startle Harley Street by riding to College on horseback. She married a solicitor named Godefroi, and when his health broke she nursed him devotedly until he died. She was then left very badly off. I am glad to say that several years later I had a letter from her, characteristically short and to the point:

'Dear Ernest,

Rejoice with me. I have won seventeen thou' in the Irish Sweep. Now, of course, long lost relations are buzzing around like flies.'

Chapter Eleven

HOLIDAYS IN DEVON
AND GERMANY

SECOND-YEAR students who had passed into the Upper School and could show a record of regular attendance and good behaviour were given certain privileges. Amongst these was the chance to compete for a scholarship called 'The Landseer' which was worth £40 a year for two years. Without telling Father I entered three works – a study of a head, a painting of a nude, and a drawing. It was a pleasant surprise for him, as for me, when I won the scholarship. Fred Appleyard won another scholarship at the same time.

Forty pounds for two years seemed to me a fortune. I could not help remembering how I had won my first shilling at the age of seven and had contemplated matrimony with Vera Beringer on the strength of it. Since then my sense of proportion had improved, and although now 'passing rich on £40 a year', I felt that matrimony was not yet in sight. I had from time to time earned a few pounds by making joke drawings at the rate of 5s. a drawing for a paper called *British Boys*, and had even tried my luck without success with *Punch*. So when an invitation came from Gussie I was able to tell Father that I could pay my own fare to Devonshire.

Cyril, of course, could not go, being tied to the City until the time came for his annual holiday; Ethel and I went together. We were up early and, reaching Paddington before 10.30, took our seats in a through carriage to Kingswear. I had never travelled on the

Great Western before, though I had studied much of its history, and had always loved its engines of dark green with shining brass-work. Great Western rolling stock, too, solidly built with cream-coloured uppers, the company's arms emblazoned on the panel and with clerestory windows, appealed to my aesthetic sense.

We settled ourselves in comfort and on the strength of my new-found wealth I booked two places for lunch in the dining-car. The main line through Westbury had not yet been built and we travelled via Bath and Bristol, stopping at each place. I knew the landmarks on the line from my study of the G.W.R. – the Box Tunnel, Clifton Suspension Bridge seen in the distance, and the flat lands before Taunton. After leaving Exeter we ran close to the sea by Dawlish, then turned inland again. The countryside with its red earth and bright spring green and its cider-apple orchards in bloom impressed me deeply and I realized why Devon had earned its title of Glorious.

As we neared Kingswear we came in sight of the Dart, with H.M.S. *Britannia* and H.M.S. *Hindustani* lying at anchor. The old three-deckers, painted black and white, were still the homes of the naval cadets, for the Royal Naval College had yet to be built.

As the train drew up at the quayside station at Kingswear I saw Gussie on the platform and beside her a small man with a fox terrier on a lead. 'That man must be Mr Rogers,' I thought. Gussie looked just the same as I remembered her nine years before: it was such a joy greeting her after all that time.

As we left the station she crossed the road and stopped at a baker's shop opposite. When she came out she told us we could leave our bags there and Mr Luckraft would bring them up when he delivered the bread. It was over a mile walk from the station to 'Coombeside' and a most delightful walk it was. Tropical trees and plants grew on the slopes down to the harbour and on the other side was the tiny church of St Petrox and the battery of obsolete guns. Groby Rogers and I walked behind the others and he pointed out the blue gum trees. Blue gum trees, he told me, grew to an immense size in South Africa. He was a quiet little man, but he had a gay twinkle in his eye and I took to him immediately.

Coombeside stood by itself on the side of a little valley running down to the sea, with a tiny cove at the bottom. There was a very small landing-stage cut into the rocks and a boat was hanging from davits. We left the road and turned into a drive bordered with bracken and ferns. The house had a pleasant loggia with french windows and a grand view across the bay to Start Point. I was quite enchanted by it.

After tea Mr Luckraft arrived with our bags and sundry groceries and bread for Groby's brother, Harry Rogers, who lived in an isolated house across the valley. Neither the baker nor the postman liked the extra walk that delivery entailed, so an arrangement was made whereby things were brought to Coombeside and collected

from time to time. Groby and I sorted the parcels and packed two baskets, Gussie's voice reminding us from upstairs: 'Don't forget the bottle of whisky and his letters. And there's a bag of saffron buns – he likes those.'

We sallied forth. A footpath down the hill brought us to the cove. Snap the fox terrier followed close at heel as he had been trained to do since, a year before, while chasing rabbits among the bracken, he

324

had been bitten by an adder. 'I saw him standing with his tongue out and whimpering,' said Groby, 'and I went across to him. I guessed what had happened immediately I saw the tiny red marks on his paw, and I ran home with him as fast as I could. Fortunately I had had experience of snake-bites and knew what to do. The dog's leg was swelling so I slashed the paw with a razor until it bled freely and then poured in whisky. He was all right in a couple of days. But it was a near thing.'

From the cove we climbed a hill by a rough cart-track and came in sight of a small house close to the edge of the cliff. It had a very untidy garden and a little greenhouse. There was a young man at work in an outhouse on some carpentry. Groby hailed him: 'Hullo, Herbert. Is Harry in?' The young man stopped work and jerked his thumb over his shoulder. Harry Rogers appeared round a corner and greeted us. He was short, like his brother, but more lightly built and his fair hair was thin on top. We had difficulty in entering the

house, for the porch was stacked with planks of various sizes. We climbed over a carpenter's saw-bench and entered a large sitting-room. The place was covered in shavings and looked like a carpenter's shop, though there was a carpet on the floor. By way of explanation, Harry waved his hand towards the mess and said: 'You see, we are getting on with the big organ.' This statement surprised and puzzled me, for there was already an organ, a small one of somewhat original design, in the corner of the room. I was soon to learn the workings of this extraordinary *ménage*. Harry was a very keen musician, and Herbert, who showed musical promise, had been more or less adopted by him and he was teaching the lad to play. But Herbert, in addition to his musical gifts, had proved to be handy with carpenter's tools, and between them Harry and Herbert had designed and built the small organ in the sitting-room. This instrument had a wonderful tone and it was a great treat for me to listen to the music which young Herbert produced from it. Now the pair were building a larger organ – hence the clutter. I was shown the drawings for the new instrument and was taken to the outhouse where the boy was lovingly fashioning the tiny wood-and-leather valves. Both men were wildly enthusiastic about their plans, and it was difficult to bring Harry down to earth sufficiently to give us his next grocery order.

In earlier days Herbert had rigged the dinghy we had seen down in the cove. Several times we went sailing in it in Dartmouth Bay, where the pilot boat lay at anchor waiting for an incoming ship. There were two pilot boats. We called them 'Penny' and 'Twopenny' because they bore 1D and 2D painted on their sails. One evening when we came back from a sail Harry Rogers was waiting in the cove. After the boat was stowed away he said to me: 'You know, I always feel a little anxious till Herbert gets back. He handles the boat perfectly – but you never know. I can never forget what happened three years ago.' Then he told me how two cadets from H.M.S. *Britannia* had come with the Vicar from Dartmouth in their sailing-boat. They had all had tea up at his house and at about six o'clock left to sail back. As the Vicar had to make a call at Kingswear the boys started alone. They knew how to handle the boat and were perfectly at home with her, and it was but a short distance to the harbour, so no one entertained qualms. Harry told me he watched the boys leave the cove and saw them wave to him as they passed out of sight round the headland. No trace of them or of the boat was ever found. Harry, his eyes full of tears, turned to me and said: 'I can never now bear to watch our boat round the headland.'

The evenings were chilly and after supper we sat round the fire at Coombeside. Groby lay on the settee in the corner with Snap curled up beside him, while Gussie showed us some of her special treasures. She talked to us of her schooldays with Mother at Queen's College. She explained, with slight embarrassment, why she had found it difficult to keep in touch with us since Mother's death. She had once met the Aunts during Mother's lifetime and had not got on well with them. This did not surprise us, for indeed Mother herself, with all her tact and sweet nature, had found it difficult to adjust herself to the conditions of Gordon Square. But now that we were with her again Gussie's friendship was to be unbroken till her death in 1922.

Took pot-shots at rabbits

327

Groby and I took long walks, with Snap at our heels, over toward Brownstone and the Beacon. We usually carried a ·22 rifle and took pot-shots at rabbits – not easy to hit with a rifle. We once went as far as Man sands under Berry Head, where it seemed Groby had sometimes found gold quartz. Having spent years digging for gold in South Africa he knew what to look for. Grubbing about among the stones, he pocketed a few to take home and break up with his hammer. He told me he had sent specimens to London to be assayed, but the analysis, though it showed traces of gold, did not offer much prospect of a fortune. He had been in the Transvaal during the unsettled times preceding the Boer War, and had always been in trouble with the Boers. He made me a present of some garnets that he had scooped up in the Vaal River while he was being shot at by a Boer farmer.

My visit to Devon had a profound effect on me. It seemed to open a new chapter in my life. Much of the happiness that I had felt when Mother was alive returned to me. Groby's friendship, which seemed to grow with the years, was a tonic to me and helped me to overcome a certain aloofness to which I was prone and which he chaffed me out of by calling me 'Grandpa'.

Groby and Gussie had known each other since childhood. At sixteen he had left home and gone to Russia, but he did not like it there and soon returned. Then, when the gold rush started in South Africa, off he went to make his fortune. He found gold all right, but not enough, and was soon on his beam-ends. He lived with the Zulus in a kraal for more than a year, learning their language and even translating 'Three Blind Mice' into Zulu. This, 'Matatu eibooni goondarni', was adopted by the young warriors as a war song. Groby, suitably clad and armed with a knobkerrie, would then give us a rendering of it, while Gussie shook with laughter and Snap barked. I learned most of the song by heart and gave a performance of it later in the corridor at the Schools – till the noise brought the Keeper on the scene.

I think that Father must have had a windfall about this time, for one evening in July he surprised us by asking if we would like to go to Germany for our summer holiday. Would we not! Cyril's holiday was due in the last fortnight of August, and our plans were made accordingly. On a Saturday in the middle of the month we found ourselves at Liverpool Street station boarding the train for Harwich. I was determined to try my hand at oil painting again and had packed my easel, camp-stool and two or three canvases. We arrived at Harwich in the late afternoon and went on board S.S. *Peregrine*. She was not an inviting-looking ship. Painted black all over, she had none of the attraction of our friend *Tamise* of two years before.

It was a thirty-two-hour voyage and the third-class sleeping quarters were in the bowels of the ship and very stuffy. Soon after leaving harbour we began to pitch and roll. Dinner was eaten in ominous silence, and Father hurried from the table before the end of the meal. I went on deck, but it was so cold that I soon took refuge in the saloon. A few men were drinking there. Ethel had disappeared. It was not long before Cyril and I too were stricken down. The dreadful atmosphere below and the signs of distress all around were our final undoing. I spent a miserable night; I had not realized sea-sickness could be so painful. I lay on the hard bunk and longed for the end of the world. In the morning Cyril went on deck, but was down again almost immediately – the smell of frying bacon was too much for him. I tried to face food at lunch-time, but in vain. Ethel, however, was by now quite cheerful; she had recovered from her attack, and she ate a hearty meal. There was no sign of Father. We had none of us seen him since he left the dinner-table the previous evening. A search revealed him lying on a settee in the third-class saloon wrapped in a rug and, mercifully, asleep. By sundown my inside was beginning to settle down and, after we had passed Heligoland and run into calmer waters, I fancied I could face a meal. Alas! I still couldn't. Feeling I had been stretched on the rack, I retired again to my bunk.

I awoke next morning to sounds of activity and the rattling of chains. Looking out of the porthole I saw that the ship was alongside a quay, which I realized must be Hamburg. By this time Cyril and I were clamorous for food. We waited very impatiently for breakfast to be served and ate heartily when we got it. Father was up, but feeling squeamish; and it was not, indeed, until he got his feet on dry land again that he recovered his equilibrium.

After very brief formalities we boarded a train for Hildesheim. It was a dull journey: flat, featureless countryside for miles and miles;

but the old town, when we reached it, was a pleasant contrast. The streets were lined with red-brick and timbered houses, many with signs hanging over the pavement. A narrow river, running through the centre of the town, gave it an almost Dutch appearance. We chose an hotel from Baedeker and it proved cheap and comfortable. The German meals were excellent. It was something new to have stewed, syrupy fruit with our meat, and rich pastries with cream to follow, but I could have done without the caraway seeds. For breakfast we had honey and delicious hot rolls.

The German people interested me greatly. The tradesmen seemed to have distinctive clothes – a square white cap for a carpenter, a top hat for a sweep. There were many soldiers in the streets and when they passed an officer they broke into the goose step, slapping the pavement with their feet. Everything in the town was very orderly and well kept, which gave the place a prosperous air. I chose a spot near the river and painted the red houses overhanging the water while Father made sketches in the church near by.

We stayed five days at Hildesheim and then moved on to Wernigerode, a dull place on the River Oder. From Wernigerode we took a trip to the Brocken. A light railway took us to the top of this so-called mountain. We passed numerous signs with 'AN DER SCHÖNEN AUSSICHT', but I could see nothing very beautiful, nor was the view from the summit impressive. Even the witches were absent – except on the postcards on sale in large numbers at a kiosk.

We did not stay long at the top, but on our way down we came to a beer garden. It looked inviting, with a waterfall in the background and coloured plaster gnomes lurking in the surrounding pinewoods, so we chose a table and sat down. The waterfall interested me; it had a suspiciously artificial look and presently Cyril and I slipped away to investigate it. We found a path that led up to the rocks above the fall and there saw that a natural stream had been diverted into a channel made to carry the water over the edge. Peering down, we could see the beer garden below with a family party gathered at each table. We decided to stop the waterfall. Collecting a number of large stones, we gradually filled up the diversion channel. Retracing our steps, we joined Father and Ethel, and we did not have to wait long before signs of consternation became evident. Stout gentlemen forsaking their beer stood pointing upwards; a waiter was sent to fetch the manager. The water diminished to a trickle and voices were raised calling for an explanation. Cyril and I quietly told Father what we had done and we all decided it was time to go. As we left, the manager, a portly man, was being assisted up the steep path by two waiters.

After three days we went on to Goslar. This delightful mediaeval town provided a complete contrast to Wernigerode. It was surrounded by a wall with gates and round bastions roofed with tiles. In the centre of the square stood a fountain topped with a bronze eagle which, it was said, dated from the tenth century. Opposite was a picturesque old inn where we inquired for rooms. Herr Bode, the proprietor, greeted us and found us accommodation, and then broached the subject of dinner. 'You will have some nice trouts, yes?' We were shown the fish swimming in a tank. Delicious trout they proved to be.

Goslar was a garrison town and there were plenty of soldiers about. The officers of artillery were particularly smart in their dark-blue frock-coats with red facings. Apparently it was a good thing for civilian pedestrians to step aside into the road when officers passed on the side-walks; the demigods of the army were treated with immense respect in the Kaiser's Germany. A corner of the dining-room at our inn was set aside for their use. No civilian ever violated the sanctity of these tables.

The bronze fountain in the square interested me deeply and I made some drawings of it. The eagle on top was a quaint bird like a soda-water bottle with wings. Water spouted from its beak. In the evening the young men and maidens gathered round it. The girls, many with fair hair plaited in twin pigtails, were wearing national dress of full skirt and short black embroidered bodice. There were no cinemas to draw young people indoors in those days.

We could not stay long in Goslar, for our fortnight was nearly over. On leaving we spent a night at Harzburg, a spa with little of interest, before moving on to Brunswick for our last night in Germany. Father had chosen from the bottom of Baedeker's list an hotel which seemed likely to be the cheapest in the city. When, however, we left the railway station and asked for it, we were directed to a smart bus which landed us at a most imposing building though on an ugly site. It appeared that Baedeker's cheap hotel had been rebuilt and was now one of the best and most expensive. Father tackled the manager, who promised to accommodate us at a reasonable figure as this was the off season. We escaped the next day, dodging the staff lined up in the hall and slinking out by a side entrance with the connivance of the under-porter.

Our arrival back at Hamburg was marked by a full-scale thunderstorm. The lightning, like streamers from clouds to earth, was an impressive sight as we sailed down the river. The deluge of rain seemed to have a quieting effect on the sea, for the return voyage was a placid one. In the afternoon Ethel entertained the passengers with a concert on the ship's antediluvian piano. Owing to our shortage of cash care had to be exercised in our choice of meals, but by pooling our resources we were just able to pay our fares back to Blackheath.

That autumn a debating society was formed at the Royal Academy Schools. The meetings were not always given to formal debates, sometimes a paper was read. As I listened I began to realize the deficiencies of my education. I had never been a diligent reader and now found myself far behind my fellow students in knowledge of English prose and poetry. The Society's meetings were held in the evenings, usually at a room in New Court normally used as a studio by two of the girls. Afterwards Philip Streatfeild and I would go out of our way to see Florence Chaplin and her sister Adrienne, also a student, to their home in Earl's Court.

The time was coming for the winter show of students' work. The prize-giving that followed was always held on the tenth of December, Foundation Day of the Royal Academy, and also, as it happened, my birthday. Our paintings and drawings were hung in the Academy Galleries, and we were able to criticize and appraise each other's work and decide which were likely to be prize-winners. The painting about which we were all agreed that year was the head of a girl in profile by Florence Chaplin; it was quite outstanding. When we were all in the Gallery I went up to her and said how good I thought it was: we walked over and stood before it. Then she said: 'I got into trouble with the Visitor, you know. He accused me of putting palette scrapings on the hair.' She gave me one of her quick smiles and added, 'He was horrified when I admitted it.' She asked to see my work, which, as no signatures were allowed, she had been unable to identify. She stood in front of it for a few moments and said, 'Your drawing is much better than your painting. You are still afraid of your paint.' 'Yes, I know,' I replied, 'I only wish you would give me a lesson.' 'Oh! I couldn't do that. I have never taught painting and should not know where to begin.' When the prize-winners were announced, Florence, to my joy, was given the silver medal.

After Christmas we made up a party to see the pantomime at

Drury Lane Pantomime, drawn at aged 13

Drury Lane. Cyril and I had been to every pantomime there for several years. No longer were Dan Leno and Herbert Campbell the main attractions as they had been for nearly ten years. Some of the best contemporary comedians had been substituted, but the effect was not the same and everyone missed the famous pair. We paid our half-crowns and fought our way into the pit. I cannot recall which of the small range of traditional pantomime stories this one was supposed to represent, but I do remember Harry Randall, robust and loud of voice, singing

> *Oh what a happy land is England!*
> *Envied by all nations near and far.*
> *Though of Gladstone we're bereft,*
> *We have Winston Churchill left.*
> *Oh what a happy land we are.*

Churchill was even then making his name – one of the angry young men at the turn of the century.

Chapter Twelve

MY FIRST STUDIO

I N England the year 1899 ended in gloom. The Boer War had started and after some initial successes the situation of the British troops had rapidly deteriorated. None of our generals was prepared for the elusive tactics of the Boer. They had never had to face an enemy armed with modern weapons, and their hidebound approach to their problems only led to the destruction of their troops. There were plenty of armchair tacticians to tell them how the war should be fought, but the wretched struggle dragged on for three years. Much bitter feeling existed in the country and outspoken criticism was uttered on all sides. In the schools we had many arguments about the rights and wrongs of the war. In spite of my love of soldiering I could not work up any enthusiasm and never felt the slightest impulse to volunteer for the Imperial Yeomanry.

With the New Year things began to look more promising, and when the news came of the relief of Ladysmith, followed by that of Mafeking, we really let ourselves go. The students of the Royal College of Art prepared a celebration in the form of a procession through the West End of London with a statue of Queen Victoria. The statue, larger than life, was constructed in a most ingenious way devised by the professor of sculpture. The seated figure was built up on a wooden foundation; the head and shoulders, an excellent likeness, were modelled in clay and placed on top; and old curtains were arranged as draperies and sprayed with plaster. The whole was placed on a large sculptor's trolley and looked most imposing.

On the appointed day the students sallied forth in their painting smocks, some of dark blue, and moved down Bond Street to meet the procession coming along Piccadilly. (Next day a paragraph in one of the daily newspapers commented: 'It was a strange sight to see a procession of butchers marching down Bond Street and turning

into Piccadilly.') When we Academy Schools students joined up with the procession, intermittent bursts of cheering encouraged our journey along Piccadilly. At the Circus we turned up Regent Street. It was a fine sight looking back from the head of the procession: fifty or sixty smocked students straining at the ropes of the trolley with the girls marching behind waving palms. It looked rather like some scene from the building of the Pyramids. There were no traffic difficulties; the police just held everything up and let us go by. We had no band, but we broke into song at intervals and were much cheered by the crowd.

At the Schools we had also our own small celebrations. These took place in the evenings when we were working in the life class, and were often staged for the express purpose of ragging the Curator. He was a plump, unctuous man named Bosdet, with a neat little beard and a manner that did not commend itself. On one occasion we formed a procession after assembling in the corridor. I got myself up as Kruger in a borrowed top hat and a Newgate frill made of cotton wool. We entered the classroom singing a funeral dirge. This

was too much for Bosdet. He rushed to the door to bar our progress. There was a short struggle and he was borne backwards, his cries of 'Gentlemen! gentlemen!' becoming fainter until, breathless, he sank into his seat. Mopping his brow he gasped: 'I shall report you for this. It is quite easy to see it is an organized disturbance.' He was still fretting and fuming when the visiting Academician appeared in the doorway. It was the American artist Edwin Abbey and he was wearing his top hat (my 'Kruger' one was stowed away under my seat). This was no coincidence, for Abbey went everywhere in his hat, though he usually removed his jacket. As Bosdet fussed up to him and poured into his ear the tale of our misdoings a broad grin spread over Abbey's face, and looking round he said, 'Waal, they seem quiet enough now,' as indeed we were and hard at work too. Nothing much came of the affair except that the Keeper, Crofts, came in the next evening and read us a little homily ending, in an undertone, with 'You must try not to annoy Mr Bosdet, you know.'

We were always glad when Abbey was the Visitor. Not only was he a brilliant draughtsman and a great teacher, but he took a continuing interest in our welfare. I had him to thank for my introduction to *Punch* four years later, while several of his other students were employed by him at his studio at Fairford when he was painting the big frescoes for the Boston Library. I never could see the object of the Curator's presence at the evening life class. On the rare occasions when Bosdet was away and the Keeper appointed a senior student to take charge, perfect quiet was preserved and no one thought of making a disturbance.

In the early part of the summer I devoted some weeks to working for a British Institution prize. This was a cash prize of £60 a year for two years and was open to students all over the kingdom. When the results were declared in July I was one of the lucky ones. This, added to my £40 from the Landseer Scholarship, would give me £100 for the next year, and I began to consider the possibility of taking a studio in town, perhaps sharing it with another student. There was to be another competition for the Creswick Prize in the summer and I wanted to paint my picture in Devon, where I knew of a subject close to my friends at Kingswear.

Philip Streatfeild and I decided to go together, so I wrote to Gussie and she found us rooms in a labourer's cottage in their valley, for which we each paid one pound a week all in. Early in August we travelled down together. Again Gussie, Groby and Snap met us at the station and Mr Luckraft's cart transported our luggage. We had the tiniest rooms, but Mrs Blake looked after us well. Within a few days we had begun our painting. Usually we worked until midday, when Groby would appear at the top of the valley and join us for a bathe in the cove.

It was a perfect summer. In Devon we had four weeks of

unbroken sunshine. The use of Harry's dinghy, he and Herbert being away on the moors, was a special amenity, and we also had the run of his home, 'The Warren'. Philip was a pianist, so we had some gay evenings at the house on the cliff. There were plenty of mackerel about and our painting was often inter-rupted by Groby shouting down the valley that the fish were in the bay. We would leave our work and launch the dinghy in no time and go off to chase the shoals. We caught dozens at a time. Sometimes we did not even need to use the boat, for the mackerel would come right into the cove, chasing the little britt which made for the rocks, and we could scoop the fish out with our hands. It was great fun grabbing the mackerel and throwing them up on the rocks. We had them for supper most nights. There are few things nicer than mackerel grilled fresh from the sea.

Regatta week came to Dartmouth at the end of the month. There were three nights of it, with fireworks to round it off. The whole harbour front was given over to merry-go-rounds, swings and sideshows. Old Hancock sat in front of the big centre tent waving the crowd in, and gnawing great hunks of meat on the bone. Two dancing girls in short tight-waisted spangled skirts and high boots danced to the rhythm of the mechanical organ. The woman at the

pay desk examined our hands to see if we could pass as workers and
so get cheaper seats. The yachting folk, ashore from their craft,

mingled with the crowds and would give a golden sovereign to the roundabout man for a whole evening's turn.

Though I had not finished my competition painting, I left after the Fair to join Father, Ethel and Cyril in Suffolk. They were staying at Wade's Farm, near Dunwich, and I was eager to go there as I knew that not far away, at Hinton, I should find Florence Chaplin. She had told me earlier in the year that her mother had a house there and that she and her sister would probably be at Hinton in the summer. I spent a night in London with my two aunts in Gordon Square. It was the last time I was to stay there, for Aunt Alicia, my godmother, died the following winter and the house was sold. Next day I took train to Saxmundham, where Cyril met me on a hired bicycle. After fixing my bag on the back of my own machine, we pedalled the four miles to Wade's Farm. It was a lonely place and not very attractive, but near enough to Dunwich to get some bathing. I felt very nervous about presenting myself at the Red House, the Chaplins' home, and as Cyril was coming with me we decided to arrive at three o'clock so that no meal would be involved. I need not have worried. We were given a warm welcome, and I was terribly flattered when Florence introduced me to her mother with, 'This is little Shepard. You have heard of him.'

Besides four girls

there was a brother, Lindsay, whom I remembered as a small boy, even smaller than I, at St Paul's; he was still at school. Florence and her younger sister had their hair done in pigtails and with short skirts looked almost like schoolgirls. We were made to stay to tea and the girls cycled part of the way back with us. I think Cyril was as taken with Adrienne as I was with her sister, and I know we were a couple of very gay young men when we reached the farm. Within a few days it became a settled thing for us to cycle over to the Red House and call for the girls to join us in an outing.

We had to go home at the end of a fortnight for Cyril's holiday was up and I had to go back to Devonshire to finish my picture. This time I stayed at Coombeside and worked in the spare room, for the weather had turned too cold and wet for outdoor work. The Academy term had already started, so after a week I had to say goodbye to Gussie and Groby and make for home.

Once back at the Schools I gave my serious attention to the problem of sharing a studio and was turning over in my mind whom I should ask when the matter was settled for me. George Swaish came up to me while we were washing our brushes and said, rather diffidently, 'I hear you are thinking of sharing a studio. Would you think of sharing with me?' I had never considered George as a possible, and was a bit startled, for I did not, as yet, know him well, but I agreed at once. I am very glad I did so, for it was really the start of our friendship, a friendship that lasted till his death in 1930. I learned from him much that helped to broaden my outlook on life.

We did not waste any time but started studio-hunting forthwith. We saw dozens, large and small, sound and leaky, and eventually settled on No. 52 Glebe Place, Chelsea. It was large with enough space for two to work. It had a tiny bedroom, big enough for two truckle beds, an adequate lavatory, a larder and a coalhole. The care-taker, Mrs Scott, lived next door and was prepared to do what cleaning was necessary. The rent was £50 per annum, £10 more than we meant to pay, but we agreed that as George would have to give up his digs and make it his home, something good was practicable. We took the studio from the Christmas quarter. As my twenty-first birthday was on December 10th, I was able to make it known to those interested that presents in the form of pieces of furniture would be most acceptable. As a result I received a studio easel from Frank Dicksee, an armchair from his sister, and Gussie, dear Gussie, wrote to say I could have her piano if transport could be arranged.

George and I went shopping. We bought our beds and bedding at Maple's, which gave customers a free lunch in those days. We bought pots and pans and a small gas-cooker in the King's Road,

and invited Cyril and Philip Streatfeild to join us in our first meal. We chose a steak, and as I knew steaks had to be beaten, I laid ours on a drawing-board and ham-mered it with a T-square. It came out quite thin, like a small blanket, and had to be folded several times to get it into the pan. We fried some onions and potato chips and the meal was washed down with bottled beer. The steak was as tough as hide.

I arranged that I would live at the studio during the week and go home for week-ends. George and I developed a regular breakfast drill: one shaved while the other stood by to see that the porridge didn't boil over. It was great fun. Sometimes we were joined by Arthur Connor on his way to Heatherley's. I was rather concerned about Arthur: I felt he was getting into a rut. He had been at Heatherley's over three years, and seemed quite content to spend the rest of his life there. George and I felt this would never do, and we joined in a determined effort to persuade him to try for a scholarship at the Academy Schools. At first he only dug in his heels, saying he was doing quite well where he was. But in the end we secured his consent. He passed, and in due course joined us as a student.

I found studio life very pleasant. When we had finished work in the evening life-class three or four of us would have a meal together. It had to be somewhere cheap, and we found a suitable

restaurant in the Brompton Road, close to the Oratory, a place patronized chiefly by cab-men. We sat round a table with a zinc top and ordered meat and two vegetables for 6d. When we were in funds we followed this with apple turnover. The serving girl was called Polly, and she always giggled when we called for 'Turnover, Polly!' A small man with a large expressionless face was part of the establishment. He seemed to spend his life washing the floor, and was usually out of sight under a table. After a particularly bright sally on our part his face would appear like a full moon, only to duck again immediately he was observed.

We held a house-warming party in the New Year. The piano had arrived and Philip Streatfeild played. Both the Chaplin girls were there; Father and Ethel came up from Blackheath; and everyone brought a small gift. Father's arthritis was now acute and even the short journey from Blackheath tried him.

About this time we began to hear disquieting rumours of the Queen's state of health. References to her condition in the press were at first guarded, but presently it became apparent that the old lady was failing rapidly. But although the public was to some extent prepared for the news of her death when it occurred on January 22nd the effect on us all was strangely contradictory. Somehow we had almost come to believe that she could go on for ever. The whole country mourned, people going about with bowed heads. The funeral procession through London was a very moving sight. George and I stood amongst the crowd in Sussex Place to see it pass. King Edward and the Kaiser followed immediately behind the coffin, which was borne on a gun-carriage. It was all very simple; only the bands playing the funeral march broke the silence. No one could fail to mark the difference from the cheering crowds of three years earlier.

After my mother's death, Father had given up his connections with the theatrical world. This winter, however, he was asked to stage a Shakespearian play in aid of the hospital for sick children in Great Ormonde Street. In the past he had produced several plays for the Irving Club, and now he wrote to some of the members, friends with whom he had played, to enlist their support. Having had experience of the difficulties in managing the front of the house, he put that part of the business in charge of an agent. *Measure for Measure* was the play chosen. The club had produced it successfully some years previously and a cast of good amateur actors was formed. Cyril and I were given small parts; mine was Verges, and I much enjoyed it. A host of Academy students, male and female, was forthcoming for the 'crowds' and the dance in the last act. We had a very good orchestra, an organ for the marriage scene, and an ex-army drummer and bugler for 'tuckets off'. Some scenery was specially painted and Nathan provided the costumes. St George's Hall in Upper Regent Street was hired and *Punch*, a staunch supporter of the Children's Hospital, provided an ornamental programme. It was all the greatest fun.

Six months later we students produced another theatrical venture of quite a different kind. It was a burlesque of 'Sherlock Holmes' written by a student from Cope's school. I was cast for the lead;

I don't know why, for though I had grown a lot and was no longer 'little Shepard', I was hardly tall enough for Holmes. But by adding something to the heels of my boots (like Wilson Barrett in *The Sign of the Cross*) I gained sufficient height. Our studio in Glebe Place was used both for rehearsals and for scene-painting. We made a lot of mess with our backcloth for the scene in the *Twopenny Tube*. As a curtain-raiser we did W. W. Jacobs' *Ghost of Jerry Bundler*, and were lucky to get Charles Rock, the actor and dramatizer of the play, to produce it for us. The show was produced at the Queen's Gate Hall in Harrington Road and was received with great enthusiasm.

After all this excitement I settled down to work again. I persuaded Ethel to sit for me. It was an ordinary portrait, but it was accepted by the Royal Academy and hung on the line at the Summer Exhibition, the only success I have ever had with a portrait. I had little time for any other outside work as the conditions of my Landseer Scholarship entailed my regular attendance at the Schools either in the morning or the evening. However, I decided to enter for a landscape competition called the 'Turner', with a subject, announced early in the year, of a bridge over the Thames in London. I chose to paint Tower Bridge; I don't know why, for it is neither beautiful nor easy. In preparation I explored the dark alleys leading to the river round London Bridge and Blackfriars Bridge, but this proved vain, for the alleys, besides being smelly, were liable to inundation at high tide. Next I thought of trying a wharf. There were a great number to choose from, but I was lucky in meeting a man who advised me to try Hay's Wharf, which stands opposite the Tower of London. It was shut when I located it, but the night watchman answered my knocking. He assured me that there would be no trouble over my painting if I came after working hours. I explained that I had a large

canvas and he agreed I could
keep it in his watch-room. His
name was Dan and I learned
much about the riverside from
him. He began by warning me
to be careful how I went about,
for lately there had been groups
of young men, known as hooligans, who were causing trouble
on the riverside and doing a lot
of damage. He told me that
only a few nights previously
they had smashed a window
in the wharf next door and
stolen a lot of stuff. On his
advice I carried my traps along
before closing time, for he said
that if the trouble-makers saw

my canvas as like as not they would poke a hole in it. For several
weeks I worked every evening until the light failed without trouble
or disturbance of any kind. Another warning Dan gave me was:
'Don't be seen talking to the police, else the lads'll be after you.'
I had noticed that the police went about in couples and I was careful
to avoid them. I often passed groups of hooligans lounging at street
corners; gradually we got on nodding terms, and even got as far
as exchanging good nights. Poor lads! They had nowhere to go to
except the pubs. No wonder they got into mischief.

Chapter Thirteen

IN LOVE

Now that we had a piano at our studio, George and I decided we ought to make use of it, so we invited our friends to come for music in the evenings. I cleaned my fiddle, bought some new strings and, with Streatfeild at the piano, we tried our hands at simple things. Two or three others joined us, Denholm Davis came with his violin, Stanley Young the sculptor – Big Ben we called him – brought his 'cello, and Mortimer Brown, another sculptor, his flute. Gradually we became more ambitious and tackled Handel. Our rendering of the Largo was unorthodox but effective; we had no music for the 'cello and Big Ben had to improvise. The standard of chamber music we attained was not high, but it gave us pleasure and we arranged to give a concert. We clubbed together and laid on a supper of bread and cheese and beer. Then we invited our men friends, adding a suggestion that anyone who could play, sing or recite would be called upon. The result was a variety programme. After a solemn start with the Largo and a song or two, Reginald Higgins gave some excellent impersonations, which were followed by a flute solo, 'Alice, where art thou?' by Mortimer Brown, and we wound up with a Zulu war dance. This brought the caretaker with a message of protest from the man next door.

Our studio grew to be a meeting-place for students of the neighbourhood. Besides Streatfeild at Trafalgar Studios, there was Gregory Robinson at the Onslow Warren in the King's Road. Gregory was perpetually hard up, and although he was a good marine painter he seldom had the luck to sell his paintings. His studio, at the top of that ramshackle block, was small and very untidy, with always the remains of a meal mixed up with the paints and brushes on the table. The room was lit by gas, and more than once we found Gregory struggling to work by candlelight for want of a shilling to put in the meter slot.

It was a great day for him when he was commissioned by a journal to make a double-page drawing of the return of the P. & O. liner from an Empire cruise with the Prince of Wales on board. The night was a foggy one when George and I decided to go round and see how Gregory was getting on with his picture. We found him working against time and almost in despair. He sat looking at his drawing. 'The bows, the bows!' he groaned. 'I can't get them right.' The thing had to be finished by the next morning and Gregory had had no dinner. First, then, he must be fed, so we hustled him out to get something to eat. Then we thought we might be able to help the picture along in his absence. Neither George nor I knew much about

ships, but even we could see that the bows were a bit odd. I remembered that there was a student who lived not far away who was an expert on ships and we decided to consult him. Off we went through the fog, found him at home, explained the situation, and brought him back with us. I can't remember his name, but I know that the first thing he said was, 'He's got the bows wrong.'

'Very well,' we said, 'that's what Gregory says himself. Put them right.'

'Oh! I couldn't do that,' he protested.

'You must,' was our answer. 'And quick – before Gregory comes back.'

He started work, and while he was busy at one end of the picture I went ahead at the other, painting the people in the boats waving to the ship, while George added flags, lots of them fluttering in the breeze. We were rather pleased with our combined efforts. When Gregory returned he sat down and stared. For a few minutes he said nothing; then: 'There's a story somewhere about fairies or mice doing something in the night, but I never knew mice who could draw ships.' He was not in the least put out, and agreed that the bows were better, but he did complain about my boatloads of people and George's display of bunting. We left him to carry on, and at about eleven the following morning he called at our studio with the picture under his arm on his way to Fleet Street. I hope they paid him adequately.

There was a lot of fog that winter. At times it was so thick that traffic practically ceased. This did not worry us because George and I always walked from the Schools to Chelsea. Sometimes Arthur Connor accompanied us, though he would never join us in dining at the 'Bug and Gluepot', as we called our haunt in the Brompton Road; he preferred to take his meal at home. One particularly foggy night we three started out from the Schools after the evening life-class. It was all right till we came to Hyde Park Corner. There it was so dense that we could not see the kerb and the lamps were dim yellow blurrs. Arthur, who had little sense of direction, bore off to the left and was lost to sight in a moment. I knew his failing and we decided he must be found at all costs. We called his name. No answer! Then, raising our voices, we shouted in unison. A faint cry of distress came out of the fog and we made for the sound. It was like navigating at sea with only the sound of a distant foghorn to guide us. The nearer we seemed to get the fainter became the bleats. Finally we struck (literally) the railings in Belgrave Square. We knew that our quarry could not be far off. Then George had a brain-wave. 'Let us,' he said, 'separate and go round the square in opposite directions, keeping to the railings, till we meet again on the other side.' I did not have to go far before I found Arthur. He was clinging to the railings thinking he was at Victoria Station. 'All right,' I bellowed at the top of my voice. 'He's found.' When we fore-gathered again we had to decide what action to take. It was out of the question to leave Arthur to his own devices, so we all made for Sloane Square, a simple job for those used to it. At the Underground we said good night to him and dived into an A.B.C. in the King's Road for some supper.

The Prize Distribution at the Academy Schools that winter was a really happy event for me. I had won a medal for a painted figure and ten pounds for a set of life drawings. But what pleased me even more was that Florence Chaplin had won the £40 Prize for a mural. The subject was 'The Procession of the Hours' and she treated it by showing the Horae as female figures. It was lovely both in colour and design and the award was a most popular one, all agreeing that it was by far the best. She was later to be commissioned to carry out

A group from the mural

the design for the nurses' dining-room at Guy's Hospital. It was a big undertaking, measuring twenty-five feet in length, and took her over a year to paint. Many years later I was able to buy back the original drawing, and it hangs in my drawing-room today.

At the prize distribution both my father and Mrs Chaplin were present. They sat together and got on extremely well: a couple of proud parents delighted at their children's successes. As Mrs Chaplin afterwards expressed it, 'Ready to burst with pride.'

After the gloom of Queen Victoria's death it was a relief when spring came to London. I worked at the Schools in the daytime, and started making studies for my riverside picture at Hay's Wharf in the evening. I did not begin work on the big canvas till the early summer, and as the days lengthened I was able to put in long hours at it. I was careful to follow Dan's advice, and never had any trouble with the hooligans.

When the Schools broke up in July George asked me to spend a week at his home at Bristol. We agreed to make the journey by cycle. It was a long haul – 120 miles – but we felt equal to it, especially if we rode at night. By starting at about nine in the evening we should reach Bristol by breakfast-time. I bought a valise to fit on my cycle and packed a few clothes. We settled our accounts with the caretaker, and on a warm night early in August we set off. I had told Florence of our plans and she suggested that we call at her home in Earls Court, which we did and were given packets of sandwiches and were waved goodbye from the front door in Penywern Road. It had been George's idea to start at night, for it meant that the worst part of the journey would be in the cool and the dark; he had tried it before, he told me, and found it worked.

We pedalled steadily along the Great West Road, traffic lessening as the hour grew later; by the time we neared Taplow we had the road all to ourselves. It was a very close night and we were glad to stop on the bridge at Maidenhead to eat our sandwiches and have a drink of lemonade. The stretch beyond Maidenhead was tiring, for the road was in bad condition; my wrists went quite numb with the jolting. George's lamp kept going out, which meant frequent stops to re-light it, until finally he ceased to bother with it and rode close behind me. Passing through Reading a policeman spotted him and shouted, 'Where's your light?' We put on a spurt and left trouble behind. As we approached Newbury a grey light promised dawn. We stopped in the deserted street. My poor legs were as stiff as pokers. Then came a few drops of rain. We waited under a wall, for the rain was not heavy enough to make us don our mackintosh capes, and after a while it stopped. We peered up at the sky, which was leaden grey. However, we decided to go on and mounted our bicycles. We had not gone a hundred yards before the rain came down in torrents. The dusty road turned to mud. We floundered on for a while but had to give it up. We crouched for shelter under a hedge and curled up close together for warmth. I promptly fell asleep. I was wakened by a passing cyclist shouting 'Good morning!' I felt it was anything but a good morning, for I was shivering with cold. Sleepily I asked George who his friend was. He looked at me in surprise and said, 'What friend?' 'That man,' I answered. All George said was, 'You must have been dreaming!'

By this time the rain was falling only lightly and we agreed to push on. Stiff and cold, we mounted our cycles and pedalled along till we came to an inn. We did not know the time, but our thoughts turned to breakfast and we knocked on the door. There was no reply, so we hammered. A window above opened and a tousled head looked out: 'What do you want?' 'Breakfast,' we called in unison. 'Breakfast!' shouted an indignant voice. 'You won't get any breakfast here – not at this hour.' And the window was shut with a bang. Wearily we remounted and rode on.

It was broad daylight when we reached Hungerford – most appropriately named, we thought – and we were lucky to find a small eating-house open. A woman served us with tea, cold ham and stale bread and butter. Refreshed, we had to make up our minds what to do. It was still raining, though not so heavily, and George said, tentatively, 'We might be able to get a train from here.' He spoke what was in my mind, though I was ashamed to admit it. 'Do you think we ought to?' George's answer was, 'We've come quite a long way and I'm soaked.' I suggested tossing up, but we agreed to go to the station and ask about a train. One was due in an hour's time, we were told, and without further hesitation we decided to take it. We bought our tickets and were doing our best to dry off in the waiting-room when the sun came out. It got warmer and warmer and blue skies appeared. 'Do you think,' I said, 'we might return our tickets and ride on?' George shook his head. 'I'm much too stiff. Sitting under that hedge was a daft thing to do.' I quite

agreed and we gave in.

It was a blazing hot morning by the time we reached Bristol, and when we arrived at the Swaishs' home in Redland Road we were almost dry and feeling more cheerful. After a late and very welcome breakfast we spent some time cleaning and oiling our cycles and then were glad to relax on deck-chairs in their garden.

George's father, a city councillor and magistrate, was the owner of several shops in the town, and his elder son Ernest was in charge of them. I had never been in Bristol and was anxious to see the town, so, later in the day, we went to have a look at the cathedral, then to the Art Gallery and ended up at the Bristol Savages Club, of which George was a member. On another occasion George took me to St

Mary Redcliffe, which I found far more interesting than the cathedral. One of the things which particularly pleased me was the famous brass lectern which was reputedly made from a life-time's collection of brass pins.

On Sunday morning I went with the family to the Baptist Chapel. I was glad to go as I had never been to a Nonconformist Chapel. I don't know what my grandfather would have thought, but I enjoyed the service and was very much impressed by the heartiness with which all joined in. George and I had often had arguments about the different forms of religious observance, for I had been brought up to regard Nonconformity with suspicion. His brother Ernest held very strong views about the hierarchy of the Church of England and a rather exaggerated view of the attitude adopted by some of the bishops. I was inclined to think that he was right. We sat and argued about it all that evening until Mrs Swaish came in and sent us off to bed.

I spent six days at Bristol and left there reluctantly to return to London and get on with my painting.

This time I cycled all the way. Starting after breakfast, I reached Chelsea late in the evening, tired and hungry, I had a meal at the 'Bug and Gluepot' and tumbled into bed.

There was still a lot of work to be done on my Tower Bridge painting, so the following evening I carried my canvas along to the wharf. Dan was sitting outside. 'I wondered if you'd be coming back,' he said. 'There's been more trouble, but they caught two of 'em at it the other night, and that's put the rest off.' Anyway, there were no more disturbances while I worked there. It was only for a few evenings, for I soon realized I could do little more to my picture on the spot. I said goodbye to Dan and carried all my things back to the studio.

But there, by myself in the evening, I could not settle to anything but wandered around feeling painfully alone in the empty studio, dissatisfied with my work and utterly depressed. I sat there long after it was dark, thinking, thinking about Florence, and hardly daring to own to myself how much I cared for her. There was no one I could talk to, for Father and Ethel had shut up the house at Blackheath and gone to Kingswear for a month. They had taken Harry Rogers' house, 'The Warren', on the cliff opposite Coombeside. I knew that Cyril was going to spend his holiday with them and the following morning I had a pleasant surprise, a letter from him. He wrote in raptures about the place and urged me to join the family there. I made up my mind to go at once and, packing my bag, I was off to Devonshire by the next train.

Cyril met me at Kingswear station and we carried my bag between us. He was full of praise for the place and spoke of his joy at seeing Gussie again. We called at Coombeside on the way. Gussie's first remark to me was: 'Why, Grandpa, what's the matter? You seem to be all eyes.' I tried to pass it off, but I was beginning to realize that I was in love. I had often been in love in a mild way before, but this was quite different and gave me no peace. It seemed so hopeless for me to think of winning Florence. I spent hours going over in my mind the times we had spent together and I could find little encouragement in anything she had said or done. There were some small crumbs of comfort here and there. I remembered how pleased she had always seemed to see me. I had told no one of my feelings, but it had taken Gussie only a few moments to realize there was something wrong with me. The next morning we started out to shop in Kingswear and, stopping at Coombeside on the way, Gussie made some excuse to call me back. I joined her in the kitchen. 'Well, Grandpa,' she said, 'I think you'd better tell me what's up.' I could

not find words to reply, so she went on: 'Come on, out with it!'
Then I told her, rather incoherently, I fear, all about Florence: how
I had known her for two years and how I had gradually grown to
love her. 'Not only is she far cleverer than I am, but she seems so
far beyond me. She must look upon me as an immature boy.
Besides,' I continued desperately,
'how many years will it be before
I can earn enough to marry, even
if she would have me?'

Gussie waited patiently while
I blundered on, then she said:
'If she loves you, she'll wait;
Groby and I had to wait ten
years.'

'It seems such cheek,' I went
on, 'that I should ever tell her that
I love her.'

Gussie flared up at this. 'Now,
Grandpa, don't talk nonsense.
No girl ever minds being told she
is loved. Where's your spirit?'

When I told her that Florence was three years older than I, her
only comment was: 'I am four years older than Groby.'

I was silent after my outpourings while Gussie went on with her
cooking. A feeling of relief came over me, relief that I had been able
to tell her and have her sympathy. Presently she came across and
kissed me. 'Don't worry, Grandpa,' she said. 'It'll turn out all right.
The sun may be shining tomorrow.'

It did not shine the next day, but it did a week later, for I had a
letter from Suffolk. It had been forwarded from Blackheath Post

Office and I hardly dared to open it. It was from Florence, asking me to stay with them at the Red House.

Dear Kipper,

If you can spare the time from your picture do come and stay with us here. You never told me how you got on in Bristol. With love from

Florence.

I tried to contain my feelings, and then, at the first opportunity, dashed across the valley to Coombeside. Gussie and Groby were in the garden. I rushed up to her, took her in my arms and kissed her. 'Um,' she said, 'Grandpa's feeling better. It must be the Devon air!' I showed her my letter. 'Well, I suppose you'll be off tomorrow,' she commented, and I was.

Gussie's last remark as we said goodbye was 'Tell Florence that if she wants a nice quiet holiday with humdrum people, adequate cooking and plenty of Devonshire cream, she is to come to Coombeside.'

'What a grand idea!' was all that I could say.

Chapter Fourteen

ENGAGED

IT was too late to travel that day so I hurried into Kingswear and sent a telegram to Florence. Then I repacked my bag and next morning I left. The night at the studio *en route* was much happier than the one I had spent there the previous week. In the morning after a hasty cup of tea I put all my things in my cycle valise and set off for Liverpool Street Station. This part of the journey did not take me long. Cycling in London before the advent of the motor car was very different from what it is now. Horse-drawn traffic moved slowly and drivers would signal with their whips before stopping or making a turn. Fast-trotting hansoms and trades-men's gigs were hazards, as were the barrows of itinerant vendors moving along by the kerb, but traffic blocks were almost unknown, and at only a few busy corners in the City and West End were police-men stationed to take control.

I had no idea what time there would be a train to Saxmundham, and when I reached the station I found I had a long time to wait, so I had a meal. Eventually I reached Saxmundham at four o'clock and half an hour later was at the Red House at Hinton.

All the family were gathered at the farm next door to celebrate the arrival of a litter of pigs and I was greeted with excited shouts but was not allowed to see the piglings. There were a lot of people at tea, various neighbours having dropped in; I was very pleased to

To celebrate the arrival of a litter of pigs

be treated almost as one of the family. They made me tell Mrs Chaplin of my experiences painting in dockland. She was a very handsome woman who had been a widow for several years. Her husband 'Jimmy' Chaplin had been a member of Lloyd's and, among other things, had had a nice taste in old furniture and a keen appreciation of the arts; he had counted a number of artists among his friends.

So Florence had been brought up in a congenial atmosphere, something like mine.

After supper I was shown the Family Album. There were all the Chaplin children, five girls and three boys. There was a picture of Florence aged four, very fat and smug, with dark curls, and another, taken at the seaside, of the three younger girls in jersey frocks. A later picture showed the girls when they were at school at Spa in Belgium. There was a daguerreotype of Ebenezer Landells, one of the founders of *Punch*, who was Mrs Chaplin's father, and another of her brother Robert, also an artist and one who had served as War Correspondent to *The Illustrated London News* during the Franco-Prussian War of 1870.

After breakfast next morning there was some talk of going in a party to Southwold, but Florence's sisters were quick to realize that she and I might like to be on our own, and they started for Southwold alone. Florence and I set off on our bicycles in the opposite direction with the intention of visiting Blythburgh. The country was a complete contrast to Devon – flat, with a wide horizon. Presently our attention wandered from the landscape. I told Florence about my stay at Kingswear and how delighted I had been to receive her letter. Thinking we had found a short cut, we followed a sandy track, but this soon petered out and we realized we had lost our way. It was rough common land and the only living thing in sight was a tethered donkey who, after regarding us for a few minutes, resumed his feeding and took no further interest in us.

Florence asked me how I got my nickname. I told her I had earned it at the age of sixteen while a student at Heatherley's. 'Arthur Connor and Chattie Wake and – ' I said. She stopped me. 'Why Chattie and I were 'friends at the Royal College of Art! We both started our training there. I remember her lovely mane of red hair. She left when I did and I haven't seen her since.' I told her that Chattie left Heatherley's to go to Rolshoven's School, and though I had not seen her for two years we still wrote to each other.

After a pause Florence said: 'I think "Kip" suits you.' And she went on: 'I have a nickname, too. It sounds rather a silly one – "Pie". I have had it since I was four years old. It was given me by my father as a kind of joke. You saw from that photo in the album how fat I was as a child. He used to chaff me about this, and make me kneel before him and say: "Pity the poor starving skelington!" I did not know what this meant, but it always provoked peals of laughter. Then he would say: "What would the poor thing like to eat?" and I always answered "Pie, please! Pie, please! Pie, please!" '

Quickly I said: 'Then I shall call you "Pie".'

'Yes, do! I like it much better than Florence, and Florrie is just awful.'

We sat on and she asked me about my boyhood. I told her of

our happy childhood before Mother's death, about the Aunts and Lizzie, and our meeting with Gussie again. 'I have a message from Gussie for you,' I said.

'For me!' She looked surprised. 'Whatever can it be?'

'It is to go and see them in Devonshire.'

'But – ' she hesitated.

I went on: 'I told Gussie – I *had* to tell her, for she guessed at once – I was in love with you. I didn't think I ought to tell you, but she said I should and that you wouldn't mind.'

I waited, not daring to look at her.

Then I said: 'Do tell me you don't mind.'

'Of course I don't, Kip. I love you, but I don't know whether I do like that.' She sat quite still, and when I looked at her I saw tears in her eyes.

'Oh, Pie!' I burst out. 'I can't bear to worry you or make you unhappy, but I do love you so much and will try never to spoil things for you.' I had a haunting fear that there might be someone else, it seemed impossible that there should not be. But I knew that I must say no more then.

After a while I went back to talking of just ordinary things – like my working down at the docks; my life with George at the studio; our cheap meals in the Brompton Road . . . Then I asked her to tell me about herself.

'It isn't very exciting,' she said.

'But you showed me some photos of Belgium last night. Do tell me about that.'

'Connie and Addie and I went to a school at Spa kept by a Madame Lecocq. We were the only English girls; the others were all German or Belgian. We had much more freedom than at an English school. I was there three years. We all learned to speak

French fluently and were very happy, We still keep up with Madame by writing. The German girls were sometimes rather a trial; they were inclined to panic on the slightest provocation. One evening we were all in the schoolroom doing our prep when we heard a scream. A German girl had been sent upstairs to fetch something and she burst in gasping, "*Ein Mann! Ein Mann!*" We all went upstairs in a body and found a dummy sitting on a chair in the dormitory. Two of the Belgians were responsible for rigging it up. We never let the Germans forget it . . .! "*Ein Mann!*" we would call out whenever anything unusual happened.'

I told Pie about our trip to Germany and how we stopped the waterfall near the Brocken. We were both laughing when the time came to cycle home.

When we reached the Red House, Pie went in but was out again almost immediately. 'I wanted to make sure the boys were out,' she said. Then: 'Come and look here!' She led me across the garden and stopped by a fruit tree laden with what appeared to be green plums. She picked several and handed me some. 'The boys think they are plums and are waiting impatiently for them to ripen. They are really greengages. Aren't they delicious?' I readily agreed they were. Then Pie went on: 'Addie discovered this last week and we have to be careful; if the boys see us eating them they'd finish the lot in no time.' The 'boys' were Pie's younger brother Lindsay and his cousin Percy who was staying in the house. It was not long before the secret was out. Pie's sister was caught in the act of picking. The boys were furious and our behaviour was described as 'caddish'!

One afternoon we cycled to Walberswick – 'Wobbleswick' as Charles Keene called it. I knew that he had often been there and I recognized the backgrounds of many of his lovely drawings. Pie admired his work as much as I did. I still have the etching, given me by Keene's brother many years later, of the old wooden jetty. I was so happy to be with Pie and to know that she liked being with me. There was always the hope that some day she might care for me as much as I did for her. But then would come the depressing thought:

'How long will it be before I can earn enough to ask her to marry me?' Well, for the time being I should see her at the Schools, though not for long, for her time as a student was nearly up. The prospect of losing her, however, was avoided by her decision to share a studio in the Fulham Road with a friend.

My Landseer Scholarship had now expired, and I was no longer compelled to work every day at the Schools. I spent more time at Glebe Place making black-and-white drawings. Then I received a commission to illustrate *Tom Brown's Schooldays*. I had a copy of the original edition (my prize won at 'Bewsher's') with the fine illustrations by Arthur Hughes and Sydney P. Hall, and I found it difficult to avoid being unduly influenced by them.

I was able to see Pie at her studio and went there as often as possible, but owing to the state of Father's health I had to spend more and more time at Blackheath. An operation he had recently undergone, though slight enough in itself, had affected his arthritis and he could now hardly walk.

Part of my time at Blackheath was spent in looking for subjects to paint and I found some in Morden College. The little chapel appealed to me particularly and I promised myself I would paint it when circumstances permitted. These preoccupations meant that I could not see Pie as often as I wished, but I was comforted by the feeling that she was growing fonder of me; I was sure, at least, that I was very much in her confidence, and I knew I was able to help her in a number of ways.

Early that spring she was commissioned to carry out her prize mural design in the nurses' dining-hall at Guy's Hospital. It was a big undertaking and she decided to do the work in oils. The huge canvas was prepared – twenty-five feet long – and fixed to the wall. As the painting was high up a movable platform on wheels was made. I went with her to see it set up. The canvas looked very big and rather frightening, but we had fun climbing up on the platform and starting to square it out. In March she came two or three times to Blackheath after working all the morning at the mural; it was easy to take a train from London Bridge. I had painted a water-colour in our garden, and she stood for me where the daffodils were coming into bloom. I called the picture 'The Eve of April'.

Father was very pleased when she came, for he knew how much I loved her and I think he hoped we might become engaged. He was growing more and more crippled and his doctor advised us to consult a specialist. The consultation took place in London, and after the examination we were told that Father was suffering from disseminated sclerosis and that there was no chance of his getting better. We must prepare ourselves for the gradual loss of control of all his limbs. This was a great shock. When we reached home Ethel, Cyril and I sat down to talk things over. We should probably need the services of a male nurse – someone strong who could lift Father. We should also need to hire a wheel-chair. The trouble was that we did not know Father's financial position. When we did find it out we were shocked. Father, always an optimist, felt sure that he could be cured by a sea-voyage, and I said I would go with him if the money were forthcoming. Of course it was not; and we arranged instead to take him to Dover for a week. He had the happiest memories of the place as he and Mother had spent part of their honeymoon there. We booked rooms in an old house on the sea-front and took him by train. He could just walk the few steps to the carriage. We hired a wheel-chair in the town, and though the weather was cold and stormy he liked to go out. We pushed his chair along the sea-front, struggling against the boisterous winds. Cyril came down for the week-end and at the end of the time we managed between us to get Father home. It was the last time he was to leave our house at Blackheath.

Back at home again our doctor found us a male nurse, a retired Irish Guardsman, a great big fellow called Howse, who was more than equal to Father's weight and who lifted him into his chair and took him for airings on the Heath. Soon Father became too feeble to go out. Old friends, including Frank and Minnie Dicksee, came to see him. His mind was perfectly clear till near the end, but he was quite helpless. Our dear old Lizzie, who had been with us for years, was heartbroken. I gave up going to town, and Ethel, Cyril and I took it in turns to sit up with Father at night. Towards the end of April Aunt Fanny came and took her share of the watching. Early in May Father died. He was only fifty-six.

The illness had cost a lot of money and there was hardly anything left. Cyril and I had a difficult interview with the bank manager, who pointed out that our best course – in fact our only course – was to sell the lease of our house. We were spared one anxiety: Lizzie's future. She told us that we need not worry about her as she and her sisters had inherited a considerable sum of money from a distant relative. It appeared that the old gentleman, about whom she had sometimes spoken, had made a fortune in the City. So the three old ladies bought a house in Streatham (and a piano) and spent their declining years in peace and comfort.

We sold our house, stored most of our furniture and moved into rooms in Hyde Vale, close to the Heath. I told George that I could no longer afford the studio and he readily agreed to take over for the last few months till our agreement terminated. I was able to start my painting in the Chapel at Morden College. I answered an advertisement for a 'tame' artist to work in a newspaper office, but this proved to be a whole-time job, and as the pay was only two pounds a week I did not think it good enough.

Though we had been poor for so many years, until now it had never seemed to matter. Living among fellow students, all as impecunious as myself, being 'hard-up' was the normal condition. One did not look ahead or make plans for the future. Now everything was different, and I must think of someone besides myself. I had come to realize how much I relied on Pie's sympathy and understanding and that I was, in fact, in danger of taking too much for granted. She fully understood how I felt about Father's death, for she had lost her own father only five years before and this had obliged her family to cut down all expenses and to take in paying guests in order to keep the house going. She had a far clearer view of the things that matter in life than I had, and, sitting beside me on the sofa in her studio, she rallied me for being so downhearted.

'I can't help worrying,' I said, 'for the one thing in life that I long for seems so far away. I am longing to marry you, but how can I ask you when I have absolutely nothing to offer you?'

She said: 'I suppose money is important.' Then she went on: 'You might sell your picture.'

I shook my head. 'It's no good relying on that. I must tout round and get more black-and-white work.'

She broke in: 'I shall have a hundred pounds when I have finished my mural.'

'But, Pie, that's *yours*! I should never dream . . .'

She cut me short: 'Surely it's a much better way for us to share everything. But – ' Here she smiled at me. 'You haven't yet asked me to marry you, have you?'

'Oh, Pie, darling . . . I . . . Will you?'

She just answered: 'Yes, Kip.'

I was so overcome I couldn't speak. I took her two hands in mine, she put her head on my shoulder and we sat there close together, holding each other, like a couple of children.

Chapter Fifteen

FINDING A COTTAGE

I WENT back to our dim lodgings in Hyde Vale that evening feeling as if the heavens had opened and bestowed a benediction on me. Ethel and Cyril were delighted when I told them. Ethel was writing a letter to Gussie telling her of the change in our fortunes and I asked her to add my good news and say I would write myself in a day or two.

Cyril and I slept together at the top of the house; our room was overcrowded with furniture, for we had kept back as much as possible to save the cost of storage. We lay in bed and talked far into the night. He agreed that the best plan was for Pie and me to find a cottage in the country, not too far from London, where we could live really cheaply. We could not be married for at least a year; that is to say, until Pie had finished her mural at Guy's Hospital. Meanwhile I must work as hard as I could. In some trepidation I wrote to my two surviving aunts. I had not seen Aunt Ellen for three years. She had left Steyning and now lived at Watford. Since Aunt Alicia's death and the sale of the big house in Gordon Square, Aunt Fanny had lived in a small house in Woburn Place near St Pancras Church, with the faithful Jane in attendance.

I knew that I must face Pie's mother, who would naturally want to know about my prospects, and I put off the interview as long as possible until Pie said I must face it. 'I don't think you need worry,' she said. 'Mother is fond of you and is quite used to having very little money herself.' So I went the next day. I think Mrs Chaplin disliked talking about money matters as much as I did, for she did not ask me if I had a settled income, or what it was. I said I was prepared to take on any work and that we hoped to be able to live quite cheaply. She said, 'There is one thing I insist on. You must insure your life.' I readily agreed; and that was about all that was said on the subject of money. We then talked of our future prospects and of my plan to find a cottage in the country. She said: 'I cannot give Florence any allowance, but I will give her some furniture when you find your cottage.' She went on to tell me she was giving up her house in Penywern Road and moving to Deal and was sure she would have some to spare. I was very grateful to her, for I was afraid she might insist on our waiting until I was earning a steady income.

I did not have to wait long for a letter from Aunt Fanny. She wrote: 'This *is* a surprise and I hope you will be very happy. You must bring Miss Chaplin to see me.' Pie had heard so much about my aunts that she was rather shy about accepting the invitation, but she summoned up her courage, put on her best dress and, wearing a new hat, joined me at Earls Court Station and we took the Underground to Gower Street. Aunt Fanny had invited us to tea and was sitting in the drawing-room with the table ready laid when we arrived. As we went in she rose and came forward to meet Pie. Taking both Pie's hands, she smilingly said: 'My niece!' Then looking steadily at Pie for a moment she kissed her. It was done so simply and sweetly. We sat down and told her of our plans. She showed no concern over the risks we were prepared to take and seemed to have perfect faith in my ability to earn a living. She said: 'I got quite cross with your Uncle Willie. When I told him about your engagement he was horrified and said you should not dream of getting married until you had a sufficient income. I said "Stuff and nonsense! They're old enough to know what they are about." ' I could feel Pie's heart warming towards my dear little aunt.

Aunt Ellen reacted a little differently. She showed some bewilderment at our rashness, but she added: 'I have lived alone and been out of touch with modern life for so long that I find it difficult to understand how you can both be brave enough to marry with such slender prospects. But, my dear boy, you have my warmest blessing. Please bring Miss Chaplin to see me if she can forgive a very deaf old lady.'

After hearing what Aunt Fanny had told me I was not surprised to receive a letter from Uncle Willie. He said he was rather shocked to hear that I contemplated marriage at such an early age (I was twenty-four) and with no settled income. He himself, when a young master at St Paul's School, had married and found it difficult to make ends meet, even though he had private means to supplement his salary. He begged me to consider the matter most carefully before I embarked on such a course.

We *had* considered the matter most carefully. One evening after dinner at Roche's we had sat at our corner table and totted up what we would have to spend on rent, food and coal. We had quite agreed that a cottage should be our home, and after Pie had assured

me that she would love to
live in the country, she said:
'I have enough clothes to last
me for ages, and it will be
fun trying to cook.'

I think it cannot have been
easy for anyone brought up as
Uncle Willie had been to
understand the courage of a
girl who was prepared to
share the life of a penniless
artist. I was earning something
with my black-and-white
drawings, though my efforts to get a drawing accepted by *Punch*
were fruitless: it was two years before I achieved that.

I spent part of every day working on my picture in the chapel
at Morden College. I was determined to finish it in time to send it
to next year's Academy. Whenever I could I went to Guy's Hospital
to give Pie a hand. There was a narrow border to her mural, a
repetitive design that was tiresome to paint, and I was able to work
on this, doing a yard at a time, while she worked on her figures.
It was a constant joy to me to watch her paint, for she was so sure
and direct and rarely had to repaint anything. As the work progressed, so the scaffold had to be constantly shifted. The nurses
helped Pie with this unless I was there, when we would manage it
between us.

Gussie's reply to my letter was prompt and characteristic. After
expressing her joy at our engagement she wrote: 'You must bring
Florence to stay with us and I would like to ask Ethel and Cyril too.
I am sure you all need a rest after the trouble you have been through.

L'ART NOUVEAU

Painting the mural—a contemporary sketch

I cannot ask you all to stay here, the house is not large enough, but I could have Florence and could get rooms at the farm for you three. Let me know when Cyril has his holiday and I will see what I can do.' This was a wonderful invitation, and when I told Pie she said she would be glad to have a fortnight off from her painting. Ethel, Cyril and I put our heads together over the cost and agreed to pool our resources for a fortnight in August when Cyril's leave was due. It was rash of us to spend the money, but the pleasure of looking forward and afterwards of looking back was compensation enough.

Neither George nor Arthur betrayed surprise when I told them of my engagement. 'This is a family affair,' said George, 'and I hope you'll ask us to your wedding.'

'No doubt about that,' I said, and went on to tell them of our plans to find a cottage in the country. Arthur was concerned about our sketchy finances; living at home, as he was, and in receipt of

383

an allowance, the spirit of adventure did not appeal to him. 'Who will do your cooking?' he asked.

'Ourselves, of course,' I said. 'I can make excellent porridge and can grill chops, and Pie is learning to cook. We shall manage and we'll invite you to a meal when we are settled in.'

Arthur looked a bit dubious about this, then he said: 'Look, I am going to paint a portrait of a cousin of mine in Surrey in June or July, and if you like I will make inquiries round about. My cousins live in Shamley Green, a village near Guildford, and I shall stay in rooms in Albury, where I have been before. There may be something in that neighbourhood.'

George suggested that it would be nice if we came near Bristol, but I explained that that was too far from London.

A few weeks later I heard from Arthur. The letter was written from Albury and asked me to join him there. He said his cousin Mrs Nelson knew of a cottage on the Cranleigh Road that was vacant. He could give me no details of the place except that it belonged to a Mrs Arbuthnot. I packed a few clothes and was off on my cycle.

Arthur's cousins lived at 'Long Acre', a house by Shamley Green. Sir Charles Crosthwaite, whose portrait he was painting, had been Governor of the North-West Province of India, and Mrs Nelson was his daughter. I found her a charming lady and most sympathetic. 'The cottage,' she said, 'is very small and has been empty for some time. I have no idea whether Mrs Arbuthnot is prepared to let it, but there is no harm in finding out.' She told me where it was and I went off to investigate.

I came to the cross-roads at Stroud Common and asked at a tiny shop on the corner. A little woman in a black straw hat came from a back room. After I had bought a packet of cigarettes for fourpence, she was quite ready to tell me all she knew about the cottage. Then

she said: 'You'd best go down the
road to Upper House and ask the
gardener there. His name is Foxall
and he has the key.' I pedalled down
the road and came to Upper House.
It had a long drive with stables on
the right-hand side. There was a
lad cutting grass with a fag-hook
and I asked him for Mr Foxall and
was directed to the garden. Mr
Foxall said that the cottage had been
empty for over a year and needed 'a

bit of doing up'. It might be to let, but he couldn't say. I had best
write to Mrs Arbuthnot. He gave me her address in London and
then we walked up the road to see the place.

I was not impressed. It was very small and square with a porch
in front and no architectural pretensions. The roof was of slate and
the overgrown garden had a railing with a gate on to the road.
Foxall produced a key and we went in. The kitchen, on the left, had
a brick floor, a decent-looking range, and a box staircase leading
upstairs. A sitting-room on the right smelt of damp and the paper
was peeling off the walls. There was a scullery with a pump at the
back and a sort of larder beyond. Upstairs were two bedrooms with
fireplaces and a tiny room under the eaves behind. The windows
were iron framed with leaded lights. 'There's no water, you know,'
said Foxall. 'There's a well, but I wouldn't drink the water, it's
mostly surface drainage.' My heart was sinking rapidly as I asked
about the sanitary arrangements. 'Oh, that!' said Foxall. 'It's out
in that shed.' Then he added: 'You can always draw water from
Mrs Wilson at the corner, they have a good well there that never

runs dry.' I kept wondering whether Pie could endure such primitive conditions. There was quite a stretch of garden at the back with two or three apple-trees and a blackberry hedge.

I asked Foxall about the rent. He said: 'Maybe you could have it for seven and sixpence a week, but I can't say – you must write to Mrs Arbuthnot.' He became quite communicative as we walked back to Upper House. He told me he had been Lily Langtry's gardener for years and found his present job mighty dull. As I left him he said: 'Mind you, I can give you no promise, but I expect the old lady will be glad to have the place occupied.'

I mounted my bicycle and pedalled about for miles to think things over. I climbed Ewhurst Hill and at the top saw a 'notice 'To Let' on a small house. Behind it was a larger house with a drive. I went along this and found the front door ajar. I knocked and pushed it open. A rumbling voice inside called: 'Who is it?' 'I am looking for a house,' I replied, 'and I see you have one to let.' 'Come in,' said the voice. I went in and found myself in a large studio. An old man was seated in an armchair in a corner wearing a dark-blue cloak draped over his shoulders and a skull-cap. There were several large canvases on easels and the room smelt of oil paint and tobacco smoke. I asked about the house to let. The rent, he told me, was £50 a year.

I thanked him and retreated. As I left he said: 'If you think of taking it, write to me. My name is Clayton Adams.' I realized that however much I might admire his landscapes I could not afford his rent.

I returned home the following day and wrote a letter to Mrs Arbuthnot telling her that I had seen her cottage and asking her if she were willing to let it. The reply she sent me was not encouraging. She said: 'I don't know what that man Foxall told you, but he has no right to make any arrangements. I have not made any plans at present about letting the cottage, as I may want it for one of my staff.'

I showed the letter to Pie and we agreed that this was not a definite refusal. The phrase 'at present' held out some hope and I said that I would return to the attack later. I had no time to go exploring again, and though I wrote to house agents in Guildford and Cranleigh the 'To Lets' they sent me were too expensive.

Pie and I were having dinner at our corner table at Roche's when I told her about the cottage. I drew her a picture of it with a plan of the rooms. She did not seem alarmed about the drinking-water or the lack of modern conveniences, but was worried about baths. 'I have got a hip bath that belonged to my aunts,' I observed tentatively. 'But we should have to heat the water for it on the kitchen range.' Pie thought this would be rather fun and was delighted at the prospect of a garden with apple-trees. 'There would be nowhere to paint,' I said, and we agreed that we must have a studio of some kind put up in the garden as soon as we could afford it.

Ethel, Cyril and I were in high spirits when we met Pie at Paddington Station for our holiday in Devon. On the journey we discussed the housing problem, toying with the idea of looking for something in Devon, but I knew that however alluring the prospect, it would not work; we had to find something nearer London. We travelled via Bath and Bristol and I was happy to point out to Pie all the landmarks on my beloved Great Western Railway. As we came in sight of the Dart, with *Britannia* and *Hindustan* anchored in the river, we leaned from our carriage window and sang like children on a school treat! Gussie, Groby and Snap were waiting on the platform at Kingswear Station and we all crowded into a wagonette and drove off, stopping at Green Park Farm where Cyril, Ethel and I were to stay. The farm was only half a mile across the fields from Coombeside, and after putting us down with our luggage the wagonette drove on with Gussie, Groby and Pie; Gussie calling back to us: 'Come along for tea. It will be ready in half an hour.'

Green Park Farm was pleasantly situated with great bushes of hydrangeas down the drive. The farmer's wife had put bowls of flowers in the sitting-room set aside for our use, and there was a lovely smell of newly-baked bread. We only waited long enough to thank our hostess before crossing the fields to Coombeside.

I was not a bit surprised to find Pie already perfectly at home. She was brimming over with excitement and eager to explore the valley. We did this after tea, climbing the path up to The Warren. We looked in through the windows and saw Harry Rogers' organ, now nearly completed and quite filling the room. Harry and Herbert were away on their annual trip to the moors and had left a message for us giving us the free use of their boat. We took them at their word and were out most days in search of mackerel. These were very scarce, but we had one good afternoon and took the catch to Coombeside, where Pie helped Gussie to cook a glorious supper.

It was a lovely holiday, and like all lovely holidays the days of it passed swiftly by. The last evening was spent at Coombeside, Groby producing a bottle of old liqueur brandy for the occasion. I had tasted brandy in France but nothing like this vintage. We all drank a toast to 'Health, Wealth and Happiness'.

Chapter Sixteen

OUR GREAT ADVENTURE

BOTH Pie and I had a lot of hard work ahead of us but our holiday had done us so much good that we were able to tackle it with renewed vigour. The mural was going well, almost half of it being finished. But as the days drew in Pie was not able to give so much time to it. Since her mother gave up the house in Earls Court she had been living with her sister Connie at Norbury. Connie was married to Henry Young, a doctor practising in Norbury and Streatham; their house was near the station, but the journey to Guy's Hospital was tedious and there were many days in winter when the light was too bad for work in the dining-hall. I had to give up painting in the chapel, partly for the same reason and partly also because the place was not warmed and was like an ice-house in the cold weather. I filled in my time with black-and-white work and was commissioned to illustrate two books.

Both were very dull. One was a story about the earthquake in Martinique and bore the title *Smouldering Fires*. I cannot think why the publishers should have chosen me as the illustrator, for I knew nothing about the place and had to spend a lot of time trying to find out. However, these small jobs brought in ten or fifteen pounds, so I was able to put something by.

The cottage was constantly in my mind, but I was too much occupied to do anything about it then. Later on I would try and get a definite answer from Mrs Arbuthnot.

I was glad when the spring came and I could finish my work in the chapel. I was not very satisfied with the result, but I bought a frame for four pounds and was somewhat reassured when I showed my work to George and Arthur, for George said: 'It's jolly well painted.' Sending-in day at the Royal Academy was at the end of March and I carried my picture to Burlington House wrapped in a dust-sheet. The thing looked very insignificant among the large and important canvases stacked in the corridor and I offered up a silent prayer as I came away. Outside in the yard the students were lounging on the bench. I did not see any familiar faces. It seemed an age since I myself had sat there with my friends. I pushed open the swing door leading to the Schools and found Osborne, the porter, in his office. He grumbled about the present-day students. 'Not the same as in your day,' he said. I fancy he may have been saying the same thing to every past student for twenty years or more. Then I went to Guy's Hospital to see Pie and forget all about my picture.

The mural was nearing completion. She was working on the central group, which included the figure of a small winged boy. Presently the nurses trooped in to their luncheon; they stood looking up and one of them asked: 'How much longer will it take?' She went on: 'We all think it is lovely and will be sorry when it's finished. We have enjoyed watching you paint so much.' Pie told me that she had heard from Sir Cooper Perry, the doctor who was responsible for commissioning the work, that an additional £50 was to be given her for her expenses. She was in high glee and said: 'I have reckoned it up and find that it has not cost me that, so we shall have something over.'

Three weeks after sending-in day I heard from the Academy that my picture was accepted and a varnishing ticket followed. Varnishing day was a great occasion, when artists were able to see their accepted pictures in the galleries – the lucky ones hung on the line. Some of the less fortunate, whose pictures were 'skied', could be seen on ladders touching up their work, piling on the colour to bring the pictures to notice; one in particular, I remember, was splashing on scarlet paint. I was one of the lucky ones, for my picture was on the line in the second room. I met several friends and one of them told me that Edwin Abbey was in one of the galleries. I promptly went in search of him and found him deep in

conversation with a fellow Royal Academician. I waited till presently he saw me and greeted me with: 'Hallo, Shepard, what are you doing here?' I told him and he went on: 'You should go on with your black and white, you know. Have you tried *Punch*?' I told him of my unsuccessful efforts. 'You must meet Linley Sambourne,' he said. 'He's somewhere about. Come along and I'll introduce you.' He took my arm and we charged from room to room.

Sambourne was talking to a friend. He was the senior cartoonist for *Punch*, having taken John Tenniel's place three years earlier. He turned towards us while Abbey, holding my arm, said: 'Here, Sambourne, do you know Shepard? A promising young artist who wants to get into *Punch*.' Then he gave me a dig as though to say, 'Now get on with it,' and left us. I stammered a few words in praise of Sambourne's work, but he cut me short and talked about *Punch*. He said: 'You want to get hold of some good jokes, make rough sketches and fire them in.' I told him of my failures. 'Of course,' he said; 'that happens to everyone. You've got to go on. Give them no peace!' He left me feeling rather bewildered. I went out to get some lunch and on my return met a student friend on the stairs. He told me Frank Dicksee was looking for me.

Frank was very tall and always wore a frock-coat, so he was easily found. 'I like your picture,' he said, 'but there is no price on it. Is it for sale?' 'Oh yes,' I answered. Frank went on: 'Hamo Thornycroft and I have been deputed to buy a picture for a colonial art gallery and we both would like to buy yours. We can only spend £100 – can you sell it for that?' My voice, I fear, was hardly audible. 'Yes,' I said, 'I shall be very glad to. Thank you so much.' Frank then said: 'I expect you'll find the money useful when you get married.' I was able to answer heartily, 'Indeed we shall!' A hundred pounds was more than I should have dared to ask. I had thought of sixty guineas, but George had advised me not to price the picture; an experienced artist had told him to wait until one's picture was hung before fixing the price. I was thankful I had followed his advice. Now the whole situation was changed and I could go ahead with the cottage. I sent a telegram to Pie, who was staying at Deal with her mother. She told me afterwards it was almost unintelligible and read as if I had made some money in a colonial investment.

When I reached home that evening I wrote to Mrs Arbuthnot. As I concocted my letter I prayed that the place was still vacant. I had to wait a month for a reply. 'I have been abroad,' she said. 'If you want to rent my cottage you had better come and see me about it.' I seized on this ray of hope and wrote asking for an appointment. Her reply a week later was written in the third person and named a day and hour at which I was to present myself at her house in Mayfair. When the day came I made my way to South Street, found the house and rang the bell. The door was opened by a maid; as I paused on the door-step and asked for my hostess, a voice from somewhere inside said: 'Wipe your feet!' I wiped my feet and passing in was shown into a sitting-room. The owner of the voice was standing by the window. She was tall and stout and wore a large hat. 'Why do you want my cottage?' she asked. I explained I was marrying a wife and wanted somewhere to live. 'It's not the kind of place *I* would want to live in,' she went on. 'I don't want to have any bother with it. If I let it you must do it up and keep it in repair, and be prepared to turn out if I want it.' This struck me as a rather one-sided arrangement, and I said I hoped she would give me at least a year's tenancy with the option of staying on. Her reply was: 'I don't want to be bothered with it, I must think it over.' I explained that I would be glad to have a definite answer as I wanted to marry in the autumn and time would be needed to do the place up. I asked her if she would take this into consideration and let me know the rent. 'Oh, the rent!' she said. 'I should not charge much – perhaps half a crown a week.' I thanked her and asked her if she would give me permission to take possession of the cottage. She replied: 'I will write a form of agreement. We need not go to the expense of a lawyer.' That ended the interview and I came away satisfied with the rent she named, but not easy in my mind about my position. Could I go ahead and

make plans with a builder to have the place done up on so vague
a promise? I consulted Cyril and he advised me to chance it. When
Pie came back to London to her sister's house we talked it over
together; she agreed with me and was all for going ahead. So I
packed my valise and cycled to Shamley Green.

The cottage looked much the same, the weeds perhaps even
more in evidence. I went to Upper House and routed out Foxall,
telling him that I had taken the cottage. I said that an agreement was
being drawn up and I had been promised the place for a year. Meanwhile I should like the key so that I could make plans with a builder
for repairs. Foxall demurred. He had had no word from Mrs Arbuthnot and could not hand over the place like that. 'She might change
her mind,' he said. 'She's done it before.' I refused to be put off and
offered to take entire responsibility for anything that might happen.
He relented at this and went so far as to tell me of a builder on the
Cranleigh Road, a small firm that might be willing to do the job.
I went off and found the builder's yard quite easily. A workman
told me to come back in an hour as the builder was out. I cycled on
to Cranleigh and had a look round and booked myself a room for the
night at an inn. The builder was there when I reached the yard again
and he agreed to go with me to see the cottage and give an estimate,
but warned me it would be a month before he could start work. He
had a trap waiting outside, so we drove in that with my bicycle tied
on the back. He spent a long time going from room to room, tapping
the walls and testing the woodwork with a penknife. He lit paper
in the fireplaces and shook his head over the damp patches in the
sitting-room. He said that if the walls were treated I might have a
nice bit of panelling fixed as a dado, but I said that papering the
walls would satisfy me. He went outside, fetched his ladder from the
trap and had a look at the roof. 'Sound enough on the outside,' was

his comment, but short of removing the
slates there was no means of inspecting
the timbers. He condemned the system
of drainage. He stood looking at the gully
by the back door and picked up a bit of
stick and poked about among the dead
leaves. 'You'll have trouble with that,' he
said. 'There ain't enough fall.' He was
right. We did have trouble, endless
trouble, with that gully. Finally he agreed
to post me an estimate within a few days.

When I reached home a letter awaited
me from Mrs Arbuthnot, enclosing a
form of agreement drawn up on a sheet of
writing paper. It was a strange document;
I don't know what a house agent would
have said about it. It stated simply: 'Mrs
Arbuthnot is prepared to let her cottage
to Mr Shepard for one year certain on condition that he does it up
thoroughly and keeps it in repair.' The accompanying note directed
me to affix a sixpenny stamp, sign the document and return it
to the sender. Though I was no business man it seemed to me
that there were some things lacking in this, but I was ready to
take a chance. The rent at least was modest – even more modest, I
decided after much calculation, than the 2s. 6d. a week Mrs Arbuthnot had suggested when I called on her: £6 a year works out at
2s. 3½d. a week. The difference of 10s. was more than enough to pay
for the stamp.

I carried the agreement with me when I went to report progress
to Pie. I had arranged to meet her at Guy's Hospital and help her

pack up her painting things. The mural was finished and at last we could see the whole thing unobstructed by the scaffolding. It looked grand, and Pie flushed with pleasure as several nurses and students

congratulated her. One of the students gave her a bunch of flowers. I went back to Norbury with her and told of the builder's verdict on our cottage and that work could not start before September so that our wedding would have to wait till the end of the month. We talked it over with Connie and her husband and had a good laugh over my 'Agreement'. The Youngs had already offered to lend their house for our wedding reception and suggested that we should be married in their parish church. This would solve a problem, for Mrs Chaplin was living at Deal and we did not want to be married there. So it was arranged, and Mrs Chaplin came to Norbury a few days later for a family conclave at which our wedding was fixed for September 28th. Already it was August, so there was not much time. I wrote to my aunts, to Uncle Willie and my near friends. Pie and I went over our lists together and chose those of our fellow students who should be invited.

I had a charming reply from Aunt Ellen, who expressed her regret that she was not able to come and enclosed a most generous cheque. Uncle Willie turned up trumps, as he always did: no longer criticizing our rashness, he wished us every form of happiness and backed it with a cheque for £25. Aunt Fannie, accepting the invitation, said that her present would be groceries from Shoolbred's. Pie had a canteen of cutlery from her uncle and aunt; the Dicksees gave me a gate-legged table; and Mrs Chaplin, besides her gift of the Suffolk Dower Press, gave us a carpet and some chairs. One of the best presents promised to us was from Annie Gregory. She had been a very close friend of my mother's, and was the wife of Charles Gregory, the painter and member of the Royal Water Colour Society. They lived at Milford in Surrey and it was outside their house when they lived in Ripley that I had disgraced myself at an early age by lying on my back in the middle of the road and screaming. She wrote offering to go to our cottage on our wedding day and prepare it for our arrival – light the fires, air the sheets and cook us a dinner. I wrote an enthusiastic acceptance of her offer with instructions where to find the key.

When the builder's estimate came in it was lower than I had expected – under £16 – so I wrote accepting it and asking for an early start with the work. Ethel and Cyril, who fully shared my excitement, volunteered to go with me and help to get the cottage ready. Cyril felt that our presence would have the effect of hurrying the builders. As he could get away only at week-ends, it was arranged that Ethel and I should pack a trunk with linen, blankets and a few stores and camp in the cottage and Cyril would join us when he could. So, a week later, Ethel and I were off. Besides our suitcases we had the trunk, a box of kitchen ware and some stores. The local 'fly' drove us from Bramley Station. We found the cottage in a rare mess, with workmen in the bedrooms distempering the ceilings and re-papering the walls. The kitchen had been whitewashed and looked fresh and clean. While Ethel unpacked the trunk I got to work on the kitchen range; the thing was choked up with odds and ends of wallpaper, cigarette packets and painter's rags. Having cleared it, I took the bucket up the road to draw some water at Mrs Wilson's well and to buy firewood. Looking into the outhouse I was relieved to see some coal had arrived. Lighting the fire was easier than I had expected, and before long it was roaring away in fine style. 'Let's have some tea!' I shouted to Ethel – and then remembered there was no milk. This meant a journey down the lane to Edginton's farm. I came back with milk, butter and eggs. We had brought a loaf of bread and some jam with us.

While the kettle was boiling I went upstairs to see how the builders were getting on. The bedroom ceiling was finished and a man was washing the floor with a rag. Lifting a gloomy face to me, he said: 'You sleeping 'ere to-night?' I said that I was. He squeezed his rag into the bucket: 'I suppose you know the place is 'aunted?' he said. 'Really!' I answered. 'Yes, 'aunted,' he went on. 'That's what they say, and that's why the place wouldn't let.' I thanked him for the information and went downstairs to pass on the startling news to Ethel. She was no more disturbed about it than I. 'If the ghost turns up,' she said, 'I shall get it to help me with the curtains.'

We had our tea sitting on the trunk, for as yet there was no furniture. That was due to come the following morning from Deptford, where it had been stored. We worked at cleaning up till nearly nine, then had a scratch supper and camped out in blankets on the sitting-room floor. No eldritch shrieks or rattling chains disturbed our slumbers. As the furniture was not expected before midday, I cycled to Cranleigh and bought a dinner service. It was of nondescript pattern and very cheap, but so strong that it lasted us for years. I still have one of the plates – nothing will break it. Packed in a small crate, the service was too heavy for my cycle and had to be left for the carrier to deliver next day. Ethel and I had a bread-and-cheese lunch and waited for the furniture. Then it began to rain. The van arrived at three-thirty; of course the men had lost their way. It was no fun carting the furniture indoors through the wet. The men were in a hurry to get back to London and our things were dumped anywhere. It was five o'clock when they left after drinking gallons of tea.

Sorting out the furniture was troublesome; we had to get at the beds and mattresses to sleep on that night. I made the kitchen quite natty with the gate-legged table, the Dower Press and four antique chairs. Mrs Chaplin's rugs looked well on the brick floor. Ethel unpacked a bundle of assorted curtains and set to work on them. There were no rods, but she cut them to fit the cottage windows and fixed them up temporarily. I spent the next afternoon laying our carpet in the bedroom. The workmen had finished upstairs and were whitewashing the scullery and larder.

Before supper I took the bucket up the road to draw some water and have a chat with Mrs Wilson. She was full of gossip and it was evident that she had never heard of our ghost. She had watched the arrival of our furniture with interest. 'They're moving in!' must have gone round the neighbourhood already, for the next morning I had a visit from an old man prepared to tackle the garden. After a look round he said: 'It ain't no good – no good at all. 'Tis all coochy.' However, he volunteered to come once a week. Soon after that the carrier arrived with my dinner service. He asked if there was anything I wanted in Guildford. I had yet to realize that the carrier was prepared to do one's shopping in the town – a practice much to be commended as he was the only means of public transport, this being before the advent of the country bus.

Cyril was due on Friday night; he had Saturday morning off. He arrived at nine o'clock, having cycled from Bramley. He was quite impressed by my cottage, which certainly looked its best at night. He brought with him a heavy and strangely shaped parcel which had been delivered at Hyde Vale by Shoolbred's van. We unpacked it and found a complete side of bacon, a present from Aunt Fanny. We hung it up in our small larder and it provided delicious rashers for months.

With Cyril's help we got things straight. Together we laid in the sitting-room the carpet from our old home which had always been a favourite of mine – it was a darkish green with a border of flowers. On Sunday I borrowed a fag-hook from Mr Wilson and Cyril got to work on the jungle in the garden while I tried to get the weeds out of the brick path in front of the cottage; Ethel cooked our meal with eggs and some bacon cut from Aunt Fanny's gift.

After supper we talked over their plans for the future. Cyril was now with a firm of Underwriters at Lloyd's and was earning a good salary. As Ethel was teaching at the Blackheath Conservatoire of Music and wished to remain in the district, the pair of them planned to rent a house in Lee or Blackheath after I was married. Next morning Cyril had to catch an early train to London. Ethel and I stayed on for a couple of days to see the work finished. Then after a last look round, I left the key with Mrs Wilson and we returned to town.

I went to Norbury the following day and told Pie of our experiences at the cottage. When I came to the ghost she was highly interested and wanted to know all about it. I explained that it could not have been a very obtrusive ghost or Mrs Wilson would have heard of it. Certainly it never had any substance as far as we were concerned, for though we lived in the cottage for six years we never saw it, nor did any of our friends. While I was away Pie had received a cheque from her godmother. Our cash presents now amounted to £45; and we also had a little money saved, so we felt quite rich. With the addition of our united earnings from painting, we could face the future with confidence.

The arrangements for the wedding were now virtually complete; even Pie's wedding dress was nearly finished. I cannot describe it though I heard reports on it from her sisters, but I do know that she looked lovely on the day. When that day came Ethel, Cyril and I were up early. Cyril, as my Best Man, put the ring carefully in his waistcoat pocket. We both wore frock-coats – though how I acquired mine I cannot now imagine. I was terribly nervous and so anxious to be in time that we reached the church much too early. Thereafter all went well. Pie's uncle, the wine importer, gave her away, and afterwards, at the reception, gave me a bottle of a rather special wine to drink at our first meal in our cottage. Aunt Fanny was in great form and was introduced to all her new relations; she and Mrs Chaplin got on famously. We had a terrific send-off from a bodyguard of our fellow students as we drove away to the station.

The train from London set us down at Chilworth. I had ordered a fly to meet us and it was waiting at the station. The evening was misty, quite thick on the common by Wonersh, and the driver lost his way, but I was able to redirect him and, as we turned the corner by Mrs Wilson's, Pie leant from the carriage window to catch her first sight of our cottage.

Lights already shone from the windows and the front door stood open. When we stopped I got out. 'Come on,' I said, 'I'm going to carry you over the threshold.' 'You are certainly not. You are much too tired. You'd probably drop me – and the wine as well.' So I gave in. Annie Gregory was waiting in the doorway to greet us, and a lovely smell of dinner came from the kitchen. 'I never thought

I should get ready in time,' she said, 'so I'm thankful you're late. Having no water laid on, and having to find everything! . . . However, it's all ready now.'

I took Pie upstairs, carrying a candle, to show her the rooms. A cheerful fire was burning in our bedroom, and there were flowers on our chest of drawers. We looked into the spare room and the little room under the eaves. Pie said: 'I think it's quite sweet. You know, it's not as small as I expected. And I love the kitchen.'

Downstairs I unpacked our bottle of wine – fortunately I had remembered a corkscrew. We had no wineglasses but I poured the wine into tumblers. Annie had laid the dinner on our gate-legged table and it looked very inviting with our four brass candlesticks, the red checked cloth and a bowl of Michaelmas daisies. We asked her to stop and share our meal. 'I can't keep the fly waiting,' she explained (it was to take her back to Bramley). 'Besides, there is the train to catch.' Then she turned to Pie: 'You and Ernest must come over to Milford soon and while Ernest talks art with Carl I can give you some tips on cooking.' Taking my hand she said: 'Carl and the girls send you their love and good wishes. Now I must be off.' We all drank to happy days and I took a glass out to the driver. We waved goodbye from our front door as they drove away.

It was quite dark by this time and the mist made it cold outside. The only sound was a pheasant squawking in the copse opposite. We turned and went into the kitchen and sat down to the first meal in our own home. We were too tired to think of washing up afterwards; I just put the things in the sink and pumped water on them. Before we went to bed we looked out the special treasures we had brought with us – the panel portrait of my grandmother by Thomas Dicksee; the charming little nude by Chaplin, the Belgian artist; Pie's enamel patch box and her tiny china mouse.

We were very happy. Pie's mural at Guy's Hospital had been triumphantly finished. I had a picture accepted by the Royal Academy, hung on the line and sold for £100. We were married, and between us we had savings and wedding presents in cash amounting to perhaps £70. What had seemed impossible a few months earlier had come to pass, and we thanked God for our cottage home.

Other books illustrated by Ernest H. Shepard
published by Methuen

THE WORK OF
E. H. SHEPARD

Edited by Rawle Knox

This volume, published to mark the 100th anniversary of the birth of Ernest Shepard, offers the best and most characteristic of his whole range of work; it also provides a balanced appreciation of the man as artist and companion.

Ernest H. Shepard, 'Kipper' to his family and friends, is perhaps best known – and loved – for the children's illustrations he did for the work of A. A. Milne and for his incomparable drawings for Kenneth Grahame's *The Wind in the Willows*. His output, however, was considerable and altogether he illustrated somewhere near to a hundred books. Over a period of fifty years he also had weekly drawings in *Punch* magazine and these too are represented here.

Contributors to this volume include H. F. Ellis, for many years assistant editor of *Punch*; Penelope Fitzgerald, author of the definitive biography of Edward Burne-Jones; and art historian Bevis Hillier. It is Bevis Hillier who has the last word on Shepard's place in the history of English illustration. 'I see him as the end of a tradition, not the beginning of one. He is the last of the great Victorian "black and white" men.'

Illustrated with over three hundred drawings and paintings, many in colour.

'... a fine book, wonderfully illustrated with well-chosen and excellently reproduced examples of Shepard's work and with a touching and clear account of his life.'
THE DAILY TELEGRAPH

THE POOH SKETCHBOOK

Edited by Brian Sibley
with an Introduction by Sir Roy Strong,
Director of the Victoria and Albert Museum

These pencil sketches and preparatory drawings by Ernest H. Shepard for the A. A. Milne Winnie-the-Pooh books have been selected from the extensive collection bequeathed by the artist to the Victoria and Albert Museum. The majority of them are published here for the first time.

The drawings, made between 1924 and 1928, have a freshness and spontaneity which complement the published work; they are superb examples of Shepard's genius as an illustrator. Through these sketches one can trace the development of many of the best-loved Pooh drawings and meet the original toys from Christopher Robin's nursery as they posed for the artist. There are also beautifully observed details of the Sussex countryside where Pooh's adventures took place. Some of the drawings are accompanied by familiar quotations from the books.

THE POOH BOOK OF QUOTATIONS
Selected by Brian Sibley

An amusing and entertaining volume of all the witty, profound, and most memorable sayings by the Bear-of-little-brain and by all his friends and relations. For ease of reference these are assembled under such headings as Thoughts on Food; Thoughts on Writing, Spelling and Long Words; Thoughts on Organizing Things and many others.

THE TAO OF POOH
Benjamin Hoff

Benjamin Hoff shows that Pooh's Way is amazingly consistent with the principles of living envisioned long ago by the Chinese founders of Taoism.

POOH'S WORKOUT BOOK
Ethan Morddan

The only exercise guide with full technical data on: The Hunny Pot Paddle, Jumping and Squeaking, The Frisk, Swimming, Bouncing and Rest Up After. Complete with Workout Hums, Heffalump Avoidance Tips, and Smakerel Chart.

WINNIE ILLE PU

A Latin version of *Winnie-the-Pooh* translated by Alexander Lenard.

DOMUS ANGULI PUENSIS

A Latin version of *The House at Pooh Corner* translated by Brian Gerrard Staples.

THE WIND IN THE WILLOWS COUNTRY COOKBOOK

Arabella Boxer

Here is a sumptuous offering for cooks and would-be cooks of all ages. A selection of mouth-watering recipes, inspired by Kenneth Grahame's *The Wind in the Willows*, range from a Riverside Sandwich to River-Banker's Broiled Chicken and Toad Hall Trifle.

The book is divided into five sections with recipes for everyday food as well as food for picnics, for storage, and for celebrations.

The pages are embellished with the beloved Ernest H. Shepard illustrations and with favourite passages from *The Wind in the Willows*.